Wounded By Reality

Understanding and Treating Adult Onset Trauma

Psychoanalysis in a New Key Book Series
Volume 6

Psychoanalysis in a New Key Book Series
DONNEL STERN, PH.D., SERIES EDITOR

Wounded By Reality

Understanding and Treating Adult Onset Trauma

Ghislaine Boulanger

THE ANALYTIC PRESS

2007 Mahwah, NJ   London

Acknowledgment is gratefully made to:

Contemporary Psychoanalysis for granting permission to use material that originally appeared in two articles published in its pages: "The Cost of Survival: Psychoanalysis and Adult Onset Trauma," 38: 17–44, January 2002. And "Wounded by Reality: The Collapse of the Self in Adult Onset Trauma," 38:45–76, January 2002.

Chapter 7 is an expanded and adapted version of "From Voyeur to Witness: The Recovery of Symbolic Function after Massive Psychic Trauma," which originally appeared in *Psychoanalytic Psychology*, 22:21–31, 2005. Copyright 2005 by the Educational Publishing Foundation. Adapted with permission.

Chapter 9 is an expanded and adapted version of "The Strength Found in Innocence," which originally appeared in *Psychoanalysis and Psychotherapy*, 20:119–136. Copyright 2003, International Universities Press.

The Estate of Mrs. Claire Blunden and PFD (www.pfd.co.uk) for permission to reproduce Edmund Blunden's poem "1916 seen from 1921" (© Estate of Mrs. Claire Blunden 1922).

The Analytic Press, Publishers
10 Industrial Avenue
Mahwah, New Jersey 07430
www.erlbaum.com

Cover design by Tomai Maridou

CIP information for this volume may be obtained by contacting the Library of Congress

ISBN 978-0-88163-430-3 — 0-88163-430-1 (cloth)

Books published by Lawrence Erlbaum Associates are printed on acid-free paper, and their bindings are chosen for strength and durability.

Printed in the United States of America
10 9 8 7 6 5 4 3 2 1

For Charles Kadushin

Contents

1916 seen from 1921

Tired with dull grief, grown old before my day,
I sit in solitude and only hear
Long silent laughters, murmurings of dismay,
The lost intensities of hope and fear;
In those old marshes yet the rifles lie,
On the thin breastwork flutter the grey rags,
The very books I read are there — and I
Dead as the men I loved, wait while life drags
Its wounded length from those sad streets of war
Into green places here, that were my own.
But now what once was mine is mine no more,
I seek such neighbors here and I find none.
With such strong gentleness and tireless will
These ruined houses seared themselves in me,
Passionate I look for their dumb stories still,
And the charred stub outspeaks the living tree.

—Edmund Blunden (1921)

Edmund Blunden, "1916 seen from 1921" from *Men Who March Away,* I. M. Parson, ed.

Acknowledgments

.

Where to start? Perhaps with the people without whom this book could never have taken shape in my mind: the Vietnam veterans I interviewed after their return from combat in the 1970s when I was part of a large research project. And this leads me to the other survivors of adult onset trauma I have found in my practice or who have found their way to me. I thank them for their trust in sharing their experience with me.

Without Donnel Stern's invitation, I would not have tackled this subject as a book, but would have left it as a series of articles. I am grateful to Don for his confidence in my project and for his great skill as an editor who pays close attention both to the large themes and the smaller details.

For more than 20 years I have met regularly with Elliot Kronish to talk about ideas and readings and cases. The articles and books we shared, many of which he was responsible for bringing to my attention, inform so many of the themes I develop here, that I can say unequivocally that this book would not be the same without him.

Robert Prince has been a wonderful friend and supporter since we met a few years ago. Bob's own pioneering work on the children of Holocaust survivors is a model of good scholarship. I count on him for his sense of humor and his good judgment. He "gets it" when others don't, yet he is an incisive critic.

For several years I have been privileged and challenged to be a member of a reading group run by Donnel Stern. To the other members of this group—Phil Blumberg, Robert Grossmark, James Ogilvie, Bruce Reis, Nick Samstag, and Steve Tublin, and of course our leader, Don—thank you all for letting me be a part of this group and for sharing ideas and texts so generously. Finding such diverse talent and laughter in one rather small room is a heady experience.

After reading drafts of the first two papers I was working on about this topic, the late Stephen Mitchell's generous and enthusiastic encouragement motivated me to keep going. Steve's work shaped much of what I have come to know as a psychoanalyst; without the changes his ideas brought to our field, this book would have been inconceivable. I am so sorry not to be able to give him a copy.

Barry Farber, director of the program in Clinical Psychology at Teachers College, Columbia University, has been generous with friendship, reprints, support, and much needed advice.

It has been a great privilege and pleasure to get to know Henry Krystal a little during the last few years. I am continually astonished by the curiosity, generosity and enthusiasm that this pioneer of the psychoanalytic study of massive psychic trauma demonstrates. Henry is always interested to hear about the most recent trends in psychoanalysis, always ready to make connections between people, always eager to share his work and his thinking. I have learned from his modesty and his kindness.

Over the years, conversations with other friends in the field have contributed so much to what I know and how I think about this topic. I thank each of them for their generosity in sharing their ideas with me and in listening to mine. I am thinking particularly of Tom McGoldrick, who does extraordinary and ongoing work with combat veterans at the Staten Island Vet Center; Mary Marshall Clark, director of Columbia University's Oral History Program, whose ability to listen and to teach others to listen is legend; Judith Rustin, who has been a welcome source of cutting edge neurobiological texts; Jeanne Wolff Bernstein, my Lacanian guide; and Karen Seeley, who shared with me early drafts of her post-9/11 field work with mental health professionals.

Students in the classes I have taught both in psychodynamic theory and in psychoanalytic theories of trauma deserve thanks for keeping me on my toes.

Many friends on Fishers Island generously fed me and my family when, during the summer of 2005, I announced I had a book to finish so I would be accepting invitations but not giving them!

I would also like to thank Paul Stepansky, publisher of The Analytic Press, for making a place for this book on his excellent list; Nadine Simms, who has scrupulously shepherded my manuscript through the publication process, and Kristopher Spring who has been a great help in preparing promotional material and offering good cheer.

To families made, families given, families found: to Katharyn Bond, Kate Durocher, Barbara and Ken Eisold, the late Hettie Frank, Joanna and Jimmy Hulsey, Matthew, Michelle, and Rachel Kadushin, Andrea Krauss, Spyros Orfanos, Elaine Richard (who also gave me invaluable editorial advice), Sophia Richman, Isaac Solotaroff, Jim Stoeri, Helena Wasik, and Alan Zaretsky, thank you all for your love and support as I have been writing this book. And finally, to my husband Charles Kadushin—who did not know what he was getting into when he invited me to join the Legacies of Vietnam project in the 1970s—my most thoughtful reader, my greatest fan, and the source of all technical assistance, thank you.

1

Toward A Psychodynamic Understanding of Adult Onset Trauma

There's no initiation either into such mysteries. He has to live in the midst of the incomprehensible, which is also detestable. And it has a fascination, too, that goes to work upon him. The fascination of the abomination—you know, imagine the growing regrets, the longing to escape, the powerless disgust, the surrender, the hate.

— Joseph Conrad (1902, p. 7)

Recently, I was teaching a course on trauma and psychoanalysis to advanced candidates at an analytic institute. I asked the candidates if they could offer examples from their own practices to illustrate cases of adults who had been traumatized in childhood and cases of adults who had been traumatized as adults. Each of them readily volunteered examples of adult patients who had suffered physical, sexual, or emotional abuse as children. Much of the time, the abuse in question was cumulative and consistent. There were also examples of sudden and horrifying violations of the trust between a caretaker and child. Others offered cases of striking emotional neglect, rather than active abuse. These are the painful and familiar narratives that we construct with patients daily, if not hourly, in the course of our professional lives. But, when I asked about examples of catastrophic stress in adulthood, there was silence. No one even asked me what I meant.

My peculiar expertise lies in the extremes of human experience, what Conrad (1902) calls "those ironic necessities that lurk in the facts of human existence" (p. 91). Although this is not where most of us locate our practices, I believe it is important for psychoanalysts and psychodynamically-trained therapists to become conversant with the chronic disorders to which massive psychic trauma can give rise, for too often they have been misunderstood. These disorders do indeed "lurk," often well beneath the surface; they are not always easy to detect. By suggesting clinicians become conversant with them, I do not mean giving a cursory glance at or even memorizing the list of symptoms of Posttraumatic Stress Disorder (PTSD) in the Diagnostic and Statistical Manual (American Psychiatric Association 1980, 1987, 1994), but developing an understanding of how these symptoms arise and the far-reaching consequences for the survivor's psyche. As Terrence Des Pres (1976) repeatedly makes clear in his work on the Holocaust, the phenomenology of adult onset trauma has been almost impossible to address in psychoanalytic terms. In this book, I intend to provide a way of thinking psychodynamically about that phenomenology.

By and large, psychoanalysis resides most comfortably in the quotidian. Reaching back to the past to search for and understand patterns that disrupt the steady flow of life in the present day, the small and not so small terrors of childhood, the errors of omission and commission carried out by those who should have known better and often wished they had known better, but did not. In the United States, until very recently, psychoanalysts have rarely found themselves coming up against the aftereffects of violence in adult life. Our training has not prepared us to address encounters with earth-shattering external events. The changes wrought by adult onset trauma have occupied a contested space in psychoanalytic theory, if they can be said to have occupied any space at all. All too often the psychoanalytic clinician will avert her gaze from these reactions, conflating them with childhood trauma, or attributing them to prior pathology or psychic conflict.

As I started to speak about the apparently very rare phenomenon of adult onset trauma to my class, one after another of the candidates looked quite shocked and hands tentatively were raised. At least half of the members of the class had such cases in their current practices. Most, if not all of them, recognized that they had treated such patients at one time or another. A couple of cases were shockingly violent: a man who had been held hostage and tortured for several days; a woman who had made a daring and very frightening escape from a life threatening situation, not knowing from one second to the next whether she would actually find her way to safety or die trying. Other candidates suddenly recalled that, earlier in their training, they had spent months working in rape crisis centers or in the Veterans Administration with combat veterans. How was it that these dramatic stories had not immediately come to mind when I asked about cases of adult onset trauma? The candidates offered several explanations. One talented clinician remembered feeling so badly about the way his work had gone that he had simply pushed it out of his mind. Another suggested that she didn't know how to think about these horrors in psychoanalytic terms.

I shouldn't have been surprised by this encounter, but I was. It was this kind of experience that led me to ask myself whether the treatment of adult onset trauma belongs in psychoanalysis, or, more accurately, whether psychoanalysts can effectively treat those who have suffered massive psychic trauma in adulthood. My answer is no ... and yes. We have the tools but not the theory, a fact born out by one psychoanalyst who commented shortly after the destruction of the World Trade Center that his own psychoanalytic treatment was immensely helpful to him as he worked with survivors, but his analytic thinking was not much help at all (Meyerson, 2001). Cohen (1985), in a volume on treating Holocaust survivors, wrote, "We are dealing with a psychotic experience anchored in reality events, one therefore that psychoanalytic theory may not be equipped to address" (p. 166).

The third candidate in my class volunteered that she and her patient had spent a lot of time speaking about the patient's terrifying experience that had initially led her to seek therapy; it was now part of the background of an ongoing treatment. It had not been dismissed, overlooked, or explained away; its aftermath continued to reverberate through the patient's sense of self, the feeling that she was in some deep and unwelcome way permanently changed by her experience. Nonetheless, with considerable courage on the part of the patient and skill on the part of the analyst, this recognition was becoming integrated into her life and into the treatment.

The adult survivor of a catastrophe—be it an airplane crash, a life threatening assault, an act of terrorism, torture, war or genocide, natural disasters, or an illness presumed to be fatal—frequently finds nonanalytic therapists and self-help groups more open to the psychological consequences of his or her experience. Psychoanalysts, for the most part, maintain an uncomfortable silence on the topic or attempt to understand the reactions in terms of developmental arrests, childhood trauma or conflict. This book considers the uneasy relationship that has existed between psychoanalysis and catastrophic trauma. It is uneasy because psychoanalytic epistemology has traditionally provided few ways of understanding the plight of an adult who has survived a life threatening trauma; it is uneasy because this theoretical shortfall has left some clinicians feeling dissatisfied with their treatment of these patients and often led patients to dismiss their analysts as out of touch; and it is uneasy because those who have worked effectively with survivors often find their own peace of mind has been seriously disrupted by the painful realities they have to entertain.

It is as if psychoanalytic theory itself has denied or dissociated the possibility of lasting reactions to late onset trauma, just as childhood seduction was also denied for much of the last century. This stepchild to psychoanalysis is properly located in Lacan's register of the Real. Events that constantly fail to secure a place in social discourse—slipping out of conscious awareness and defying memory's attempts to register them, leaving instead a gap where understanding might be, or a sense of confusion where clarity might be—belong to the Real. The Real is at work in every act of destructive violence that is rapidly normalized, every instance of genocide that is overlooked, every war whose combatants find no socially acceptable avenue in which to describe their experiences and so are condemned to silence.

Despite the uneasy relationship that has existed between psychoanalysis and adult onset trauma, I hold that among mental health professionals, psychoanalysts should be uniquely situated to work with massive trauma. "A brute appeal to reality can never be the explanatory end of the line," writes Lear (2000, p. xiv). Indeed, there is always a relationship between the survivor's psychodynamics, the psychological impact of the traumatic event itself, the psychological consequences and meaning that event assumes, and current symptoms. To overlook any of these variables and their interaction with one another is to fail the patient. The trauma must be contextualized; if it is given short shrift, as has been the case too often in psychoanalysis, the patient feels misunderstood and blamed, her ordeal minimized. On the other hand, if the trauma is emphasized but its psychic consequences are not considered and understood in and of themselves, which is too often the case in trauma therapy or grief counseling when the patient is given some formulaic explanation for her catastrophically altered perceptions and feeling states, the patient continues to be overwhelmed by aspects of internal experience that have not been articulated and that therefore remain inchoate and incomprehensible. Without words and concepts to capture the inner experience, the patient continues to be silent about subjective aspects of the ordeal, and silenced by the ordeal, fearful and confused. The sense of being alone and isolated—a consequence of the trauma and the legacy of her encounter with the Real—is confirmed rather than repaired by the treatment. Davoine and Gaudillière (2004) emphasize the further dangers of not recognizing and treating adult onset trauma when it is first manifest. The cases they describe trace the passage of catastrophic trauma through the psyches of several generations until it emerges in treatment. Perhaps it is not surprising that these authors are French; they work in a country that has been subjected to wave after wave of hostile occupations and wars affecting civilians as well as soldiers, giving Davoine and Gaudillière all too many opportunities to analyze previously unrecognized wartime trauma as it precipitates out during the treatment of a daughter or grandson.

My purpose in the first half of this book is threefold. First, to make a distinction between childhood and adult onset trauma. Second, to consider why, as Meyerson (2001) previously quoted put it, our analytic thinking is no help at all in this area. And finally, to offer a way of conceptualizing adult onset trauma in psychoanalytic terms that facilitates questions, a way of framing the experience that helps patients feel sufficiently understood so that they are prepared to begin the often terrifying work of coming to terms with the meaning of this catastrophic event that has, in fact, taken meaning out of their lives.

Before turning to psychoanalysis itself, however, it is worth taking a brief detour into psychiatry to see how diagnostic practices have changed in relation to massive psychic trauma. In the late 1970s, an unlikely alliance of Holocaust survivors, Vietnam veterans, and women's movement activists (see Boulanger, 1990; Herman, 1992) lobbied for the inclusion of the diagnosis of Posttraumatic Stress Disorder in DSM III (APA, 1980). An earlier diagnosis of Gross Stress Reaction had been introduced in DSM I (APA, 1952), where it was noted that this reaction "differs from neuroses or psychoses chiefly with respect to clinical history, reversibility of reactions, and its transient character. If the reaction persists," the editors warned, "this term is to be regarded as a temporary diagnosis to be used only until a more definite diagnosis is established" (p. 40). This point of view clearly reflects Freud's (1920) claim, made after World War I, that "most of the neurotic diseases which had been brought about by the war disappeared on the cessation of war conditions." In 1968, with publication of DSM II, the diagnosis of Gross Stress Reaction was subsumed under the category of Transient Situational Disturbances. The editors reiterated that "if the symptoms persist after the stress is removed, the diagnosis of another mental disorder is indicated" (p. 49). Although DSM I and II note that individuals "without apparent underlying mental disorders" (1968, p. 49) could develop acute reactions to overwhelming environmental stress, the emphasis is on the fleeting quality of these disorders. It is an interesting footnote to history that in 1968, the year that DSM II was published, Archibald and Long (1968), among others, confirmed the persistence of stress reactions among combat veterans twenty years after the conclusion of World War II. Subsequent studies with World War II veterans and surveys of combat veterans from Vietnam have found posttraumatic reactions lasting up to thirty years after their return from the war.

The question of whether predisposition plays a role in posttraumatic stress reactions has been the subject of considerable speculation, and different editions of the Diagnostic and Statistical Manuals have taken different positions. Epidemiological studies (Grinker and Spiegel, 1945; Kadushin et al., 1981; Card, 1983; Boulanger, 1986; and Bromet, Sonnega, and Kessler, 1998, among others) and clinical experience (Krystal, 1968; Kardiner, 1969) suggest that, regardless of character type and prior psychopathology, a specific set of symptoms arises in many adults in response to life-threatening trauma, that the likelihood of a psychological reaction increases in proportion to the intensity and duration of the trauma, and that the reactions can last indefinitely. These conclusions are at variance with the psychoanalytic and diagnostic mainstream.

The criteria necessary for the diagnosis of Posttraumatic Stress Disorder listed in DSM III, IIIR, and IV (APA, 1980, 1987, 1994) do not do justice to the pervasive nature of this disorder.[1] The symptoms include

---

[1]The symptoms of Posttraumatic Stress Disorder fall into four categories:

A. Exposure to a traumatic event in which the person experienced, witnessed, or was confronted by an event that threatened death or serious injury, or a threat to the physical integrity of others.

B. The traumatic event is persistently reexperienced through recurrent and intrusive recollections including images, thoughts or perceptions, and nightmares. The person acts or feels as if the event were recurring. There is intense psychological distress at exposure to internal or external cues reminiscent of the event. There is physical reactivity on exposure to these cues.

C. Persistent avoidance of stimuli, including thoughts, activities, and conversations reminiscent of the trauma. Inability to recall aspects of the trauma. Diminished interest in activities that were previously significant, a feeling of detachment from others and restricted range of affect.

D. Symptoms of increased arousal such a sleep disturbance, irritability, difficulty concentrating, hypervigilance, and exaggerated startle reactions. (APA, 1994, pp. 424–429).

recurrent, unbidden thoughts; intrusive visual, and occasionally auditory, memories and dreams about the trauma. Sometimes a memory is
so vivid that it temporarily blots out present reality, causing the survivor
to behave as though she were reliving the trauma. Although the often
catastrophic content of these memories and thoughts are experienced
as uncontrollable, it is not unusual for those who experience them to remain silent about their obsession for fear of being condemned as crazy,
or, by talking about them, increase their intensity. To the survivor, these
memories are frequently more real than the present moment; consequently, she feels out of touch with the world, as if the daily concerns of
other people have little meaning in the face of the momentous and very
private experiences she is constantly reliving.

In an attempt to restore balance to the psychic economy, events that
might trigger memories of the trauma, such as movies, particular loca-
tions, or groups of people who have had similar experiences, are often
avoided by survivors. The survivor is not always aware of this avoidant
behavior; it is locked out of consciousness, along with the significance
of the trauma.

Despite the considerable media attention given to this topic in recent
years, and its increased visibility since the 2001 terrorist attacks in the
United States, it is not uncommon to hear survivors deny that the disaster
they survived had or should have had any impact on their lives. The overall
effect of these symptoms is a determined disregard for what was the most
shattering event in the survivor's life. Paradoxically, in her attempt to belong and to forget, the survivor becomes increasingly disenfranchised.

One of the most difficult aspects of detecting the symptoms of massive psychic trauma is that they are not immediately observable and they
are rarely volunteered. Many patients fail to mention intrusive imagery,
fearing that they are hallucinating. The avoidant symptoms and denial
are passive symptoms; often the survivor does not recognize a pattern
of avoidant behavior or feels too self-conscious to mention particular
phobic behaviors, unless these behaviors are directly inquired into. As
my early encounters with Ellen, described in Chapter 6, attest,
posttraumatic responses are easy to overlook. Furthermore, the longer
the symptoms go untreated, the more entrenched they become, over-
laying and interacting with earlier character traits and conflicts, becoming chronic in themselves, giving rise to depression and hopelessness as
the survivor finds she has become unrecognizable to her former self.

Although the introduction of the diagnosis of Posttraumatic Stress
Disorder in 1981 was an important milestone in acknowledging the

long reach of adult onset trauma, with overuse and misuse the diagnosis is in danger of becoming a cliché. Since its introduction, it has given rise to a veritable industry of research, an avalanche of papers based on that research, national and international organizations devoted to the study of catastrophic trauma, and the commodification of trauma therapy and training in a range of treatments from Eye Movement Desensitization and Reprocessing (EMDR) to Critical Incident Stress Debriefing (CISD) to grief counseling. At the time the diagnosis was introduced, psychoanalysts appeared relatively aloof to the phenomenon. This book is not about Posttraumatic Stress Disorder *per se*, but there is some overlap between the syndrome described in DSM III, IIIR and IV (APA 1980, 1987, 1994) and the far-reaching consequences of adult onset trauma.

As a graduate student in clinical psychology in search of a dissertation topic, in 1976 I joined a team of social psychologists, sociologists, political scientists, and anthropologists who had been asked by a small group of Vietnam veterans to undertake an epidemiological study of Vietnam veterans and their civilian cohort. It was an ambitious undertaking at that time, comparing the postwar adjustment of Vietnam veterans with their nonveteran peers in terms of social and marital relations, educational and occupational achievements, substance use and abuse, and psychological problems. A grant from The National Institutes of Mental Health enabled the first 300 men to be interviewed, and six months later the Veterans Administration asked us to add a further 1,000 men from several key urban, suburban, and rural sites across the country (Kadushin et al., 1981). I was particularly interested in what had caused the psychological breakdown of so many Vietnam veterans on their return home; I wanted to understand this Post Vietnam Syndrome, as it was called at the time. My plan met with considerable resistance from the chair of my program, who said that this topic was not appropriate for a clinical psychologist; it should be left to social workers and sociologists. Although I prevailed, I was left with the feeling that the topic I had picked had marked me as an outsider; it was slightly off color. I wavered between fascination with what I was discovering about the veterans whose transcripts I read and a sense of shame about this fascination. Shame is a fertile breeding ground for the Real. I now know that this sense of shame is not unusual among psychoanalytic researchers and clinicians that push beyond the accepted epistemological boundaries in their search for understanding.

At the time, I did not intend to push beyond the accepted epistemological boundaries. Consistent with my traditionally psychodynamic graduate training, I was sure that I would find predisposing factors leading to the psychological disorder I was attempting to measure. The working papers for DSM III (APA, 1980) were made available to me, listing the symptoms of the proposed diagnosis for Posttraumatic Stress Disorder. I constructed a scale with these symptoms and others listed in a study of World War II veterans, *Men Under Stress* (Grinker and Spiegel, 1945), those I gleaned from reading *Massive Psychic Trauma* (Krystal, 1968), and from the work of Kardiner (1969). When I analyzed the data, I did find a statistically robust syndrome that measured long-term stress reactions as distinct from anxiety and depression. I also found an interaction between certain levels of predisposition and exposure to low or moderate levels of combat. That is to say that at low levels of combat, those with the greatest vulnerability developed symptoms of long-term stress reactions, and at moderate levels of combat those with moderate levels of vulnerability also developed symptoms. But, in the end, my hypothesis was wrong: at the highest levels of combat, predisposition played no role in determining who would later develop stress symptoms (Kadushin et al., 1981, Boulanger, 1985, Boulanger and Kadushin, 1986). As Grinker and Spiegel (1945) concluded their World War II classic *Men Under Stress*, "every man had his breaking point" (p. 44).

Trying to understand these findings led me to reevaluate what I had been taught about the durability of psychic structure and the importance of interpreting external events through the lens of the drives and their derivatives, and set me on a course to formulate an understanding that would do justice to the subjective sense of psychic collapse with which so many survivors I interviewed struggled, and to which some of them submitted.

Anna Freud (1967) warned against confusing a traumatic event with traumatic neurosis. The word trauma presents a hermeneutic conundrum signifying both an event and the reaction to which that event gives rise. The conflation of stimulus and response, of the external event and its internal consequences, appears to anticipate psychoanalysts' own reluctance to privilege external events, for classical psychoanalysts have consistently argued that it is the meaning or the response to an event that is traumatic, not the event itself. Thus, they switch their gaze from the external world of occasional uncontrollable and unanticipated violence to an internal world of fantasies and associations that can be safely interpreted and, hopefully, tamed. And yet this semantic instability is oddly prescient for, in fact, massive psychic trauma does collapse the distinction between the world without and the world within; nightmares and violent fantasies suddenly find their equivalent in external events, leading to the collapse of psychic space and foreclosing the mind's ability to reflect. In Chapter 7, I explore the consequences of being struck thoughtless in this way and the therapeutic engagement necessary to promote the recovery of symbolic function. Further, trauma, this indeterminate term, seems to hover between the need to define the event and the impossibility of words, let alone measures, to capture its meaning.

The very word trauma has been stretched so thin in psychoanalytic circles as to have become almost meaningless. It is used to designate events of widely differing significance. Drawing attention to the careless overuse of the word in psychoanalytic circles, Anna Freud (1967) asks whether trauma means that an event is "upsetting, that is, significant for altering the course of further development," or whether the word should not be reserved for those events that are "shattering, devastating, causing internal disruption by putting the ego function and ego at risk" (p. 238)? Similarly, Krystal (1978) comments on the frequent error in psychoanalysis when that which is pathogenic is confused with something shattering. In this book, I use the terms trauma, catastrophic trauma, massive psychic trauma, and adult onset trauma interchangeably to signify what Krystal refers to as "extreme circumstances of traumatization—disasters, catastrophes and overwhelming social situations" (p. 1). In Chapter 2, I explore other ways in which the term is used by psychoanalysts and further refine the way in which I intend it.

On September 11, 2001, the terrorist attacks on the World Trade Center and the Pentagon changed the relationship of many New York psychoanalysts to adult onset trauma. An interest in disasters and the extremes of human experience—that had at best appeared arcane and at worst irrelevant in the apparently orderly and often elitist world in which many psychoanalysts in the United States of America practiced—suddenly became frighteningly relevant. Psychodynamic clinicians threw themselves into the immediate postterrorist attack work, rising to the overwhelming need to offer support to survivors, to the families of the missing, and to relief workers. In New York, there were constant appeals for mental health volunteers to meet with families as they searched hospital records for missing relatives. Licensed professionals were sought to support husbands, wives, children, and parents as they came to terms with the fact that there would never be a body to bury, that only a death certificate and perhaps a small urn containing ashes from Ground Zero would bring some type of closure to this period of uncertainty. Volunteers spoke with firefighters or police or medical examiners overwhelmed by their personal losses and the grisly tasks that they were being asked to perform. Other professionals were invited to debrief corporations trying to get on with business as usual, where managers and workers alike feared that the world would never be usual again. This painful work came on top of the ongoing treatment of regular patients, some of whom had previously experienced other, more private, catastrophes in their own lives. For them, the analytic work took on new urgency. With other patients, the struggle was to incorporate some acknowledgment of this new reality into ongoing work, even while the analysts themselves shared their patients' terror of imminent destruction.

Since the terrorist attacks, many psychoanalytic books and articles have been published describing work not only with the immediate survivors of the attacks or with the survivors of those who died or with first responders, but also with bystanders, with New Yorkers who understandably felt particularly vulnerable, if not panicked, following the attacks. Already I find that I must refine my definition of adult onset trauma. Certainly the work with these bystander patients often changed in the aftermath of the terrorist attacks. Articles published shortly after the attack (Goldman, 2002; Goldman et al., 2002; Cabaniss, Forand, and Roose, 2003; Frawley-O'Dea, 2003; Stimmel, 2003) described the impact on the treatment when both patient and analyst had experienced the same trauma. Sometimes the process of treatment accelerated, bringing the defenses into sharp relief, increasing dependency, changing the nature of the transference, at least temporarily, when patient and analyst both acknowledged their sense of danger, perhaps demonstrating a mutual caring that the work had not previously revealed.

The destruction of the World Trade Center was, indeed, a shocking event for most New Yorkers, as was the destruction of the Pentagon in Washington. Indeed, the impact was felt throughout the world, although New Yorkers and Washingtonians felt most immediately implicated. Whether they saw the attack from close by or from afar or, dumbstruck, followed the events on television in real time, only to get caught in a perpetual feedback loop, for weeks on end the traumatic scenes intruded into every waking moment via television, radio, newspapers, and daily social encounters. For many the acrid smell of the smoke mixed with the sweet smell of death was a dreadful reminder whenever there was a temptation to imagine that life could return to normal. We were terrified. We no longer lived in a safe and predictable world. However, *we were shocked; we were not traumatized.* I reserve the term trauma for those who were actually caught up in the terror at Ground Zero and thought that they were in danger of losing their lives, for the families of those who were killed, and for the first responders who were exposed to the carnage at Ground Zero.

Although some authors failed to distinguish between being confronted with death and the fear of death, others reassuringly normalized the experience. Stimmel (2003) wrote of her belief that the memories of September 11 would find an unconscious context among the memories of other "less heralded days on which, for example, siblings were born, relationships ended, unwanted sexual and sadistic wishes intruded" (p. 11). It is a comforting belief that the effects of massive psychic trauma can be reduced to sibling rivalry or the pain of separation. However, it is my thesis, to be developed in the course of this book, that being confronted with the unimaginable terror of annihilation (not a symbolic death but actual and sudden extinction) is a different order of psychic experience from sibling rivalry or separation anxiety. And it demands a different level of understanding.

Psychoanalysts are not alone in their overly inclusive definitions of trauma. Social scientists, medical researchers, and epidemiologists also make the common error of confusing bystanders to a catastrophe with first responders and those who have survived the catastrophe itself (see, for example, Galea et al., 2002). Other researchers, for example Bonano (2004), use the word trauma to refer both to exposure to a violent and life-threatening situation and to the (presumably nonviolent) death of a close relation. Blum (2003) warns against this common temptation of confusing natural object loss and shock trauma; "The predictable and temporal phenomena of grief and mourning may overlap with the effects of psychic trauma, but are quite different. Trauma without object loss is a different clinical syndrome with different intrapsychic processes, though with overlap and interwoven features" (p. 423).

It would be unfortunate to leave the impression that no psychoanalysts have tackled this difficult subject. Many have worked effectively with such patients for years, but for the most part they have worked in isolation. I am aware of colleagues who treat political refugees seeking asylum in this country and others working with victims of police brutality, with women who have been raped, and with parents whose children have been murdered. Those working with Vietnam veterans have gained striking insights into the long term impact of both meting out and witnessing violence; others, returning from the former Yugoslavia, are formulating the experiences they had in working with survivors there. Some of this work is undertaken in traditional individual and group settings, but sometimes the practitioners have used less traditional ways, such as art therapy and theater, to get their patients to explore the psychodynamic consequences of their ordeal.

In this book, I propose a psychodynamic understanding of the corrosive effects of massive psychic trauma. I draw on the pioneering work of a few classical psychoanalysts who bravely tackled this subject in the shadow of the Shoah and World War II, on the rash of publications that have appeared since the terrorist attacks, on work that colleagues have shared with me, and on my own work with a range of patients that I have treated or whose cases I have supervised in the last twenty-five years.

In the next chapter, I contrast the various uses to which the word trauma has been put throughout the lifespan, but with particular attention to adult onset trauma. This book is based on the premise that psychoanalytic theory and practice have made a serious error in eliding the consequences of massive psychic trauma experienced in adulthood with early childhood experience. As Reisner (2003a) puts it, "the story of childhood trauma is the Ur story of psychoanalysis" (p. 280). However, acknowledging childhood trauma should not preempt the study of adult onset trauma.

In reexamining the consequences of childhood trauma, relational analysts have returned to the notion of dissociation, which played such a brief role in the early history of psychoanalysis that it is not even mentioned in the LaPlanche and Pontalis (1973) lexicon of psychoanalytic terms (Blum, 2003, p. 418). Chapter 2 contrasts the consequences of dissociation in childhood with catastrophic dissociation in adulthood. The difference between the two has far reaching implications for self-experience, for the experience of self with other, and for the storage and retrieval of traumatic memories. Just as dissociation plays a powerful role in forming a child's perception of the world and her objects, it de-forms an adult's self-perception. Memory takes a different path, dependent on whether the trauma occurred in childhood or adulthood. And traumatic experience is metabolized differently in children, where it is absorbed into different self states, whereas in adults the traumatic memory is not metabolized but often remains psychically indigestible. This chapter also explores the intimate relationship between the fear of annihilation and adult onset trauma.

Chapter 3 reviews the ways in which the symptoms of adult onset trauma have been misunderstood in analytic theory and practice. Classical metapsychological assumptions about where a traumatic event originates, about the role of agency, the place of contingency, the durability of psychic structure, and the authority of the past, render adult onset trauma virtually incomprehensible to many psychoanalytic practitioners. Thus, the costs of survival are born not only by the patient, who has been through a catastrophic event, but also by the clinician, who struggles to find a way of acknowledging her patient's experience.

Relational psychoanalytic practice, with its emphasis on dialectical construction and multiple meaning, with its increasing willingness to give contingency its due, and with its questioning of the psychoanalytic imperative that locates all powerful experience in the past, appears to be in a unique position to undertake the analysis of adult onset catastrophic states. In Chapter 4, I review these theoretical changes and describe recent research into the chemical and biological consequences of trauma. Together with advances in developmental and cognitive psychology, these findings offer a different perspective on the psychodynamics and consequences of abrupt changes in adult life.

There are many lenses through which to view the symptoms of adult onset trauma. Some refer to a collapsed self, an ego in tatters; others point to the destruction of internal ties; others focus on the loss of the capacity to fantasize, the concrete and repetitive dreams, the unnameability of experience. The survivor has exchanged the sense of a more or less continuous self or selves for an unfamiliar mortal self for whom time stands still. She has lost the capacity to experience a range of affects, of senses on which she could rely. She has given up her capacity to reflect for concreteness, her ability to relate for a restricted and treacherous emotional field. In Chapters 5, 6, and 7, the loss of these functions and their consequences, both individually and for treatment, are considered.

In Chapter 5, I identify several fundamental aspects of self experience that are essential to psychological development, and that are constantly rearticulated and elaborated throughout the developmental process (and beyond). These senses are mutually dependent on one another, and contribute to the maintenance of homeostasis. When the senses of agency, physical cohesion, psychosomatic collusion, affectivity, and continuity come under attack during the actual trauma, catastrophic dissociation becomes an assault on the core self. Once the core self's support systems have been disconnected during the trauma, survivors frequently find that they cannot be reconnected seamlessly. This disaggregated self experiences a chronic sense of paralysis, numbness, disruption of the sense of time, and a feeling of rupture with the self who existed before the crisis.

In focusing on the profound impact of catastrophic trauma on the internal object world, Chapter 6, which is also the first of four clinical chapters, considers psychodynamic work with survivors of adult onset trauma. For the relational analyst, therapeutic action lies in the intersubjective, yet intersubjective space is often rendered uninhabitable by catastrophic trauma. Survivors who live in an internal world populated by persecutory part objects, who have lost their belief in the possibility of benign ties, and whose sense of their own subjectivity has been seriously compromised, enter treatment with little hope of recovery and little notion of what recovery means. How can these patients, who are so fearful of developing new ties, be engaged in a treatment that they fear will expose them to further harm?

Chapter 7, the second clinical chapter, deals with the difficulties for both analyst and patient when the Real invades and deadens the thinking process, when symbolic thought is compromised by massive trauma. Survivors of massive psychic trauma frequently experience deficits in symbolic functioning affecting the capacity to dream, to entertain fantasies and to think productively. Clinicians working with survivors can also find themselves struck thoughtless, unable to reflect on the horrors their patients describe. I suggest that the clinician's initial incoherence might be a necessary condition of the healing process when analysts work with this population. It is in the struggle to overcome this state and to become thinking professionals again that they can start to bear witness to the patient's experience. Through this work with the clinician's containing presence, the survivor ceases to be a mute observer to her own losses, recaptures her thinking self, begins to inhabit her own narrative, and becomes a witness to her own survival.

Although it has become fashionable to speak of the analyst as bearing witness to the survivor's experience, I consider the implications of bearing witness whether as an analyst or survivor. I argue that this necessary aspect of the recovery process must not become its endpoint; it is equally important to move beyond this witnessing to a life that acknowledges the trauma but is not lived by it.

Finding a way to speak about trauma without sounding hysterical or overly intellectual, or minimizing it in some other way, presents patient and clinician alike with an ongoing challenge. In Chapter 8, I distinguish between safe and lifeless narratives, that numb clinician and patient alike, and therapeutic narratives, that come alive and grow. Whether it is in a memoir, a biography, or a narrative spoken to a therapist, finding the words to describe a catastrophe, to relive it, and ultimately to engage its many meanings is no small feat. This chapter considers the difficulty of using words when words themselves threaten to retraumatize. How do patients move from being voyeurs, separated from their own experience, to witnesses who can speak meaningfully and fully about that experience? In this third clinical chapter, I describe a patient who believed she could not share her experiences with anyone for fear of doing to them the damage that she had sustained; at the same time, she needed to preserve her memories in order to honor those she had witnessed dying. An extended transcript, recorded over the course of several months, demonstrates the way in which narrative can move from a lifeless and deadening repetition to one that is full, almost unbearably full of personal meaning.

In working with the survivors of massive psychic trauma, the psychoanalytic clinician often meets with considerable resistance from her patients. Technically, the term resistance is reserved for those words and actions that impede the expression of unconscious material; however, survivors are frequently resistant to reliving the traumatic experience. For every form of resistance the survivor can summon, the analyst has to struggle against her own resistance, against the fear of facing up to her own vulnerability to psychic trauma. This countertransference can take many forms. Chapter 9, the fourth and final clinical chapter, identifies several different types of countertransference that clinicians experience in the face of their survivor patients' resistance. Sometimes the countertransference is unconscious, masked by a strict adherence to theory or technique, at other times it is conscious, born of the conviction that the survivor has already suffered enough or that the suffering is contagious.

The final chapter will consider the larger field of psychological politics, battles fought around metapsychology, distance, closeness, gratification, and control. Little appears to have changed in the years since Kardiner (1969) wrote of the utter confusion that massive psychic trauma generated in psychiatric circles: "There is practically no continuity to be found anywhere, and the literature can only be characterized as anarchic" (p. 245). In this concluding chapter, I consider the ways in which the diagnosis of posttraumatic stress disorder has been put to commercial and political use, frequently demeaning the experience of survivors and distorting treatment options. Whether it is research that concludes that treating survivors is unnecessary and potentially damaging or, at the other extreme, companies that insist that all their employees exposed to a "critical incident" must be debriefed, or the Department of Defense vacillating between calling traumatized veterans cowards and arguing that there is a means of preventing the disorder among combat troops, the field is characterized by confusion and conflicting agendas. I consider our responsibility as psychoanalysts to the survivors of massive psychic trauma. How do we enter these debates and what can we contribute to them?

I begin the next chapter with the case of Jonah and follow his story through several chapters. Jonah's is, by no means, the most horrifying story that I have heard, but that is precisely why I start here. The police raid on Jonah's building did not make headlines in the local papers; very few people were aware of this incident of police brutality. In the neighborhood where it happened, it was rapidly swallowed up by subsequent news about gentrification and drug raids. Although this book is being published several years after the terrorist attacks first alerted many psychoanalysts to the importance of being able to work with adult onset trauma, it is important to remember that cases like Jonah's, or Ellen's that I describe in Chapter 6, often present themselves in our practices. It does not take a national disaster to fall prey to adult onset trauma. In later chapters, I describe several patients and the work that I did with them. I follow several of these patients from chapter to chapter as different aspects of their treatment become germane to the discussion. In each case, I have taken pains to conceal the identity of the patients and, where it has been possible, I have obtained permission to discuss the work that we did together.

2

Catastrophic Dissociation and Childhood Trauma: Some Distinctions

At present there is no way of conceptualizing the nature of infantile trauma and its relationship to the adult form.

— H. Krystal (1978, p. 81)

Jonah, a 41-year-old, moderately successful businessman, had been living in New York for five years when he came to my office. He was referred by friends, who were troubled by his sudden moodiness and uncharacteristic isolation. Eighteen months earlier, Jonah had been attending a party on the roof of his upscale apartment building in the East Village. Towards the end of the evening, the partygoers watched as the police battered down the door of an abandoned building in order to evict the squatters who had taken up residence there. When he was told that the police had now turned their attention to his own building and were battering down the front door, Jonah, the president of his building's co-op, left the roof in order to go downstairs to "straighten things out." As he reached the fourth floor, he heard "the noise of soldiers, many boots stamping." Suddenly he was facing dozens of policemen in riot gear who pushed him up against the wall; some held guns to his head, cursing him and screaming that he shouldn't move, while others demanded that he lie down. "I didn't know what to do, they were out of control. I thought if I lie down they will shoot me and if I keep standing the others will shoot me. This is the end; I'm going to die here," he recalled thinking. After several police hit him with nightsticks, another crashed a riot shield into his head and threw him down to the next landing. He was crouching there, hoping to crawl to his own apartment, when he saw the building's young handyman literally flying toward him, his eyes wide with terror. "That's what I keep seeing over and over again," he told me, "the terror in Fred's eyes and the guns pointed at my head. I see them in my sleep, I see them during the day; these scenes just come into my mind. If someone says 'East Village' or if I hear of any violence, I feel it happening again."

As he was telling me of his ordeal, Jonah lost eye contact with me. His breathing became perceptibly shallow, but his affect was quite flat. The memory of the event appeared to have been seared into his mind's eye. "I can't cast a shadow over it," he said. For Jonah, as for many other adult survivors of massive trauma, the memories are not mediated by subsequent events; they remain intact, in an endless feedback loop, as if time has stood still. "Time has gone," is how Jonah described his life since the assault. "I am in a dead end. It's like you are walking along and suddenly you hit a wall. You can't go back and you can't go forward; you keep hitting the wall. I used to be more interested in what is going on. Now I don't go out. I don't read the paper in case I read of violence. I don't watch television … I have lost hope of things being different. … I am emotionally devastated. … I have lost my soul."

Before the police broke into his building, Jonah appeared to have been functioning well. He had a good job in which he was advancing "on schedule;" he had a circle of close friends; he was thinking of proposing to a woman he had been dating for 18 months; he was an athlete who played team sports and had run in marathons for several years. Now, a year and a half later, he is a recluse. His job gives him no satisfaction and he is getting a reputation for being unduly irritable; his girlfriend has broken up with him; his closest friends treat him like an invalid.

Jonah was deeply ashamed of his collapse and made the appointment to see me with reluctance. He could not understand what had happened to him. He was not sure if this dramatic change in his sense of self could really be attributed to the assault. If it could, he felt unmanned by it. He believed he should have been able to rise above it. Despite the traumatic change in his sense of himself, his symptoms were very private; few people recognized the extent of the crisis he was facing.

How am I to understand Jonah's condition? If I subscribe to Arlow's (1984) definition that psychoanalysis is fundamentally a psychology of conflict and that the psychoanalytic situation "is skewed in the direction of facilitating the emergence into consciousness of derivatives of persistent, unconscious conflicts that originated during childhood" (p. 525), I have few choices. Rather than attending to Jonah's detailed account of the beating and his subsequent symptoms, the intrusive imagery, the conscious avoidance of any stimuli that remind him of his attackers, his hypervigilance, and profoundly altered sense of self, I would assume that the assault reactivated an unconscious conflict whose psychic reality outweighs current reality and that it is this conflict alone that is, in fact, immobilizing him. For example, I would ask myself if the assault unleashed a conflict about his aggressive impulses that, until that time, had been successfully repressed. Did the beating at the hands of the police represent an earlier traumatic scene, one that had perhaps been successfully repressed or dissociated? Did the apparently successful course he had been on—a high paying and interesting job, a wife, eventually a family—represent an oedipal victory over his depressed father who had been less successful in love and work? These are among the choices that psychoanalytic epistemology has offered clinicians treating adult survivors of violence and horror whose reaction lasts much beyond the termination of the traumatic circumstances. Furst (1967) summarized the decision many analysts come to about how to proceed in such cases when he wrote, "Adult trauma can best be approached as a later edition of the childhood model and the same metapsychological variables may be applied to both" (p. 36).

Jonah's symptoms are typical of the posttraumatic state: intrusive memories of the beating and consequent avoidance of anything that might remind him of it, recurrent dreams that replay the events of that evening exactly as they occurred, the disruption of his sense of time and of his interpersonal relationships, feelings of numbness and loss of interest in the world around him. Today analysts working with patients who, as adults, have confronted almost certain death—be it an airplane crash, a life threatening assault, an act of terrorism, torture, war, genocide, or "an act of God"—often hear their patients claiming that their lives have been profoundly, and sometimes irreversibly, changed. In general, these analysts find that taking adult onset trauma seriously not only challenges many of the fundamental assumptions on which psychoanalytic theory is based, but also their own preconceptions about the durability of psychic structure and the nature of psychic reality come under careful scrutiny.

Adult onset trauma turns our attention to the outside world and suggests that psychic experience can be profoundly altered independently of dynamic conflict, motivation, structural defect, and developmental arrest.

Despite recent advances in the recognition and treatment of the traumas of childhood, adult onset trauma continues to be overlooked in psychoanalytic metapsychology. Throughout this book, I argue that it is important not to conflate the consequences of traumas that occur in childhood with those faced by adults who have survived catastrophes.

One way in which traumatic experiences in adulthood and in childhood mutually implicate one another in classical theory is through the concept of *nachtraglichkeit*, later interpreted by Lacan as *après coup*. According to this concept, a current traumatic event suddenly throws an earlier experience, one that had not originally been experienced as traumatic, into sharp relief. The "future and past condition signify each other reciprocally in the structuring of the present" (Baranger, Baranger, and Mom, 1988, p. 115). I do not question the workings of *nachtraglichkeit* when a particular loss or disappointment in adolescence or adulthood throws a different perspective on an earlier experience, one that has previously not been available for analytic reflection. However, when the trauma in adult life involves terror rather than anxiety, *nachtraglichkeit* is not sufficient to understand its impact. Earlier experiences of anxiety do not find their equivalent in later experiences of terror. In the previous chapter. I cited Stimmel (2003), who invoked the concept of *après coup* to argue that the reactions of those who had been traumatized by the terrorist attacks would fade into earlier hurts. I argued that Stimmel was making a common error in her formulation by failing to distinguish between separation anxiety and sibling anxiety on the one hand and the real life terror of annihilation on the other. Schermer (2003) calls this "clinical whitewashing" (p. 204).

Subjectively and metapsychologically, then, adult onset trauma requires careful consideration in its own right. If this position is not clearly understood, adults who have survived catastrophes are in danger of being situated beyond the reach of effective psychoanalytic practice. Furthermore, the consequences of unacknowledged and untreated adult onset trauma can be passed from parent to child, rippling through later generations, gaining rather than losing toxicity, as they get further and further from the original source of trauma.

One of the difficulties in defining trauma as a psychoanalyst is that the nature of what is considered traumatic varies throughout the life span. For a baby, breaks in the continuity of maternal care can, depending on the duration and frequency of these breaks, become catastrophic losses with serious consequences for the developing child and developed adult. Despite increasingly sophisticated infant observation and experimental studies, we imagine—for we have no way of knowing what the baby is actually feeling—that the baby feels helplessness and despair. (This is what Piers, in press, calls "frontloading," that is "positing starting conditions of mind, often in post hoc fashion, to account for emergent phenomena,"). Depending on our orientation, we argue that the threat of annihilation experienced at this moment is overwhelming and will echo through later moments *in extremis*. In words that capture the traumatic state certainly as adults describe it, but also as he intuited infants experience it, Winnicott (1974) most graphically describes this condition. He writes of the "primitive agonies", feelings of falling forever, of falling to pieces, losing the relationship between body and mind, the loss of continuity and, to these he later added, having no means of communicating with another. I consider these feelings as they are manifest in adult onset trauma in Chapters 5 and 6, but here I focus on the fate of the traumatized infant and child as distinguished from the traumatized adult.

For close to seventy years, analysts (Freud, 1926; Krystal, 1968, 1985, 1988; Greenacre, 1967; Rangell, 1967; Tarantelli, 2003; to cite only a few) have compared the adult's subjective experience during a trauma to the state of helplessness in infancy. Greenacre (1967) addresses the theory behind this when she points out that the traumatized adult has fallen back on pre-ego mechanisms since the ego is temporarily unable to function due to the overwhelming nature of the trauma. However, Anna Freud (1967) makes a crucial distinction and one that I adopt here: "the infant is an undifferentiated being, *he experiences distress, not trauma* in the strict sense of the word. But this distress of the infant is probably identical with the older being's helplessness before recovery from the trauma" (pp. 231–232, italics added). Phenomenologically, then, Ms. Freud is arguing that the experience of helplessness may be the same, but we should bear in mind the difference between the infant's undifferentiated state and adult's ego that, to use her words, "has been shattered out of commission" (p. 238) by the trauma. This is an important distinction because, as I argue, the adult ego is indeed shattered and cannot be reassembled as it was originally. Blum (1986) and

Tarantelli (2003) both stress the importance of distinguishing between the adult experience of catastrophic trauma and primitive traumas where the organism has undergone an experience which endangers its existence without having the capacity to structure a defense. "Prior to ego differentiation the concept of psychic trauma may not be applicable, it would be more appropriate to think of organismic trauma and distress" (Tarantelli, 2003, p. 25). Yorke (1986) further suggests that the term infantile helplessness does not do justice to the internal disruption an adult experiences, and, like Ms. Freud, he argues that "when the [adult] ego is overwhelmed in traumatic neurosis, it is not simply flooded with pervasive anxiety. It is totally knocked out in a flood of excitation" (p. 3).

Krystal (1988) traces the shift from the infant to the adult form of trauma, pointing out not only the difference that comes from increasing cognitive ability but also the different defenses that come into play. He writes, "The adult form of psychic trauma comes to the fore with the development of ego functions and the ability to mobilize such defenses as denial, depersonalization, and derealization" (p. 167). However, Krystal is distinguishing between the feelings of helplessness to which infants may be subject and the terror adults feel when confronted with traumatic situations, in this instance he is not directly addressing the situation of children who are traumatized. Later, making the distinction between children and adults, Krystal points out that, intellectually, an adult can appreciate the danger of an unavoidable situation and its potential consequences. Recognizing the terror of the situation, the adult automatically retreats from the sense of helplessness by numbing physical and psychological pain, whereas children are overwhelmed by the intolerable affect to which the situation gives rise.

THE SEDUCTION OF CHILDREN

When Roberta first sought treatment, she was concerned about her failure to find a satisfying relationship, and she remarked that she was feeling increasingly "spacey" during the day. Roberta was a full-time graduate student working part time to augment her student loans. A strikingly beautiful 30-year-old woman, Roberta had had a series of intense love affairs. These affairs ended either with the man walking away in disgust from the neediness Roberta could not hide and which she loathed in herself, or when she "went on the attack," suddenly finding herself enraged at some flaw in the man's character. Roberta was tenderly attached to her sickly mother and quite fearful of her violent father, although she also knew that he admired her spunk.

Within a few weeks of beginning treatment, Roberta became panicked when her boss came up behind her suddenly to ask her something. Barely managing to make an excuse, she ran out of the office and was terrified to return. In the sessions that followed this encounter, she began to piece together a jumble of memories and a recurrent dream, occurring with more frequency now, in which a shaft of light falls on her bed, waking her with a feeling of dread. She remembered that, as a very little child, she had slept in her parent's bed with her father, while her mother went to sleep in the guest bedroom. She remembered her mother's towering rages at her and at her father, and she started to have physical sensations between her legs and in her anus and vagina. Roberta had been orgasmic as long as she could remember. The first time she discovered the feeling was when she was riding her rocking horse in her nursery and found that, by gripping with her thighs just so and rubbing back and forth while the horse rocked, she could feel wonderful.

Over a number of sessions, we were able to construct a picture of the time Roberta and her father spent in bed together. Although we would never know for sure what happened, corroborating evidence came when Roberta was told for the first time, later that year, that her father had molested her slightly older female cousins. As her cousins' children were now approaching the age they had been when their uncle had started to "play games" with them, their own memories of abuse had surfaced. They created a family feud when they confronted their parents and uncle to ensure the safety of their own children.

Graduate studies represented an area of conflict-free functioning, but when it came to her relationships with men Roberta felt increasingly out of control. From a safe distance, she longed for them, saying she felt like a tiny child seeking their protection. But when she met a new man, she would become very fearful. Exchanging a smile or a couple of innocuous sentences at the supermarket or in the gym would lead to elaborate fantasies about their plans to follow her home and rape her. She would break out in a sweat, leave the gym or supermarket as quickly as possible, sometimes even abandoning her shopping cart at the checkout counter, rush home, lock the door and refuse to answer the telephone or the door bell for a couple of days until she had calmed down. At other times, when she was confident that she had won a man's devotion, she would become haughty, contemptuous, and cruel, taunting him with his desire for closeness and sex, forcing him to beg. In one self state, she was a temptress whose sexual competence enhanced her self esteem. In another, she was a needy child looking for a strong man to father her responsibly, or a defenseless child waiting to be preyed upon by a relentless predator. In yet another self state, she was a disgusting child whose mother had understandably turned away from her, and in the complement to this, she was her mother gazing in disgust at anyone who expressed neediness.

Like the story of Jonah, I describe this case not because it is the worst case of childhood sexual abuse, but because it contains elements that are common to many such cases. There is the betrayal by a caretaker, the failure of another caretaker to offer protection, confusion about what was being asked of her and what had, in fact, happened. Finally, as I briefly describe, there is an uncanny way in which the key elements of this story are enacted repeatedly in other relationships and in the transference.

In attempting to define the parameters and consequences of childhood trauma as opposed to states of infantile distress, psychoanalytic metapsychology has gone through several reversals in the course of its history. When Freud (1914) denounced his seduction theory, privileging the role of fantasy over the role of the environment, or, to use Ferenczi's (1933) word, over *exogenous causes*, for many years, as Laplanche and Pontalis (1973) point out, the term trauma became synonymous with frustration in the life of children. When the word trauma was used in psychoanalytic literature for much of the 20th century, most often it referred to cumulative (Khan, 1975) or childhood trauma, indicating a profound sense of helplessness, fears of abandonment, narcissistic injuries, early losses, and—in the past twenty years—early sexual trauma.

The relational turn in psychoanalysis was, in part, driven by a number of psychoanalysts who wrote cogently about confronting the realities and consequences of sexual abuse in childhood (Davies and Frawley, 1994; Alpert, 1995; Gartner, 1997; and Bromberg,1998; among them). Indeed this rich and informative body of work has reintroduced trauma to psychoanalysis, reminding us that our field was initially constituted by Breuer's and Freud's (1895) observations about the psyche's failure to metabolize an external event.

When the concept of dissociation was reintroduced into psychodynamic discourse by these same psychoanalysts, ending almost a hundred years' banishment, it quite literally turned analytic theory on its ear. This concept suggests that instead of repressing unacceptable thoughts, feelings, and experiences horizontally in the unconscious, these thoughts, feelings, and experiences are split off and stored vertically in multiple, discontinuous self states.

Using dissociation to understand childhood trauma has revolutionized the psychoanalytic treatment and understanding of adults who were abused as children and, at the same time, paradoxically returned psychoanalysis to its roots in Freud's and Breuer's (1895) earliest psychoanalytic investigations. Relational analysts (Davies and Frawley, 1994; Davies, 1997; and Bromberg, 1998; among them) contend that when a child is abused, she defensively dissociates in the face of her terror, her confusion, and the unmanageable stimulation she is experiencing, forming split-off self states encapsulating the entire set of traumatic self and object representations, leaving other self states free to engage a less threatening world. Thus, Roberta achieves considerable success in graduate school; she experiences herself there as effective and in charge. But around men she is successively the seductress who is, nonetheless, seeking a strong father; the confused child who is being asked to give more than she can understand; an adult woman, identified with her mother and disgusted by a man who expresses any needs. In this way, part of the child's developing mental structure comes to represent the traumatic experience, and her subsequent dealings with the world bear the trauma's thumbprint. Memories of the traumatic encounters are manifest in the constellation of object relations particular to the abused self state. In treatment, as Davies (1997) points out: "We don't hunt for traumatic memories but attempt to reengage traumatic object relationships" (p. 7). Roberta and I worked our way repeatedly through many of these shifts in self states as I became alternately the punitive mother to her pained child, the pained child to her punitive mother, the frightened child to her exploitive father, or the exploitive parent to her bewildered child.

However, this particular view of dissociation can be confusing when it is applied to patients who have survived catastrophes as adults. There is a distinction between dissociation as it occurs in childhood and catastrophic dissociation that results from massive psychic trauma in adulthood. In childhood, dissociation is "an adaptive hypnoidal capacity" (Bromberg, 1993, p. 164) that is both defensive and adaptive as the child and later adult assumes roles that protect her from further injury. In adulthood, the dissociative process in the face of trauma does not create further splits in a developed personality but defends against terror, leaving an indelible memory of the dissociative experience itself. Provisionally catastrophic dissociation offers protection from terror, but ultimately it leaves the survivor in a state of confusion and anomie. In this it is not adaptive.

Here I quote Krystal (1985), one of the few psychoanalysts to address the differences between childhood trauma and adult onset trauma, because my clinical experience is in accordance with his: "The essential point about the consequences of the modification of consciousness [in traumatic circumstances] is that while it is an inevitable and necessary response to stress, it is also a major aspect of the adult catastrophic traumatic state" (p. 150).

Krystal (1978) points out that the difference in subjective experience between children and adults arises because adults have developed an observing ego that adds to their understanding of the danger they are in. He asserts that, in the face of trauma, overwhelming affect leads children to experience "unbearable distress" and "mass stimulation" (p. 113). By contrast, in adults the response "is initiated by surrender to inevitable danger consisting of a numbing of self reflective functions, followed by a paralysis of all cognitive and self preserving mental functions" (p. 113). In other words, recognizing the tremendous danger and overwhelmed by the terror of annihilation, the adult self, unable to act in its own best interests, loses its capacity to reflect on what is happening, growing numb and lifeless. This seems to me to be an accurate description of catastrophic dissociation, not the defensive and adaptive process of dissociation as it occurs in childhood, where the terror of the moment is pushed aside and stored in different self states, but the adult's subjective experience of catastrophic dissociation in which everything that is psychically familiar—agency, affect, the sense of time and bodily intactness, the object world, self reflection and cognition—is abruptly called into question. In Chapters 5, 6 and 7, I demonstrate that the consequences of this massive dissociation, this "surrender" as Krystal calls it, become the familiar and enduring posttraumatic symptoms of which Jonah complained. Reviews of current epidemiological research (Shalev, 1996; Solomon, Larror, and McFarlane, 1996) support this view, establishing that adults who dissociate during a traumatic event are more likely to develop long-term symptoms of stress. Their findings suggest that those who confront trauma without dissociation do not develop such symptoms.

To summarize these distinctions between the effects of trauma occurring during childhood and in adulthood: When a child is overwhelmed by fear, contingent selves form as a paradoxical protection against fragmentation; the trauma is embodied in these different self states—unwelcome, sometimes unfamiliar, but nonetheless part of the personality. In childhood, trauma becomes part of self-experience. In adulthood, it causes the collapse of the self. In subsequent chapters, I discuss further consequences of these differences as they manifest themselves in treatment and in countertransferential enactments.

The different pathways taken by the dissociative process in children and adults have consequences for the storage of memories. Under normal conditions, memory plays a key role in integrating experience: "An episode appears to enter into memory as an indivisible unit. The different pieces, the attributes of experience that make up an episode, such as perceptions, affect, and action, can be isolated from the entire episode of which they are attributes. But in general the episode stands as a whole" (D. N. Stern, 1985, p. 95). Not so with trauma. There is nothing integrating about the role memory plays in trauma. Memory, "the key to the soul" as Hacking (1995, p. 64) describes it, that drives the self's sense of coherence and continuity, is transfixed by catastrophe. Volumes (Davies and Frawley, 1994; Alpert, 1995; Gartner, 1997; among others) have been devoted to the difficulties inherent in reconstructing memories of childhood sexual abuse. Depending on the age of the child and her relationship to her abuser, memories, as such, may never have been formulated, but are rather stored in dissociated self states. The fact that most sexual abuse happens in private, often with threats about the consequence of disclosing what has happened, allows room for distortion and further contributes to the shame, uncertainty, and self doubt that many survivors of childhood sexual abuse—and their analysts—have to endure. For these patients, the refrain is frequently, "Did this really happen to me?" Which often translates into, "Can I bear, or do I dare to take this seriously?" As impressions of her sexual relationship with her father began to take shape in treatment, Roberta vacillated between rage at me for "forcing" such thoughts into her mind, turning me into the abusive father, and feelings of terrible shame over what had happened to her, not allowing herself to fully come to terms with the violation, betrayal, and losses it represented.

When a trauma is survived in adulthood, the refrain is more likely to be: "I should have gotten over this by now." Or "I'm not in danger any more. What's the matter with me?" Alternatively the lament is, "I shall never get over this. I am marked for life." When shame is present, and it frequently is, it is not so much about what one has survived, but that one has not survived psychologically. The memory is often indelible and, unlike other memories, it is unchanged by the passage of time.

Traumatic memories are repetitive and indigestible, but the form these memories take can differ depending on when they are acquired. The memories of childhood are enacted in self states as we see repeatedly with Roberta. In adulthood, the memories are assaultive. As Jonah put it, "that's what I keep seeing over and over again. I see it in my sleep; I see it during the day; these scenes just come into my mind."

Although there are cases of traumatic amnesia in adulthood, and aspects of the trauma may never be fully recalled, most adult survivors of a catastrophe know the experience happened. While they may attempt to deny its impact, it has become the marker, the sole point of reference, the rule by which all subsequent experience is parsed. For adults, in disrupting the present, catastrophe simultaneously calls into question past certainties and future possibilities. Just as the survivor was originally assaulted by the external event, or series of events, she is now assaulted by memory. Awake and asleep, vivid and repetitive images, sensations, thoughts, behaviors, and fears concerned with the trauma plague adult survivors not simply in the immediate aftermath but, for some, for many years and, for others, for the rest of their lives.

To reiterate the distinction between the dynamic consequences of childhood abuse and adult onset trauma, but this time from the perspective of memory: Memories of childhood trauma are frequently unconscious or not fully formulated, lodged in dissociated self states and acted on without awareness. Even when they have been brought into consciousness, they are often shrouded in uncertainty. For the adult survivor of a catastrophe, the memory is unequivocal and unyielding, a catastrophically altered sense of self bears witness to its tenacity.

ANNIHILATION ANXIETY

There is a final and critical distinction between childhood and adult onset trauma. To the survivor of adult onset trauma, death is not a theoretical issue. Nor, for that matter, is it for the clinician who would work with this survivor. Green (1997) describes "indifferent reality" as those events that cannot be altered by values or wishes, facts that are indifferent to life and death. Unlike the private realities and frequently uncertain details of childhood sexual abuse, there is nothing uncertain about the catastrophes adults survive; the "unambiguous facts" (Hoffman, 1998, p. 20) are incontrovertible. Thus, for adults who have survived catastrophes, the difficulty in treatment is not dealing with uncertainty, but in coming to terms with contingency and in understanding the meaning of that lingering state of helplessness. Ogden (1997) puts this dilemma starkly: "We are incapable of both maintaining our sanity and genuinely experiencing our own mortality" (p. 18). For analyst and patient alike, facing up to indifferent reality that has smashed into their otherwise constructed world means dealing with fallibility and facing their mortal selves.

Since 1926, when death anxiety was omitted from Freud's list of the four basic anxieties—the fear of loss of the object, loss of the object's love, fear of castration, and fear of superego disapproval—the subject of death and mortality in general has been downplayed by psychoanalysis until very recently. Hurvich (1991) suggests that the reason death was omitted from the list of basic danger situations is because Freud argued that the unconscious is incapable of representing its own death and that, therefore, it cannot be grasped analytically. Nonetheless, Hurvich argues that a close reading would reveal that annihilation anxiety, which Freud equates with overwhelmed helplessness, constitutes one of the basic dangers to the developing child. Whether annihilation anxiety was explicitly excluded from or implicit in his final statement on anxiety, Freud continued a trend that he had begun when he rejected the seduction hypothesis, denying external causes a role in the unconscious, and consequently excluding them as an appropriate topic of psychoanalytic speculation. Although this *lacuna* is particularly problematic when we attempt to consider the place of adult onset trauma within psychoanalytic theory, it also presents a challenge for any clinician who must inevitably consider, if not directly address, the issue of her own death and that of her patients in the course of her analytic work. One analyst who has recently commented on this peculiar omission in a craft that is dedicated to engaging the deepest and most intimate facts and fears of human existence is Robert Langs. Langs (2004) argues that the classical psychoanalytic focus on infantile development and early sources of emotional symptoms appears "to have served on one level as a means of avoiding looking toward the future where personal death inevitably lies" (p. 34). But, more than this, he argues, Freud was unable to focus on and deal with external or environmental sources of death anxiety. Among several forms that death anxiety can take, Langs singles out "predatory death anxiety" as the conscious and unconscious dread of annihilation. He cites clinical and psychobiological evidence to indicate that predatory death anxiety is "in all likelihood the single most powerful psychodynamic dynamism in present day emotional life" (p. 32).

Although Langs' criticism of the classical emphasis on development as an avoidance of death anxiety is pointed, relational and interpersonal analysts with their emphasis on attachment and the power of human interactions are not immune from his judgment. He argues that the relational analyst's emphasis on meeting relational needs distracts both therapists and patients from considering the impact of "immediate and prospective traumatic realities" (p. 34). He further points out that the relational turn has maintained an "almost exclusive concentration in psychotherapy on the mind of the patient. Reality and actual events continue to be afforded a secondary position in their psychodynamic formulations which are centered on how a given person responds mentally to external impingements" (p. 35). This is, indeed, an interesting twist; claiming privilege for the role of empathic understanding pits the analytic relationship against the power of the Real. As I develop my argument in later chapters, I maintain that although relational ties can inoculate against the state of traumatic aloneness, under extreme conditions, they are not sufficient to provide complete coverage.

Hoffman (1979, 1998) has also taken psychoanalysts to task for this failure to consider the role of death in their work with patients. In contrast to Becker's (1973) belief that it is virtually impossible for human beings to sustain an awareness of or full comprehension of their own mortality, Hoffman argues that in psychic experience there is a dialectic between the sense of being and the anticipation of nonbeing—one is figure, the other ground. Meaning and mortality exist in dialectical tension with one another, he points out. "The very annihilation that jeopardizes our sense that anything we care about matters, paradoxically, is what infuses caring with the meaning that it has" (Hoffman, 1998, p.18). I note here, and discuss in more detail in the following, the fact that Hoffman uses the word annihilation to stand for the end of life in general, whether it comes from natural or unnatural causes. Hoffman suggests that relegating both the growing awareness of mortality and its accompanying affect to the unconscious fosters a "narcissistically comforting belief in immortality in consciousness" (p. 43). Alternatively, he suggests that the affect alone could be disowned, so that a conscious claim of disbelief in immortality could be, in fact, merely an intellectual defense concealing a well-guarded fantasy of immortality held in defiance of a still more deeply buried acknowledgement of the painful inevitability of one's own death. In the average expectable life—and death—these defenses would, indeed, appear to describe the internal dance steps that we repeat as we approach and draw back from death's inevitability and the luxury, if such a word can be used in this context, we have, in an ongoing life, to try out these dance steps.

I have pointed out that Hoffman appears to give equal weight to the growing awareness of death as an inevitable fact of life and the sudden threat of annihilation experienced by those who face massive psychic trauma, but others make a sharp distinction between these two experiences. Kohut (1984) differentiates between death *per se*, of which he says "however deeply melancholy [it] is comparable to a fulfilled parting" (p. 18), and death of the self under traumatic circumstances. Hoffman criticizes Kohut for what he calls an "idealized, even mystical concept of healthy adaptation to mortality" (p. 56). But Kohut is not alone in making this distinction; referring specifically to the confrontation with mortality that massive trauma involves, Krystal (1978) writes, "Having experienced its own mortality and helplessness, no living creature is quite the same again" (p. 158). Here there is no gradual approach and withdrawal from an increasingly less abstract idea, as Hoffman describes it, but a sudden encounter with the reality of death that robs life of its vitality, that exchanges the reality of life for the certainty of death. It is a certainty that defines all future life.

Hurvich (1991), who has written extensively on annihilation anxiety, makes a similar distinction between death anxiety as a future event and annihilation anxiety that is imminent destruction. He agrees with Klein that annihilation anxiety is a universal potential. In Klein's theory, annihilation anxiety colors the baby's first experiences of life. In the paranoid schizoid position, the baby feels herself to be under attack from persecutory part objects that she herself has expelled into the world. Later unsettling experiences can mimic this state. Many patients become immobilized by annihilation anxiety at some time in their treatment. Maybe the transference has evoked a smothering mother. Or sometimes a sharp increase in anxiety leads to feelings of helplessness and fear of fragmentation. Rage at an analyst's failure to live up to an ideal established in the patient's mind can give rise to homicidal fanta-sies. The loss of a job or the prospect of divorce suddenly evokes terror that existence will be extinguished; the patient believes she can no lon-ger exist without these defining relationships. Slochower (2006) de-scribes her patient, Ken, who had a mild heart attack and lost his job around 9/11. He temporarily became overwhelmed by annihilation anx-iety that utterly disrupted his sense of protection. Slochower maintains that although September 11 was a trauma for Ken, its major impact was as a symbolic embodiment of unexpected dangers. It is precisely this ability to find a symbol to embody his fears that sets Ken's condition apart from those who have dissociated in the face of what they believe will be imminent death. The adult survivor of a trauma does not have the luxury of finding a symbol to signify his distress, but instead his abil-ity to fantasize and to deal in symbols collapses into a state of psychic equivalence, and he is forced to accept the world quite literally on its own terms. As Des Pres (1976) writes, "when death itself is the determinant, then behavior has no meaning in a symbolic or psycholog-ical sense" (p. 155).

In general, psychoanalytic theory, whether from the classical or from the object relations tradition, maintains that annihilation anxiety expe-rienced in adulthood is an indication of a "boundary weakness, inade-quate internalizations ... weakness of the defense organization and various features in the integration of structures including both self and object representations" (Hurvich, 1991, p.151). Depending on the ana-lyst's particular affiliation, then, when annihilation anxiety is manifest in psychoanalytic treatment, it is thought to arise in response to a sense of helplessness from growing tension due to need; from the fear of merger, the traumatic failure of selfobject function, or the repetition of an earlier experience of helplessness. Hurvich mentions, almost as an aside, that annihilation anxiety can also result from "adult onset psychic trauma" (p. 152).

Reporting on his personal and clinical experiences after Septem-ber 11, Strozier (2002) introduces a different term to describe the fear of sudden death. "Apocalyptic anxiety" is based on the concept of a nuclear threat that "alters the ground of our being. It changes our whole relationship to death and therefore the self. It cannot be easily symbolized" (personal communication 6/25/2003). After the terror-ist attacks in New York City, Strozier (2002) described "zones of sad-ness" in decreasing order of magnitude radiating out from Ground Zero, reflecting the apocalyptic power of the destruction of the World

Trade Center. He argues, "The apocalyptic exists in a realm that extends beyond what Kurt Vonnegut wistfully called 'plain old death' and embraces a comprehensive vision of collective death, of vast suffering, of the very end of the world" (p. 365). I would note that at least the first of Strozier's zones of sadness might be more accurately called a zone of terror, but that is exactly the point of my argument. Although there are similarities in the anticipation of a violent and untimely death, there are important distinctions between apocalyptic anxiety and the terror evoked by adult onset trauma. Apocalyptic anxiety implies a group phenomenon, a set of beliefs that may or may not be accompanied by the immediate experience of a catastrophe. Adult onset trauma, even when it occurs in groups, is an individual phenomenon triggered by the immediate and very real terror of immediate extinction. Strozier agrees that only those in the first zone of sadness were at risk for adult onset trauma, although apocalyptic trauma rippled out through the other zones (personal communication 6/23/2006). Jill, whose case is discussed in more detail in later chapters, spoke of "crossing over" as she went from Strozier's first zone of sadness, where the immediate threat of death and destruction gave way to the zones where, in her experience, people had watched without being in danger of their lives. "It was like going into another dimension; they couldn't understand what I was thinking or feeling, there was no sense in talking to them."

In the previous chapter, I argued that most of us in New York who witnessed the terrorist attacks were not subject to massive psychic trauma. I was referring to the fact that few of us had reason to believe on that day that we were in imminent danger of being killed or that our loved ones were in imminent danger. Certainly, many of us were afraid that the political situation would deteriorate and that it might come to that, this would be an example of Strozier's apocalyptic anxiety, but few of us actually looked death, our own immediate death, in the eye on that day. When I speak of adult onset trauma I mean to imply that someone has actually and precipitously been confronted with their own death or that of someone very close to them. This is the River Rubican that those who survive massive psychic trauma have crossed. The die has been cast," *jacta alea est*, as Caesar said of crossing the Rubican. There is no going back; they have stepped beyond the limits of the familiar world. Every adult survivor of massive trauma will say, in so many words, at some point during treatment, "I thought I was going to die at that moment." Jonah thought to himself, "This is it. I am going to die here." Jill, who fled her home at Ground Zero with her toddler in a stroller, convinced that the towers were about to fall on top of them both said, "That's the red hot center of it; I thought we were going to die right there. And what's worse, if it happened to me again I don't believe I would survive." Others, even more poignantly, will say, "I died that day." In her account of her recovery from a brutal rape in France, Brison (2002) found herself saying "I was murdered in France last year" (p. 35).

It will be argued that I am being very concrete in insisting on this narrow interpretation of adult onset trauma. I am. In *The Survivor: An Anatomy of Life in the Death Camps*, which is, in effect, a meditation on the phenomenology of survival, Des Pres (1976) has a word of caution specifically for psychoanalysts who seek to diminish the survivor's experience by placing it in a larger symbolic context and thus misunderstand the survivor's dilemma. Distinguishing between the contrary realms of civilization and extremity, he insists that the rules that obtain when psychoanalysts work with patients from the general population do not apply when the patient has physically escaped from but psychologically continues to inhabit, "a world ruled by death" (p. 99). This intimate knowledge of death sets survivors apart from the rest of us, demanding that we clinicians suspend our normal practice. We must move out of the realm of psychoanalytic omnipotence, and only by fully letting our patients know that we understand their experience is there a possibility that we can eventually move back into a world of meanings and symbols.

I am concerned that this appeal to reality will immediately be seen as turning away from psychic reality. This is not my intention. In the moment of terror, psychic reality and external reality are one. Only when the survivor feels that this is understood is she free to explore other meanings of her experience. Almost from its inception, psychoanalysis has promoted the illusion of agency, which has been constructed against any belief in contingency, yet we must suspend this illusion when we work with survivors of massive trauma.

A few years before Des Pres published *The Survivor* (1976), Becker (1973) wrote in *The Denial of Death*, "culture is produced against natural reality and mortality" (p. 19). Becker did not have psychoanalysis in mind when he wrote those words, but, as I discussed in summarizing the work of Hoffman (1979, 1998) and Langs (2004), our psychoanalytic culture has almost never found a way of accommodating mortality in theory or in practice. It is precisely this failure that Des Pres questions so eloquently, and in so doing he becomes a spokesman for every survivor who has met with a lack of understanding in therapy, whose experience has been dismissed or diminished by therapists unwilling to grasp all the implications of survival. For those who narrowly escaped the terrorist attacks, fighting their way downstairs, thinking at any moment they would be suffocated by the smoke; for those who fled from the collapsing buildings believing they would be crushed; for those rescue workers who handled the dead and dismembered; for others who witness or survive acts of violence individually or in groups, and those who are diagnosed with a fatal illness, death assumes an entirely different dimension.

Whether it is called "anomic terror" (Berger and Luckmann, 1966), "disintegration anxiety" (Kohut, 1984), or "annihilation anxiety" (Klein, 1977), or "infinite dying" (Langer 1991), Kohut describes the psyche's reaction to imminent destruction as follows: "What is feared is not physical extinction but loss of humanness: a psychological death in which our humanness would permanently come to an end" (p. 16). Felman and Laub (1992) are even more explicit in their definition: "the loss of subjectivity, therefore the loss of the capacity to witness to oneself and thus to witness from the inside is perhaps the true meaning of annihilation, for when one's history is abolished, one's identity ceases to exist as well" (p. 82). I think of Jonah saying to me, "I have lost my soul."

Catastrophic trauma introduces the fear of annihilation, a sudden encounter with a mortal self, and in so doing frequently triggers the catastrophic dissociative process. For the adult, dissociation in the face of a catastrophe is tantamount to annihilation. The natural being/not being dialectic that Hoffman (1998) describes collapses, as if this confrontation with near death excludes the possibility of going on being. "Being alive is no longer natural" writes Tarantelli (2003, p. 925). Shatan (1973) captures the process in this passage from a letter written to him by a Vietnam veteran: "Death is the reality now. You yourself feel unreal, to feel real again, you must embrace the ever-presentness of death by wrapping it in yourself and poisoning your sense of self with a reservoir of evil and destructiveness. Only in that way can inner and outer reality feel one again" (p. 172).

I began this chapter by exploring the differences between childhood and adult onset trauma. Children who have been abused will develop self states in which the victim self fears that she is in terrible danger, and these fears may be relived in particular relationship situations and constellations in adult life, but in other self states and relationships the adult survivor of a childhood trauma continues unaffected by the earlier traumatic violations.

Lacan (1977) has an expression that fits the psychic reality of the survivor of adult onset trauma; he locates her in the space between two deaths, *entre deux morts*. There is natural or biological death on the one hand, which is part of the "cycle of generation and corruption, of nature's continual transformation" and, on the other hand, "absolute death" (Zizek, 1989, p. 134), which is in itself a symbol for death. The place between natural and absolute death is an emptiness that cannot be contained or defined or reasoned away. When Antigone was banished from Thebes for disregarding Creon's edict and giving her brother, Polyneices, an appropriate burial, Lacan argues her banishment represented a symbolic death, her exclusion from the symbolic community, from a world of common meaning. In this empty place, she awaits her biological death. Brison (2002) uses similar words in describing the aftermath of the rape she survived, in which she was left for dead. She writes of the difficulty she found in getting others to understand how utterly changed she had been by the experience, "I had ventured outside the human community, beyond the realm of predictable events and comprehensible actions. A particularly difficult place for a philosophy professor" (p. xii).

Survivors of massive trauma who have faced annihilation and experienced catastrophic dissociation and its devastating consequences are situated within this gap. Their biological death has not happened, but they, too, feel themselves to be outsiders; intimate knowledge of mortality has robbed them of their citizenship within the ranks of the living. As Zizek (1989) puts it, "absolute death is always the destruction of the symbolic universe" (p. 135). When these disenfranchised citizens turn to psychoanalysis for treatment, the challenge is to find a way of entering this space with them.

Catastrophic dissociation in face of the sudden threat of annihilation embodies the fear of the death that did not happen and the symptoms to which that fear gave rise. It is "the death that happened but was not experienced" (Winnicott, 1974, p. 106). Caruth (1996) asks, "Is the trauma the encounter with death or the ongoing experience of having survived it?" (p. 7). I would answer that the space between two deaths is the traumatic space; it is never clear that the trauma has been survived.

In this chapter, I have suggested a number of ways in which the overuse of the word trauma among psychoanalysts can lead to theoretical confusion. The most terrifying manifestations of the word are obscured when it is used to describe both a baby's feelings of helplessness and an adult facing almost certain and sudden death. This is not to deny the pain caused to the baby and the painful consequences that can reverberate through the child's life, which lead us to speculate that adults who experience this kind of helplessness are experiencing annihilation anxiety. However, searching for a historical forerunner to the adult state encourages us to avert our gaze from the dangers of contingency in adult life. I have further suggested that adult onset trauma results in catastrophic dissociation not in the construction of different self states as trauma does in childhood. In childhood the self is more malleable, less fully structured, than it will be in adulthood. Because of that, trauma in childhood can be dealt with by building the self around it. Trauma shatters the nascent self, and some of the resulting shards (self states) come into being as ways of containing the trauma and protecting other states of self from being directly affected. As long as these states of self can be kept apart from one another—as long as the experience they would make possible is felt in other self states as "not me"—the defense holds, and the trauma is isolated in mind. "Not me" inevitably comes to be enacted with others, a problematic consequence of the dissociation, but the dissociation at least protects the sufferer from the havoc that would be wreaked if he had to consciously acknowledge these self states. The upshot is that childhood trauma scars some parts of the personality, but leaves other parts less affected. As is described in detail in Chapters 4, 5, and 6, adult onset trauma has a different effect. Because the self is already formed, the reaction to trauma cannot be isolated in a "not me" self state. Instead, the trauma affects the entire personality. The resulting dissociation can only be described as catastrophic. One ironic outcome of this understanding is that, contrary to what we are used to in psychoanalysis, adult onset trauma can actually be more damaging than trauma in childhood. But that ignores the main point of this book, which is that trauma-induced dissociation takes different forms in adulthood and in childhood and that it is a serious mistake to confuse them with one another.

In the next chapter, I consider the metapsychological problems implicit in classical and object relations theory when an attempt is made to describe the consequences of adult onset trauma.

3

The Cost of Survival: Historical Perspectives on Adult Onset Trauma

Survival is the twin brother of annihilation.

— Winston Churchill (1955)

In the last chapter I described Jonah, a previously high functioning man in his early 40s, who was referred for treatment eighteen months after having been violently and senselessly assaulted by a battery of policemen in the hallway of his apartment building. Throughout the assault, he had feared that at any moment he would be killed. This chance encounter left him in a posttraumatic no man's land.

Listening to Jonah's words, watching him struggle to articulate what had happened to him, I was reminded of the concluding lines from *All Quiet on the Western Front,* where Remarque (1928) is describing the psychological devastation that awaits those who physically survived combat during World War I:

> We will be weary, broken, burnt out, rootless, and without hope. We will
> not be able to find our way any more. ... We will be superfluous even to
> ourselves, we will grow older, a few will adapt themselves, some others
> will merely submit, and most will be bewildered; —the years will pass by
> and in the end we shall fall into ruin. [p. 254]

As psychoanalytic theory has been elaborated recently in response to shifting philosophical currents, new theoretical trends, and clinical feedback, the hegemony of drive theory has waned while the psychoanalyst's lens has widened to accommodate a socially constructed worldview. Nonlinear dynamics, unformulated experience, the unthought known, experience-near phenomena, a multiplicity of self states and the complexity of gendered experience, constitutional, biological, neurological, and cultural factors have become grist for theory making and clinical meaning. Yet one area remains curiously unfocussed and unexplored: the psychological effects of traumas that occur in adulthood. There is currently no way of locating adult onset trauma in psychoanalytic discourse except in the margins, no theoretical framework in which to fit Jonah's reactions without recourse to prior pathology. There is no way of making sense of Remarque's weary, broken combat veterans without appealing to overwhelming aggression and the death instinct, to intrapsychic conflict, or to developmental arrests.

I argue in this chapter that this oversight is not a mistake; it is built into the very fabric of early psychoanalytic metapsychology. Indeed, Laplanche and Pontalis (1973) maintain that actual neuroses, whose origin lies in the present as distinct from psychoneuroses whose origins are found in infantile conflicts, "cannot be treated psychoanalytically because their symptoms do not have a meaning that can be elucidated" (p. 10). This chapter explores the reasons why considering the impact of adult onset trauma as an event in itself, capable of causing serious and lasting disruption in even the most stable personality, offers a challenge to psychoanalysis. I examine the metapsychology that underlies various psychoanalytic theories in order to understand why the contingencies of the real world, historically negated by psychoanalytic formulations, continue to pose a problem for psychoanalysts who choose to work with the survivors of catastrophic trauma. Further, I question why the notion of contingency appears antithetical to the entire psychoanalytic endeavor.

If psychoanalysts are prepared to enter these turbulent waters, two questions must be asked: First, how can posttraumatic symptoms be understood psychodynamically and worked with in a way that does justice to the patient's experience? And, second, why have most psychoanalysts resisted the challenge to describe these symptoms in dynamic terms? Bergmann and Jucovy (1982) and Laub and Auerhahn (1989) comment on the impossibility of applying classical psychoanalysis to traumatic neuroses. The theory does "not appear sufficient to conceptualize and explain the bewildering array of symptoms presented by the survivors" (p. 8), Bergmann and Jucovy write. They conclude that "these formulations seems to omit the possibility of trauma having a psychologically deleterious effect on the adult" (p. 9). Indeed, taking adult onset trauma seriously challenges many of the fundamental assumptions on which psychoanalytic theory, be it drive theory or some version of relational theory, is based.

CONCEPTUAL BARRIERS

In order to establish the context and explain how a theory of adult onset trauma might challenge many of the assumptions on which psychoanalytic metapsychology is founded, particularly among those of us in America who practice in the shadow of Ego Psychology, it is necessary first to review the epistemological dilemma we find ourselves in when we are faced with the survivors of late onset trauma and the preoccupations they bring to treatment.

These conceptual problems fall into several mutually implicating categories. Broadly speaking, the first concerns the significance and the role external events play in psychoanalysis. The second concerns how external events are represented or structured within the psychoanalytic subject, and whether psychoanalytic discourse with its emphasis on childhood experience and internal conflicts, on agency, on the use of symbols, and on the importance of rationality can develop a vocabulary that does justice to the survivor's irrational, unmediated, and impossible-to-symbolize experience. Included among this second set of concerns is the common psychoanalytic assumption of psychic stability to which those who have successfully negotiated the shoals of childhood with the help of good-enough parents are believed to be entitled.

In recent years, psychoanalysts have been criticized for not paying sufficient attention to the outside world. Layton (2004) argues that psychoanalysis unlinks the psyche from its social context. And Greenberg (1991) suggests that the "significance and subtlety of social experience" (p. 69) has represented a challenge to drive theory for some years. The kinds of events that unleash adult onset trauma could hardly be called subtle, and yet, for all their obviousness, it might even be said that because of their obviousness our theory strives to deny their impact on the adult psyche. If psychoanalysts are to treat adult onset trauma, they can no longer afford to divorce themselves from the social context. Massive psychic trauma turns our attention to the outside world and suggests that psychic experience can be profoundly altered independently of dynamic conflict, motivation, structural defect, and developmental arrest.

In recent years, relational theory has offered an alternative pathway to and view of the psyche, one that might be more conducive to the analytic treatment of adult onset trauma. Indeed, relational analysts have been criticized for relying too heavily on conscious, interpersonal experience and de-emphasizing fantasy, dynamic conflict, and the unconscious (Arlow, 1984; Bachant and Richards, 1993; Mills, 2005; among others). But, as I describe in subsequent chapters, adult onset trauma can be equally challenging to the relational analyst, for catastrophes uproot central aspects of self experience, profoundly altering the psyche's relations with its objects, and thereby contaminating intersubjective space.

The Exogenous Factor

Over the last century, psychoanalysis and trauma have enjoyed a tumultuous courtship with all the consequences of uneasy intimacy—infatuation, repudiation, estrangement, and reconciliation. To Breuer and Freud, writing *Studies on Hysteria* (1895), psychoanalysis was constituted by the psyche's failure to metabolize trauma. Indeed, trauma seemed to inhere in the very concept of psychoanalysis. But, when Freud (1914) turned from the seduction theory, denouncing it as an obstacle "that was almost fatal to the young science" (p. 51), a decision that has been subjected to considerable deconstruction and criticism in the last twenty years (Masson, 1984; Ulman and Brothers, 1988; Alpert, 1995; Davies & Frawley, 1994; among others), trauma became an event *non grata* in the new dynamic psychoanalysis whose emphasis was on pressures within the psyche not on happenings without. Arlow (1984) somewhat wryly comments that when Freud renounced the seduction theory, he might have rewritten his famous line "hysterics suffer mainly from reminiscences" as "hysterics suffer mainly from thwarted instinctual drive wishes" (p. 522). In his recent biography of Freud, Breger (2000) suggests that Freud retreated from the real life losses and humiliations that he had experienced as a little boy in favor of an internal world that could, at least in theory, be analyzed into submission. In this preferred narrative, he emphasized, instead, his oedipal victory over his ineffective father.

When Ferenczi (1933) famously noted that an "insufficiently deep exploration of the exogenous factor leads to the danger of resorting prematurely to explanations, often too facile explanations, in terms of 'disposition' and 'constitution'"(p. 196), and detailed the devastating effects of childhood trauma, he suffered virtual banishment. Freud quite literally turned his back on him. Jones questioned Ferenczi's sanity and blocked English language publication of *The Confusion of Tongues* for close to twenty years. "Completely regressed ... stupid ... inadequate ... harmless" were some of the defensive and contradictory comments with which Freud dismissed the ideas contained in this paper (Bonomi, 1999). Paying attention to exogenous factors bore serious consequences. It is true that Freud's (1914) complemental series directs the classical analyst to consider external events, but only in terms of the compromises the psyche effects in the face of increased drive derivatives. Although Anna Freud (1967) does note that, at the extreme end of the complementary series, "there may be events of such magnitude that they can cause pathology on their own," she adds, "but we have no certainty about this" (p. 232). Ms. Freud cautions that it is important to "apportion pathogenic responsibility to the right quarters, but, clinically, no other demand is as difficult to fulfill" (p. 13). Reluctance to give the social context its due inevitably led early psychoanalysts to search for causes among familiar psychoanalytic phenomena.

After his experience treating World War II soldiers and veterans, Kardiner (1969) attempted to find a compromise to this forced choice of constructing traumatic events as either internal or external. He wrote, "In a manner of speaking, the traumatic neurosis is a kind of persecutory delusion. The persecutor is, however, the outside world" (p. 256). Hoffman (1998) points out that emphasizing dichotomies such as external versus internal is as integral to objectivist thinking and essentialism as emphasizing dialectical relationships is to constructivism. Taking a dialectical constructivist approach to adult onset trauma would require resisting the pull to locate the source of the trauma either in the individual or in the event itself. It would require giving up comfortable convictions about being strong enough to withstand catastrophic reactions to trauma in adulthood. Psychoanalysts have too often been pulled in this latter direction. On the other hand, trauma therapists and grief counselors, to whom survivors often feel drawn in order to avoid the blame that potentially awaits them in a psychoanalyst's office, often err in the other direction. When patients sense that they have been offered formulaic explanations for their catastrophically altered perceptions and feeling states, which is always a danger when dichotomies and objectivist thinking govern practice, they continue to be overwhelmed by aspects of the catastrophic experience that have not been articulated.

It is not only the presence of an external event that creates problems for the psychoanalyst trying to locate adult onset trauma within her theoretical canon. Object relations, despite Klein's *a priori* object world, and more recently, the contributions of attachment theory, self psychology, interpersonal and relational psychoanalysis—all of which emphasize interpersonal relationships and the social context (add to this the recent emphasis on childhood sexual trauma)—all weigh in on the side of external events and their impact on the *developing* psyche. The *developed* psyche remains implicitly, and often explicitly, relatively impervious to outside events.

Psychic Structure, Conflict, and Late Onset Trauma

Most psychoanalytic metapsychology includes some reference to psychic structure. The notion of structure has consistently militated against any flexibility until now. The very word structure implies something fixed, a solid, indeed an immutable, edifice. When this structure is in place, so the theory goes, it cannot be shaken; if cracks do appear, they must have been there in the first place. This aspect of our metapsychology seems to have been adopted wholesale from the construction industry; if cracks appear in a building then the foundation must be faulty; too much sand was mixed in with the mortar to withstand this particular freeze and thaw. According to this line of reasoning, I should interpret Jonah's response to his experience with the police as a propensity to react to violent encounters with authority figures in a particular fashion. Or I should assume that, in some way, Jonah invited the attack in a desperate reenactment of an earlier trauma. Or I should follow the suggestion made by many earlier psychoanalytic writers and see the moment of trauma as representing infantile helplessness, locating Jonah in psychic infancy and equating the police raid with an unpredictable mother.

In contrast to this view of fixed personality structure, some psychoanalytic writers (Loewald, 1980; S. Mitchell, 1993; Bromberg, 1998) propose a more flexible approach. They view personality as fluid, a river rather than a building, which, in its ebb and flow, is constantly subject to the exigencies of experience. In describing the paranoid schizoid and depressive positions as alternating and/or simultaneous modes of experience, rather than developmental stages to be attained and maintained, Ogden (1990), too, offers a more flexible approach to counter the traditional notion of fixity. Chodorow (1996) celebrates this move from a metapsychology based on structural thinking and from explanations founded in "putative developmental determinants" to a "clinical emphasis on contingency and the ambiguity of emergent personal meanings" (p. 33). Phillips (1994) also advocates finding a way to include contingency, "the enemy of fixity" (p. 8) in contemporary psychoanalytic metapsychology.

CLASSICAL APPROACHES TO TRAUMATIC NEUROSES

Phillips (1994) continues, "War is a way of getting uncertainty back into the picture" (p. 7). The two World Wars of the 20th century provided Freud and Fairbairn with opportunities to address that uncertainty and to analyze its impact on the soldiers' fixed psyche. Freud and Fairbairn specifically address the consequences of being in combat but they sharply disagree about the significance of the object world, and, by extension, of external events, on the developing psyche. For heuristic purposes, therefore, a comparison of their metapsychological positions offers us an opportunity to consider a range of classical and object relations theories on this topic.

It has frequently been suggested that *Beyond the Pleasure Principle* was Freud's (1920) attempt to account for the brutality and perversity (R. Clark, 1980; Gay, 1988) of World War I, but *Beyond the Pleasure Principle* also demonstrates the pressure Freud felt to restructure the psychic economy so that it would better accommodate the "dark and dismal subject of the traumatic neuroses" (p. 14). These were not just dark and dismal, however. Freud (1919) also states that traumatic neuroses were "the puzzling disorders" that presented several challenges to his metapsychology, or, as he put it, "where much is diverted from its purpose"(1920, p.13).

Freud's (1920) familiarity with posttraumatic symptoms is clear from his discussion of repetitive dreams and the avoidance of events that reminded the survivor of the original trauma, but curiously, as Gay (1988) also notes, "the reassuring intimacy with clinical experience" (p. 380) is absent. There are no case histories in *Beyond the Pleasure Principle*. R. Clark (1980) tells us that, unlike several of his contemporaries, Freud did not choose to work with shell-shocked veterans in Vienna. Yet all three of his sons were "warriors," as he wrote to Lou Andreas Salome (cited in Gay, 1988). Martin and Ernst spent several years in the trenches. Because Freud's propensity for drawing on personal experience and the experience of family members is well known, his failure to provide firsthand examples of traumatic symptoms is interesting, particularly as he does use a family member to illustrate the repetition compulsion first described in this paper. In his description of the ego's attempt to master overwhelming external experience, Freud turns from war to a description of his grandson's *fort da* game. In this game, the little boy repeatedly casts away and retrieves a spool on the end of a piece of string as a way of mastering his mother's brief absences.

The repetitive nightmares combat veterans can suffer night after night were the first opportunity Freud had to note an exception to his proposition that dreams are the fulfillment of unconscious wishes. In a radical departure, he proposed, instead, that traumatic dreams were part of a repetition compulsion driven by a death instinct. Before drawing this conclusion, however, he entertained a number of explanations for traumatically induced psychic events, particularly for the repetitive quality of dreams. On the one hand, the constant and faithful repetition of traumatic memories in dreams might be an attempt to gain mastery over an event in which one was previously a passive victim; by repeating the event one is taking the active role, he argued. In the case of children's play, he wondered, too, whether the repetition does not go beyond mastery to express an unconscious wish to actually revenge oneself on the other who made us the passive victim of her will.

Even while he is developing this narrative, Freud is continuing to argue for a sexual component to war neuroses. Somewhat tentatively at first, he writes in his *Introduction to Psychoanalysis and the War Neuroses* (1919), "if the investigation of the war neuroses (and a very superficial one at that) has not shown that the sexual theory of the neuroses is correct, that is something very different from showing that the theory is incorrect" (p. 208). But within a few years of the publication of this book, Fenichel (1954) argued much more forcefully that World War I offered many examples of the way in which trauma causes infantile sexual conflicts to flare up, "whether because the trauma is unconsciously regarded as a castration and consequently upsets the balance of the repressed instincts and the defensive forces or because it operates as a temptation for unconscious sadistic tendencies" (p. 66).

Many classical analysts (including Freud himself, 1926; for another example see the Freedman case described in Chapter 9) have found these more familiar, more compelling—and internally coherent—arguments than the appeal to the death instinct Freud proposed in *Beyond the Pleasure Principle* (1920). Anna Freud (1967) states this preferred position very clearly: "External traumas are turned into internal ones if they latch on to, or coincide with, or symbolize the fulfillment of either deep seated anxieties, or wishes or fantasies" (p. 229). In other words, trauma must have its roots in psychic conflict to be experienced as traumatic. In a more recent example of this particular view, Adams-Silvan and Silvan (1990) describe the case of a Vietnam combat veteran whose repetitive dreams focused on the terror of being blown up as he was loading a mortar. The authors interpret this dream as symbolizing the patient's repressed wishes to keep repeating the forbidden excitement and guilty pleasure he experienced in having defended his mother against his brutal stepfather when he was an adolescent. From their account, it is not clear to what extent the analyst informed herself about the veteran's actual experiences in combat.

If Freud (1920) had been content with any of these explanations for traumatic neuroses, he would not have had to reach beyond the pleasure principle, because the pleasure principle is clearly served by active mastery, or by the realization of an unconscious wish. But he did go beyond the pleasure principle, introducing the idea of a second "more primitive" (p. 17) instinct, admittedly a "far fetched speculation" (p. 24), a death instinct whose "least dubious instance" (p. 23) can be seen in traumatic dreams. He turns to the metapsychology originally developed in the Project, some twenty-five years earlier, to explain that, because of its protective shield, the conscious system is generally less impressionable to outside stimuli, but it is exquisitely sensitive to internal stimulation from the unconscious. Once the system is breached by an unanticipated external force, however, repetitive dreams attempt to master the stimulus retrospectively. The principle that drives this compulsion to repeat, Freud hypothesized, must be independent of pleasure, because what is repeated causes the ego unpleasure. Rather, the death instinct represents "the most universal endeavor of all living substance, namely to return to the quiescence of the inorganic world" (p. 33).

In *Beyond The Pleasure Principle*, Freud (1920) leaves an incomplete picture of the war neuroses, conflating them with his grandson's play, raising more questions than answers, moving closer and closer to a biological justification, rather than dynamic explanation. He continued to rework his theory of trauma in several papers over the rest of his life (1923, 1926, 1933, 1939b), apparently never satisfied that he had found a way of incorporating the facts of the traumatic neuroses into his overall metapsychology.

The notion of a death instinct driving the repetition compulsion leaves most classical analysts at a loss (for example, Cohen, 1985; Cooper, 1986). However, Laub and Lee (2003), who have written most eloquently about traumatic reactions among survivors of the Shoah, insist that Freud's "return to quiescence" does, indeed, evoke the enduring experience of trauma for many survivors; "a return to emptiness and obliteration, a dearth of structure and image, a continued absence" (p. 15). Although his own psychoanalytic theory of motivation does not include the death instinct, Greenberg (1991) recognizes that Freud's death instinct works to pull away from relatedness and connection, an experience with which trauma survivors are painfully familiar, and which is explored in greater depth in subsequent chapters.

Despite the global proliferation of catastrophes and genocide, many of those who have sought to apply drive theory to trauma categorically reject the concept that catastrophic events might breach the stimulus barrier, the quantitative or economic argument that Freud proposed in *Beyond the Pleasure Principle* (1920). Speaking for many classical analysts, Brenner (1986) writes:

> What is traumatic is the subjective experience of the traumatized individual. It is what the event meant to the individual. It is the impact of the external stimuli, how they heightened fears, intensified sexual and aggressive wishes, resonated with feelings of guilt and remorse. [p. 203]

In effect, new experience, no matter how threatening, cannot alter what has already been established; structure is impervious to contingency.

OBJECT RELATIONS APPROACHES TO TRAUMA

Moving from drive theory and the particular set of epistemological problems that a metapsychology revolving around these constructs entails, a psychoanalytic model that allows external events a greater role in psychic development might better accommodate the impact of trauma in adult life. But the move from pleasure seeking (or death seeking) to object seeking does not offer much recourse for the adult trauma survivor and the psychodynamic practitioner.

Like Freud (1920) before him, who commented that at least "This terrible war has put an end to the temptation to attribute the cause of shell shock to organic lesions of the nervous system brought about by mechanical force" (p. 12), Fairbairn (1952) hailed the change in terminology from "shell shock" to "war neuroses" as a "remarkable scientific achievement" (p. 279). It was an achievement because it implied that the symptoms of shell shock or battle fatigue were essentially psychological, not neurological. Similarly, both noted that traumatic neuroses are not confined to wartime. Freud (1920) specifically refers to the traumatic neuroses of peace, but Fairbairn was not prepared to consider any class of traumatic neuroses distinct from regular neuroses, because, he argued, they "possess no distinctive features differentiating them sharply from the various psychoneurotic and psychotic states which prevail in time of peace" (p. 256).

Fairbairn (1952) was an army psychiatrist during World War II and, as such, treated many patients who had broken down in combat. At the end of that war, he bluntly concludes that "the chief predisposing factor in determining the breakdown of a soldier is infantile dependence upon his objects" (p. 79).

Fairbairn's (1952) endopsychic structure is the result of fragmentation of the pristine intact ego, the destruction, if you will, rather than the erection of structure. It is ironic that this structure, acquired in response to the caretakers' traumatic handling of the baby and young child, develops into such a closed system that there is no way psychically to acknowledge or experience a catastrophic event in adulthood. According to Fairbairn, such events are always a reflection of earlier exciting or frustrating patterns of behavior to which the child was subjected by her original caretakers. Fairbairn consistently notes that, once fixed, the personality cannot be altered; endopsychic structure is a closed system that cannot be breached from the outside. This ironclad endopsychic structure can be dismantled by health and recovery, but not by massive psychic trauma. Responding to traumatic events in adult life as if they are traumatic only occurs inasmuch as these events match early structured experience.

In a frequently quoted distinction between the neurotic, who takes in reality and makes it conform to his internal world, and the psychotic, who makes the outside world conform to his internal world, Fairbairn (1952) has no way to account for the patient who has been exposed to a reality that does not synchronize with his internal world. In his system, there is no way to account for a reality that overwhelms any prior experience, to account for irrational reality. Indeed, Fairbairn himself makes little distinction between relatively mundane and life threatening events.

> Investigation reveals a remarkable range of traumatic experiences, as may be illustrated by the following examples chosen more or less at random ... being blown up by a bomb, being trapped in the cabin of a torpedoed ship, seeing civilian refugees massacred, having to throttle a German sentry in self-defense, being let down by an officer in a tight corner, *being accused of homosexuality by another soldier, being refused compassionate leave to go home for a wife's confinement, and even being shouted at by the sergeant-major.* [p. 259, italics added]

It is true that being accused of homosexuality, being shouted at by a supervisor, and not being allowed to attend the birth of a child might be considered humiliating or enraging experiences, leading to potential disorganization, but to equate them with being trapped in the cabin of a sinking ship, witnessing a massacre, or throttling another human being to death seems to deny any weight to external circumstances. This is exactly what Fairbairn intends. External situations must acquire the significance of repressed memories involving relations with bad objects and force the release of these objects into consciousness in order to be experienced as traumatic. When such an escape of bad objects occurs, the patient finds himself confronted with terrifying situations that have hitherto been unconscious. "The repetitive dreams of the traumatized soldier, being chased, or shot at by the enemy, being bombed by hostile aeroplanes" (p. 76), must represent the release of bad internal objects if they are experienced as traumatic.

In Fairbairn's (1952) metapsychology everything is subordinated to failing objects. As Greenberg (1991) points out, Fairbairn's subject is passive to the core, "there are no active strivings, the infant and adult alike only need and want to be taken care of" (p. 75). It is not surprising, therefore, that the soldier who breaks down is described in terms more appropriate to a needy infant than to a man who has been trapped in a sinking ship, struggling desperately to save his life. In general, the Fairbairnian analyst is an exorcist "whose task is to cast out devils" (p. 70). When Fairbairn (1952) writes that "it is rare to find a case [of traumatic neurosis] in which evidence of pre-existing psychopathological characteristics cannot be detected" (p. 257), it is as if he is saying to the traumatized soldier, "Your devils are only bad parents who don't have control over you any more." How much more reassuring these words are for the analyst, rather than having to acknowledge that the world and reality as this man has known it will never be the same. But, even if the analyst's theory does not permit recognition of this fact, the patient knows intimately that the world contains death and destruction.

In sum, it becomes clear repeatedly in the previously cited examples that, both in drive theory and in object relations theory, the notion of fixed psychic structure and elemental conflicts offer a particularly difficult challenge to the psychoanalytic clinician seeking to understand the changes that occur to the adult personality after experiencing massive trauma. Structure is predictability. It is created and maintained by it, unchallenged, unseen, built out of countless ongoing encounters with a world of givens, of regularity, and consistency—or shattered by the lack of it. According to our theories, this structure is created in childhood and becomes a given in itself. I argue throughout this book that when trauma occurs in adult life, it disrupts the predictable in a way that makes it impossible for some to recover or reestablish the familiar.

PREVIOUS FORMULATIONS OF ADULT ONSET TRAUMA

It would be misleading to leave the impression that other analysts have not addressed the topic of adult onset trauma. Under the pressure of world events, notably the two World Wars and the Holocaust, Bergmann and Jucovy (1982), Kardiner (1969), Krystal (1968, 1978, 1985, 1988), Cohen (1985), and Laub and Auerhahn (1989; among others) with varying degrees of success offered psychodynamic solutions to the problems of the traumatic neuroses, as Freud named them. Among those within the classical tradition, Bergmann and Jucovy (1982) focus on the superego pathology that dogs the psychic footsteps of survivors, arguing that massive assaults of hostility from an external source overstimulate whatever sadistic fantasies or retaliatory wishes may have broken through from within the individual psyche. With this change, they maintain, comes the loss of basic trust and healthy narcissism, and hostility is readily turned against the self. This formulation captures the general anhedonia and loss of interpersonal ties that are observed among survivors, but it does not do justice to the ways in which the survivor's psyche appears stalled in the traumatic moment; it does not account for the pervasive intrusive imagery.

Krystal (1968, 1978, 1985) echoes Freud's (1926) assertion that the subjective experience of helplessness determines whether a situation will become traumatic. As was described in the previous chapter, he proposes that for the adult caught in catastrophic circumstances, helpless submission to unavoidable danger with concomitant affective shutdown or alexithymia is at the root of catastrophic traumatic reactions. Cohen (1980, 1985) argues that the traumatic state leads to the absence of structure and representable experience in the region of the self, a regression to what he terms a pre-ego state or "primal repression." Laub's comprehensive theory, described in a series of papers (Laub and Auerhahn, 1989; Felman and Laub, 1992; Laub and Lee, 2003), addresses the meaninglessness and attack on relational ties found among survivors of adult onset trauma.

Among self psychologists, Kohut (1984) notes that the concentration camp experience destroyed the survivor's sense of self, but he does not develop his theory further. Ornstein (1986, 2001) takes issue with the emphasis that so many psychoanalysts placed on rage among survivors which, she argues, continues their dehumanization. Rather than focusing on pathological outcomes, she stresses adult survivors' resilience. She insists that adults confronted with catastrophe have the capacity to call on defensive operations that prevent the psyche from fragmenting. This capacity, she argues, depends on the relative cohesion of the nuclear self, the more cohesive the less fragmentation.

In an admirably comprehensive and carefully argued position, Ulman and Brothers (1988) maintain that traumatic events shatter archaic narcissistic fantasies central to the organization of self experience. They hold that the unconscious meaning of the traumatic event lies in subsequent defensive and/or compensatory attempts to restore these fantasies. However, these authors do not make a distinction between the consequences of adult onset trauma and the seduction of children. Further, their formulation appears to rest on the notion that a healthy adult, one who is not prone to break down under traumatic conditions, would be expected to have an uncompromising and clear-sighted understanding of the world and of her fragile place within it. Several analysts (Fairbairn, 1952; and Winnicott, 1958; among them) suggest that some illusions or areas of omnipotence, are necessary, even in healthy adults, to protect them from untenable anxiety. Even Freud, in his extensive and sometimes contradictory oeuvre makes reference to illusions that "spare us unpleasurable feelings and enable us to enjoy satisfactions instead." He continues, "we must not complain, then, if now and again they come into collision with some portion of reality and are shattered against it" (1915, p. 280).

The issue of personal omnipotence is one of several implicit assumptions underlying psychoanalytic theory and practice that make the cost of survival almost impossible to calculate in metapsychological terms. I turn next to these assumptions.

NECESSARY ILLUSIONS, AGENCY, AND THE REAL

As Lacan (1977) has recast the world of psychic experience, there are three realms. The Imaginary is a world of images, conscious and unconscious, perceived and imagined. The realm of the Symbolic represents the relationship between the signifier and the signified, between words and what they stand for. This is the realm in which meaning is fashioned and refashioned. Traditionally, psychoanalysts and their patients inhabit this realm. Thirdly, there is the realm of the Real "before which the imaginary falters, … over which the symbolic stumbles" (p. x). A cursory reading of Lacan can lead readers to come away with the impression that the Real can be verbalized into submission (see also Zizek, 1989; D. B. Stern, 2000). However, in Lacan's later, more nuanced and more disquieting interpretation, the Real is the unsymbolizeable and unbridgeable gap at the heart of traumatic experience. The Real is ineffable; by definition it can neither be captured nor given meaning, because it is the "horror that cannot be put into words" (Barratt, 1997). To Rose (1982), the Real is the "moment of impossibility on to which symbol and image are grafted" (p. 41). To Grotstein (1992), it is objectlessness. To Lacan, the Real is that which always returns to the same place; in other words, it defies exploration, it cannot be altered or signified, it stands for itself and by itself, a point of endless return. I think of Jonah saying to me, "I have gone into a dead end." There was no escape from the thoughts and images that beset him and no way of making sense of them. Trauma inhabits the Real. In the previous chapter, I described Lacan's notion of the gap in experience that exists between symbolic and biological deaths. The Real, suspended in time, defines and is defined by this space. In effect, the Real is not available for analysis because this would be an "attempt to describe the indescribable" (Kohut, 1984, p. 16).

Existing within the space between psychoanalytic theory and practice, the "fact" of trauma and its resistance to symbolization and fantasy presents the greatest problem to clinicians confronted with a patient who has survived a catastrophic and life-threatening event. What most nonsurvivors might imagine, fantasize, or have nightmares about, Des Pres (1976) writes, "Survivors must go through in spirit and in body. In extremity, states of mind become objective, metaphors tend to actualize, the word becomes flesh" (p. 172). Symbols and the symbolic lose their currency. If meaning cannot be attributed to trauma because it exists only in and of itself, then how can psychoanalysts, who trade in symbols and multiple meanings, bring trauma into analytic discourse?

THE REALM OF INTERPRETATION VERSUS THE EMPIRE OF CONTINGENCY

Traditionally, as we have seen repeatedly in this chapter, psychoanalytic epistemology has dealt with this dilemma by conflating external events and internal experience. Trauma is implicated only in the response, rather than being inherent in the external situation. "What constitutes trauma is not inherent in the actual event, but rather in the individual's response to a disorganizing, disruptive combination of impulse and fears integrated into a set of unconscious fantasies" (Arlow, 1984, p. 533). Historically, the traumatic event itself has not been at issue, only the reaction that it evokes in the survivor. Thus, the significance of the exogenous event and the necessity of exploring it are overlooked, while the individual response becomes the focus of treatment.

It has been our conceit as children of the Enlightenment that we have agency, that we can and do have control of our destiny in an orderly and lawful world. But we are not alone in this conceit. From one age to the next, from one country to the next, "culture is produced against natural reality and mortality" (Becker, 1973, p. 32). And our psychoanalytic culture is no different; agency is built into the psychoanalytic script. "I intend therefore I am," is how Grotstein (1992, p. 65) characterizes this particular aspect of our thinking. Our metapsychology has found several ways of extending the "realm of interpretation" and thereby diminishing the "empire of contingency" (Phillips, 1994, p. 15). In fact, in making a virtue of agency, it is as if psychoanalysts seek to magically and omnipotently deny the presence of contingency and, worse, to pathologize those who fall prey to accidents and disasters.

Whether it is called natural reality (Becker, 1973), factual reality (Freud, 1914), social reality (Hoffman, 1991), or external reality (Arlow, 1984), the perceived world is always filtered through a lens ground by unconscious fantasies, by drives and their derivatives, by earlier formative interactions, or it has been socially constructed through a combination of these forces as they meet in intersubjective space. In short, as we are frequently reminded in this postmodern era, there is no general consensus about what constitutes reality, but there is a consensus that however it is construed, culture, the socially constructed world, is fashioned in such a way as to buffer those who live within its embrace from terror. As Hoffman (1998) puts it, "The construction of any reality always requires blinders: it is always, partially at least, a defensive operation" (p. 16).

Green (1997) has used the phrase indifferent reality to describe those "unambiguous facts" (Hoffman, 1998, p. 20) that cannot be altered by values or wishes, facts that are indifferent to life and death. Indifferent reality presents a particular challenge to social construction, which I discuss in the next chapter.

In several paradoxical twists, depending on the metapsychology through which her psyche is constructed, the psychoanalytic subject struggles to achieve equilibrium by denying her lack of agency in an indifferent world. The Freudian subject, by bringing the drives under conscious control, achieves agency. Through sublimation and insight, she learns to tame those forces that appear out of control, thus achieving freedom from them. In this Freudian version of the Augustinian notion of free will, reason and the rational win out over the drives, the forces of evil contained within. The battles waged against oneself carry far more weight than indifferent reality; indeed, they conspire to draw attention away from this same indifferent reality.

Analysts have too often confused reason with reality, arguing that the irrational exists within the psyche, not in the external world. Trauma crystallizes the struggle between rationality and indifferent reality. The hegemony of reason, as Charles Taylor (1989) described it, that has dominated Western civilization since the Enlightenment, clearly informed Freud's ideal of psychological health. For Freud (1933), "our best hope for the future is that intellect—the scientific spirit, reason—may in the process of time establish a dictatorship in the mental life of man" (p. 635). In Freud's day, the emphasis on rationality over emotional expression went unchallenged, but by the end of the 20th century, as S. Mitchell (1988) has pointed out, we question whether rationality should be the goal of psychoanalysis. Since Freud made those comments, we can point to numerous occasions in which reason has been used destructively, occasions when the Real was at work in the guise of reason. The Holocaust is the most frequently cited example, but any clinician who works with survivors of domestic abuse, assault, genocide, terrorist attacks, or political torture knows that these abuses of reason work on an individual level that can be equally devastating. It is hard to reconcile the classical psychoanalytic emphasis on rationality with the need to come to terms with psychic trauma. As Prince (1985) points out, "there is nothing rational about trauma" (p. 54).

Freud's failure to consider death anxiety as an emergent, irreducible danger situation (Hoffman, 1979, 1998; Langs, 2004; Frommer, 2005; Chapter 2) has left a singularly confusing legacy. If the drives or our internal objects affect our perception of reality, then they are more powerful than reality. In a particularly convoluted twist, the death instinct, that analytic version of original sin, that pull toward entropy, was introduced to explain traumatic neuroses induced by an encounter with indifferent reality. This same death instinct denies the indifferent reality of the very state it proposes to simulate by bringing the death drive into our psyche, theoretically within our control. Freud (1920) himself made a similar observation. Even as he introduced the concept of the death instinct, he wondered whether "this belief in the internal necessity of dying is only another of those illusions that we have created to bear the burden of existence" (p. 39).

Object relations provides several versions of these buffers against indifferent reality. Winnicott's (1958) growing baby bases her sense of security and trust on the illusion that she can magically produce her mother's breast when she wants it. As Winnicott puts it, she learns to have "a belief in reality as something about which she can have illusions" (p. 154). Indeed, to Winnicott, reality is something about which we *must* have illusions if we are to live without crippling anxiety. "The strength found in innocence," is how Des Pres (1976, p. 13) describes this "necessary illusion" (S. Mitchell, 1988, p. 189).

Des Pres (1976) insists that the survivor's vision of the world is different from the "rest of us lucky ones because it is not clouded by sheltering illusions. They do not suddenly, in the ambush of crisis, discover their mortality, for in order to remain alive they must at every moment acknowledge the centrality of death" (p. 21). Survivors, then, in the very act of surviving have lost the shield built into their psyches that protects them from terror. How do we analysts acknowledge that loss without being disoriented both in our theory and in ourselves?

Fairbairn's (1952) subject has taken a similarly self-protective approach to the harsh reality of depending on uncertain objects. At considerable cost to her own sense of psychic integrity, she has constructed a world that is safe and lawful by splitting her ego and repressing harmful objects over which she has no control, reasoning "it is better to be a sinner in a world ruled by God than to live in a world ruled by the devil" (p. 66). As Fairbairn comments, "if the objects are good and himself bad the child is rewarded with a sense of security that an environment of benign objects confers" (p. 65). For Fairbairn too, only when the illusion that we live in an orderly world is supported can we live life fully.

In one way or another, it is as if psychoanalytic theory has been constructed specifically to deny and avoid the experience of being "wounded by reality" (Felman and Laub, 1992, p. 69), from which the title of this book is taken. Our perception of a safe and orderly world in which we have agency comes to us through one of several psychic sleights of hand that shield us from apprehending the harshest facts of life. There are no accidents in this psychoanalytic world, only intentions (Phillips, 1994), although the intent may require psychoanalytic interpretation to be understood. To the extent that they have any place in this world, disasters and catastrophes appear to belong to the same realm as accidents, jokes, and slips of the tongue, something that we have brought on ourselves. By this token, the psychoanalyst, attempting to make sense of a survivor's symptoms, struggles with such interpretive clichés as suggesting that a raped woman had been sexually provocative; believing that a Vietnam veteran who dreamed of being blown up in combat was reacting to an earlier battle with his stepfather; or establishing that Jonah, ambushed by the police, was looking for trouble.

When indifferent reality cannot be assimilated or altered psychically, when it cannot be symbolized, it becomes traumatic reality. It is a reality that sticks in the psychic craw and cannot be dislodged. The survivor is always choking on the fact of it, always fearing a repetition of the breakdown that has already happened (Winnicott, 1974), and often gives up any hope of finding relief.

At the beginning of this chapter, I raised two questions: Why have most psychoanalysts resisted the challenge to describe traumatic symptoms in dynamic terms, and how might this task be undertaken? In attempting to answer the first, we begin to question whether the second is a proper pursuit for psychoanalyis. So many features of psychoanalytic epistemology render adult onset trauma literally incomprehensible; in the Freudian canon, ontogeny (the primacy of the drives) over exogeny; in both classical and object relations theory, the centrality of fixed psychic structure; the privileging of agency and the power of the rational, and the necessity of being able to use symbols are all challenged in working with survivors of adult onset trauma. Given this theoretical shortfall, it is not surprising that psychoanalytic practice is similarly hampered in the face of catastrophe. As the different theories are examined, time and again they return to the idea of a fatal flaw in the psyche, like original sin, that accounts for adult survivors' reactions to their ordeal. In their emphasis on psychic reality, in returning always to the point of departure, these theories describe a circle around the Real. Adult onset trauma becomes the black hole in the middle of psychoanalytic theory, negating its ability to give meaning to experience.

In this chapter, I have described several problems in traditional psychoanalytic epistemology that make the consideration of adult onset trauma virtually impossible: the primacy of the drives, the insistence on a systematic unconscious that is privileged over environmental input, the centrality of fixed psychic structure, the contention that a trauma in adult life is experienced as a recapitulation of an earlier trauma, the emphasis on meaning within this narrow definition of mind, and the assumption that rationality is the highest psychic achievement. In the next chapter, I review some of the changes that the relational initiative has introduced which, together with advances in developmental, cognitive, and neuropsychology, make it possible to consider adult onset trauma in its own right. I also describe some of the ways in which this more inclusive viewpoint, nonetheless, fails to do justice to the complexity of the adult onset traumatic reaction.

4

Wounded by Reality:
The Relational Turn

Survival is an experience with a definite structure, neither random nor regressive nor amoral.

— Terrence Des Pres (1976, p. v)

This is how Jonah came to describe his impressions as he looked down the barrel of the policeman's gun:

> It was like nothing I had ever felt before. I knew they were going to shoot me, like a firing squad. I could hear the words they were saying, but I lost their meaning. I thought I was going blind, things were getting smaller, moving further away; there was blackness around them as if they were disappearing into the blackness. I was paralyzed. I thought my body was already broken, shot through with a thousand bullets, but I couldn't feel anything at all. It seemed to go on and on. I had no hope for it to end. It was just a void filled with terror.

Derealization, depersonalization, the loss of agency leading to a feeling of paralysis, the fear of physical fragmentation, the loss of affectivity and meaning, disruption of continuity, and fear of annihilation, these are the "primitive agonies" (Winnicott, 1958, 1965) Jonah experienced at that moment and that, in one way or another, continued to hold him in their thrall.When Jonah told me, after a long painful silence, that he was afraid he had lost his soul, I was struck by the extraordinary poignancy of his words and challenged to find a way to help him search for, if not recover, his lost soul. I asked myself where to begin this work. Mills (1998) suggests that "the pursuit of the soul is quintessential to the psychoanalytic quest to understand oneself" (p. 167). So Jonah and I needed to embark upon a journey to understand how he lost his self. This idea is not unfamiliar to those who have worked with traumatized adults. Kohut (1984) notes that the concentration camp experience destroyed the survivor's sense of self; Herman (1992) maintains that the self is undone during trauma; Shatan (1973) describes the tattered ego of survivors; Laub and Auerhahn (1989) write that psychic structure is dismantled by trauma; and Lifton (2005) refers to decimated psyches. But little attempt has been made to deconstruct the actual process by which the adult self is destroyed, dismantled, decimated, undone, shattered, or left in tatters during this disastrous confrontation. Drawing on contributions from relational psychoanalysis—together with recent findings in cognitive, neurological, and developmental psychology—this is the task I have set myself in this chapter and the three that follow.

I suggest that for adults, in the traumatic moment itself, in the very act of surviving, in the state of being wounded by reality, the self experiences its psychic foundations in ways that do not happen in the average expectable life. In that moment of savagery, Jonah lost the comforting familiarity of a self on whom he had come to depend. He found himself stripped to his bare and unfamiliar psychic bones. And in the aftermath of that loss, he could not regain his psychic footing. Technically, an aftermath is the second crop of grass sown in the same season. The survivors of massive trauma who have dissociated in order to survive find the second crop of dissociative phenomena to be more enduring, and consequently more alienating, than the first. Jonah had suddenly become unrecognizable to himself; he felt as if he had lost his soul.

Donnel Stern (2000) sounded a clarion call to relational analysts when he wrote: "It is time for relational psychoanalysis to bring into its theory the more arbitrary, random, traumatic and unintelligible parts of life" (p. 768). Relational psychoanalytic theory emphasizes dialectical construction and multiple meanings. It is increasingly willing to give contingency its due, and consequently privileges dissociation over repression. It questions the psychoanalytic imperative that has located all powerful experience in the past. It would appear, therefore, that relational psychoanalysis is in a unique position to undertake the analysis of adult onset catastrophic states that represent the "more arbitrary, random, traumatic and unintelligible parts of life," as Stern describes them. In essence, this approach means leaving the familiar realm of drives, interpretation (and certainty) for the necessarily unknown empire of contingency (and uncertainty; Phillips, 1994).

In addition to the greater flexibility afforded by the relational turn, recent contributions from cognitive and developmental psychologists, neurologists, and neurobiologists further our understanding of the ways in which organisms accommodate change. Taken as a whole, these initiatives support the view of a constantly evolving self informing and being informed by biological, neurological, autobiographical, and contextual changes. Whether these texts further deconstruct the mother–infant relationship; or reveal the developmental phenomena that are constitutive of mind, affect, and the perception of reality; or whether they emphasize the dynamics of emotional or implicit memory, and contribute to our understanding of protosymbolic experience; they offer a way of assembling a theory of mind and body in context, an embodied, emergent, and contingent mind, as Damasio's (1994, 1999) experiments reveal, that begins to answer Stern's call.

STRUCTURE OR PROCESS

In the evolving relational metapsychology, developmental phases are no longer conceived of as linear, following one another in a neat progression, but as events that recur in different guises throughout the life cycle. In his seminal paper, "Object relations theory and the developmental tilt," S. Mitchell (1984) warns us to avoid the common mistake of believing that earlier is necessarily more meaningful or more painful. He urges us to free ourselves from the common psychoanalytic mistake of conflating powerful and primitive feelings with infantile arrests that require the correct interpersonal conditions to make development possible.

Chodorow (1996) and Kulka (1997) suggest that contemporary metapsychology privilege process over structure, that the psyche should be seen as constantly defining itself experientially. Describing the link between the liquid nature of matter and its emergence as a solid, manifest entity, Kulka (1997) recommends that analysts focus on experience, rather than structure. Maintaining the tension between experience and the organization of experience makes it possible to conceptualize adult trauma in its own terms. Following this recommendation, trauma is both in the situation and in the experience of it, the reaction is both in the moment of impact and mediated by previous and subsequent experience. In a similar vein, Chodorow (1996) proposes that a clinical emphasis on contingency and the ambiguity of emergent personal meaning allows for indeterminacy, an escape from the authority of the past, and putative developmental determinants.

Approaching issues of structure, process, and contingency from the perspective of developmental psychology, Thelen and Smith's body of work (1993, 1996) adds to the growing evidence that the human mind is always embodied and that no single innate cause, no essence, no drive, and no single environmental event can bring about a particular behavior. In their nonlinear dynamic systems theory, Thelen and Smith focus on soft assemblies of neurological, musculoskeletal, and perceptual pathways that are acquired under the influence of specific environmental stimuli. These neural pathways carve out attractor basins whose depth and consequent stability—or rigidity—depends on the frequency of use. This rigorously nonessentialist theory stresses the fundamentally idiopathic nature of development, pointing out that new forms of behavior can always arise in a self organizing manner in response to environmental contingency. "Although behavior and development appear structured, there are no structures. Although behavior and development appear rule-driven, there are no rules. There is a multiple, parallel, and continuously dynamic interplay of perception and action, and a system that ... seeks certain stable solutions" (1996, p. xix).

However, these stable solutions are subject to disruption. Psychoanalysts who have incorporated nonlinear dynamic systems theory into their own work emphasize the transitory quality of psychic structure: "There is a point in nonlinear systems at which change in a particular input will change the basic dynamic of the system" (Seligman, 2005, p. 281). Seligman continues, "Once new adaptive processes are set in motion, they can reinforce themselves as different parts of the system respond to each other and/or to the changing environment" (p. 281). Within this system, it can be argued, the long-lasting biological, neurological, behavioral, and consequently psychic effects of catastrophic dissociation, set in motion by a terrifying external event, become self reinforcing as the traumatized individual withdraws further and further from the danger that the world has come to represent.

Galatzer-Levy (2004) describes the benefits of working within a dynamic systems framework rather than the classic psychodynamic epigenetic model that has led psychoanalysts in the past to minimize the significance of adult onset trauma. "The focus of investigation shifts from the limited search for latent continuities to questions such as whether, in appropriate circumstances, people's minds can become significantly disorganized and then successfully reorganized, or whether, in a particular circumstance a dramatic shift in underlying function has occurred" (p. 435).

The emphasis on process, on ongoing experience, and the capacity for—indeed the inevitability of change in response to environmental stimuli—prepares the psychoanalytic clinician to approach the shattering and enduring effect of catastrophic experience in adult life in a more open frame of mind.

THE ROLE OF MEMORY AND SOCIAL CONSTRUCTION

In recent years, neurologists have consistently noted the failure of the prefrontal cortex under extreme stress and the subsequent difficulties of laying down coherent explicit memories of traumatic events. Under normal conditions, the fluid ebb and flow of experience integrates a host of implicit and explicit memory systems; the senses come together with perception and with movement, with thought, and with affect. In one way or another, Edelman (2004), LeDoux (1996), Thelen and Smith (1996), and Damasio (1994, 1999) describe the process in which small adjustments occur in the brain and body as they interact with one another and with the environment, continuously maintaining homeostasis. But when the brain detects danger, there is a "profound departure from business as usual" (Damasio, 1994, p. 224). LeDoux (1996), van der Kolk, McFarlane, and Weisaeth (1996), and van der Kolk (2002) describe the "cascade of biobehavioral changes" (van der Kolk, 1996, p. 218) that occurs in individuals exposed to trauma. Multiple levels of biological functioning, from the regulation of internal homeostasis to perceptual, higher cognitive, and analytical functions, are chronically affected.

Of particular interest to the clinician working with a patient who has experienced a trauma in adult life are the neurophysiological changes that set conscious traumatic memories apart from memories acquired under regular conditions. LeDoux (1996) describes two systems involved in traumatic memory: conscious or explicit memories linked to the hippocampus, and unconscious or implicit bodily memories mediated by the function of the amygdala.

In extreme stress, the increased secretion of norepinephrine disrupts hippocampal functioning necessary for the consolidation of memory. Traumatic memories, therefore, are quite literally short circuited and stored as somatic sensations, visual images, and auditory traces in the amygdala rather than being integrated through the mediation of the hippocampus and prefrontal cortex. Linguistic memory is frequently inactivated during the trauma; thus sensory, affective, and motor memories are often divorced from a conscious knowledge of what prompted them. These amygdala-based catastrophic memory fragments are much more easily aroused and, unmediated by the symbolic function of thought, they are frequently acted upon blindly, thus providing a biological explanation for the intrusive images common to posttraumatic states.

Although cortisol released during a stressful event can damage the hippocampus, leading to the fragmented and uncertain memories previously described, the situation is further complicated by the paradoxical nature of the process. At the first sign of danger, an increase in adrenaline can strengthen explicit memory, which leads to flashbulb memories; those very clear and explicit memories of parts of the traumatic event that many survivors retain and keep seeing in their mind's eye. But, as the stress continues, the adrenaline ultimately devastates the explicit memory (LeDoux, 1996, p. 207). Thus, the survivor's memory can consist of moments of terrifying clarity and equally terrifying impressions of events that, on reflection, do not appear to hold together. As Jonah attempted to describe the sequence of events that led to his being thrown downstairs by the police, he found that there were many sequences that did not make sense to him, and actual gaps in his memory where he could not account for his actions. However, other moments, such as watching the building's handyman being thrown over the banister, were indelible and unchanging. Further, particular expressions, "East Village" for example, or certain sensory impressions, the way the light fell on some evenings, would, inexplicably it seemed to him, elicit feelings of panic as the memory fragments stored in the amygdala were stimulated, but no explicit memory accompanied them.

These neurological findings are consistent with the current emphasis on dissociation among relational psychoanalysts. In the previous chapter, it was instructive to trace how contemporary psychoanalytic discourse has shifted from the explanatory power of repression to that of dissociation in understanding the consequences of abuse in childhood. In emphasizing repression, and consequently maintaining the possibility that past events could be accurately reconstructed, the classical psychoanalyst's work was informed by a clear theory of mind and a conviction about the correctness of the underlying assumptions. Traumatic memories were repressed because the events themselves caused conflictual wishes. The goal, simply enough, was to recall the events and uncover the conflicts. Blum (1986) puts the solution that classical psychoanalysts sought most succinctly, reconstruction determines "where the truth lies" and helps uncover the repressed "historic truth within the patient's fabrication and fantasies" (p. 23). To the classical analyst, emphasis on manifest content does not resolve the real injury associated with the trauma; that lies in the symbolic meaning of the intrusion.

Donnel Stern (1997) has provided relational analysts with an alternative way of thinking about unconscious phenomena. Rather than imagining the unconscious as a repository for repressed ideas, he describes an unconscious that is made up of unformulated experience and unformed ideas. This unformulated experience is experience that has been dissociated for a number of reasons. Either the organism was too immature to register it cognitively, or the experience was left vague for defensive purposes because the affects associated with it were too overwhelming, or because there were insufficient conceptual frameworks into which it could be fitted. In everyday life, unformulated experience intrudes in apparently inexplicable enactments, impressions, "new" thoughts and affects. The clinician working with this kind of dissociated experience is less certain about her ability to discover the truth of what happened to her patient, but struggles to make sense of the dissociated impressions, enactments, and memory fragments. In this very different psychoanalytic paradigm, clinicians do not search for repressed meaning; there are no truths to be recovered here, but rather they seek to understand the impact of the traumatic experience itself. This dramatic change in emphasis challenges us to engage our patients in finding ways of describing their subjective experience, an experience that takes shape as the words are found to describe it. These clinicians are, in effect, constructing with the patient an experience that may have been brought in bits and pieces into the margins of consciousness, only to be banished before it reached the level of coherent thought.

In a passage that combines the experience of social construction with the neurological network findings previously described, Rustin and Sekaer (2004) write:

> Memory never exists in pure form. Whether it is a personal memory of an episode with a friend or factual knowledge of the world, it is both activated and transformed with input from the retrieval cue. ... Each activation of a memory is an amalgam of the patient's inner network and the analyst acting as a retrieval cue. ... A new construction is created, ... which revises and extends the network that encodes the memory. [p. 77]

However, in the case of adult onset trauma, if the analyst adapts a stance of extreme relativism, social construction presents a particular challenge and can prove as destructive as a search for truths about underlying psychic conflicts. As Moore (1999) puts it, "Trauma represents the most severe test for a constructivist psychoanalysis" (p. 166). A traumatic event in adult life is usually indisputable; whether it is a life threatening accident, torture, a terror attack, or a more private assault, the harsh facts—a word I use advisedly in this context—lie beyond the reach of social construction. Yet the survivor's dissociated experience can lead her to question her response to the event and even the severity of the event itself, fearing that she overreacted, or that she imagined it, or in some other way fabricated it out of whole cloth. It is dangerous and demeaning and further undermining if the clinician does not recognize that this uncertainty has a neurological basis that also functions as a defense against realizing the full horror of annihilatory terror. Primo Levi spent many years struggling with his need to tell the world about his experience in Auschwitz. In his memory, this need was constantly juxtaposed with the words of an S.S. officer who jeered at him that if he survived the concentration camp, no one would believe the story he had to tell. For Levi (1958), worst of all, was his own doubt: "At this very moment, as I sit writing at the table, I myself am not convinced that these things really happened" (p. 161). Similarly, Appelfeld (1994), describing his own experiences during the Shoah, wrote, "It is unbelievable. You relate it, but you don't believe that this thing actually happened to you. This is one of the most shameful things I know" (p. 181).

Clinicians are challenged to find a way of acknowledging adult onset trauma with patients whose ability to reflect on it has been overwhelmed by the influx of stimuli. When external reality and the process of dissociation has collapsed the self and its ability to subjectively recall an event, when the mind's ability to reflect is compromised by terror,

and when reality testing has collapsed in the state of psychic equivalence—that is, when the external world bears close resemblance to the
internal world of nightmares and terrifying fantasies—the clinical task is
first to re-establish a sense of reality before constructing an understanding of what the patient has experienced. "Historical reality has to be reconstructed and reaffirmed before any other work can start," Felman
and Laub assert (1992, p. 69). As Moore (1999) puts it, "with massive
trauma, the process of construction can be said to roll in reverse, the
external world disintegrates the process of construction" (p. 165).

CORE SELF/MULTIPLE SELVES

The postmodern emphasis on multiplicity can make for further difficulties in understanding the collapsed self in adult onset trauma. For all its
explanatory power, multiplicity can be theoretically confining. Flax
(1996) argues that even in relational psychoanalysis there has to be a
place for nonrelational minds, a place "for mental life not constituted by
particular internalized self object dyads as evoked by the interpersonal
past or present" (p. 582). The place for a nonrelational mind is crucial to
the understanding of adult onset trauma. Across the postmodern divide, the psychoanalytic self is constituted not only by psyche and soma,
but it is also defined severally, relationally, and contingently. In Chapter
2, I reviewed the shift that occurred in psychoanalytic discourse when
contemporary analysts introduced the concept of multiple discontinuous self states, each one pressed into service during moments of shame
and fear in childhood, thus accounting for experiences in adult life that
both bear the imprint of childhood and accommodate the contingencies of adulthood. But the accommodation does not stretch far enough
when catastrophic trauma strikes in adulthood. To the adult, dissociation in the face of massive psychic trauma does not result in a further
split off traumatized self state, but in a potentially permanently altered
sense of self. In adult onset trauma—although details of the trauma may
be discounted or distorted, stripped of their affective charge and their
significance denied—the sense of a collapsed self, a mortal self first encountered during the catastrophe, permeates every aspect of the adult
trauma survivor's conscious and unconscious life; it is manifest in each
self state.

  Speaking of the catastrophic shift that occurred in her experience of
herself and in her relationships with other people, Carla, who barely
survived imprisonment and torture at the hands of her ex-husband said,

"Every day I have to remind myself that I am not dead. Nothing is the same any more. And I feel different from everyone else. Even if I seem to forget it for a moment, when I'm listening to the kids at dinner or helping them with their homework, I'm still uneasy. I've lost something irreplaceable. I don't recognize myself."

It has been argued that with the introduction of multiplicity, relational analysts turned away from the interior sense of a core self. The very relativity of continually constructed experience would seem to contradict the idea of a core self; in fact, it would suggest that fragmentation is the order of the day and that a traumatized adult could escape from her mortal self into a more reassuring self state under favorable conditions. Yet Carla seems to be referring to a fundamental fear that does not yield in the face of contrary experience, a fear that underlies all her actions. "I have to remind myself that I am not dead," she says. Like Antigone banished from Thebes, Carla inhabits the netherworld between two deaths, *entre deux morts,* the frozen place where, having narrowly escaped one death, she can no longer fully engage in the world of the living. If catastrophic dissociation had prepared her to enter another self state, she would certainly escape from this painful condition when she is interacting with her children or singing in the church choir, but she cannot. Instead she acts "as if" she is among the living. Even when she is in a routine moment of mothering, the unremitting subjective experience of loss echoes in the background, a reminder that something is seriously amiss. This cannot be explained by multiplicity. Reis (1993) points out that dissociative patients are always, to one degree or another, simultaneously in the present of other ego states as well as in the present day. He makes an analogy to driving a car and listening to the radio, having one's mind on both tasks simultaneously. Thus, Carla is aware of her traumatically and chronically disrupted subjectivity, even as she performs and experiences the familiar routines of motherhood. Or Jonah feels a constant yearning for his lost soul as he interacts with business colleagues who are unaware of the sense of rupture from which he cannot escape.

One of the questions contemporary psychoanalysts have attempted to resolve is how, indeed whether, to synthesize the apparently disparate notions of a true self containing a singular identity on the one hand with variable, shifting, and contextual selves on the other. Some shun the very notion of a core self, focusing instead on contingent self states that account for much of the fluidity—and stuckness—of adult life. Fairfield (2001) and Reis (2005) point out that this ideological argu-

ment, this "unnecessary forced choice" (Reis, 2005, p. 91) between seeing the self as multiple or singular is just that: a battle of ideologies. "To
say that a cohesive self is a fiction or illusion is to assume that a multiplex
subjectivity is not," Fairfield (2001, p. 226) points out conclusively. Offering a solution to this problem, Frederickson (2000) and Mills (1998)
suggest that the concepts of core self and multiple self states should not
be seen as mutually exclusive but complementary; that multiplicity does
not rule out the idea of a singular unifying and integrating agent that is
"a necessary and universal condition of subjectivity" (Mills, 1998, p.
165). Indeed, as S. Mitchell (1993) points out, the experience of self as
singular and constant serves an important adaptive psychological purpose. "There is a sense of self that is independent of shifts over time,
connected with the function of self reflection, providing continuity
from one subjective state to the next. …even when I am not myself I experience a continuity with previous subjective states" (p. 107). This is
what Mitchell calls "the capacity to take oneself for granted" (p. 114).
And it is just this ability to take one's *self* for granted that is destroyed
during catastrophic dissociation.

Damasio (1994, 1999) offers a neurological solution to the debate
about single selves versus multiple selves. He proposes an ever-chang-
ing biologically based core self—"not so much that it changes, but
rather that it is transient, ephemeral, remade and reborn continuously"
(1999, p. 216)—and a consciously-based psychological self composed
of memories of the past and plans for the future, the fundamental facts
that make up an individual's biography. In understanding the effects of
adult onset trauma, Damasio's core biological self is a foundational
must. It takes precedence evolutionarily and individually over extended
consciousness. The core self is employed constantly in monitoring signals from the environment, monitoring its own responses to these signals, and integrating the results as a way of maintaining a steady state.

The unconscious sources of the self, as they shape and are shaped by
the core biological self, are more far reaching than has previously been
taken into account. Bucci (2001), whose work integrates the concepts
of psychoanalysis, cognitive behaviorism, and the neurosciences, describes subsymbolic systems comprised of the tactile, motoric, visual,
sensory, and affective senses. Understanding how these systems function provides clinicians working with the fundamentals of emotional experience, a way of envisioning the nexus between body and mind, affect
and neurophysiology. The subsymbolic systems are central to the
knowledge of one's body and emotional experience but, as the name

makes clear, they are not conscious (although, some argue, they provide the basis for symbolization in the course of time.) To paraphrase Damasio's (1999) poetic description, the core senses and sensory system constitute the flow of life as it wanders in the journey of each day. Bucci points out that although these systems underlie symbolic experience, they are not archaic, as Freud would characterize them; their importance does not wane with the advent of verbalization; they exist alongside and inform the symbolic system. Their parameters are familiar to us, and even though they cannot be directly verbalized they become the stuff of stability and provide a basis for metaphoric speech. Lakoff and Johnson (1999) maintain that proprioceptive and somatosensory metaphors are instantiated within language and abstract reasoning. They represent part of the unformulated unconscious experience that, in the case of trauma, becomes central to the sense of a collapsed self.

By incorporating these neurological and sensory data into an understanding of human subjectivity, it is possible to conceive of shifting self states embedded within a core self. The underlying core self establishes broad physiological and psychological parameters while the shifting self states are informed by the relative durability of the core self or—in the case of adult onset trauma—by the traumatically undermined core self. Despite the exigencies of daily life, the moments of shame, humiliation, anxiety, and sometimes panic that occur in every life, there is little reason to question that the core self lies in established patterns of physiological, affective, and behavioral regulation. These established patterns grant continuity to experience as they adapt to developmental changes and accommodate contextual ones. Under normal circumstances, this self is constantly evolving through experience.

The discovery of the "contingent self," the core self that has been previously resistant to, indeed the self that is antithetical to psychoanalytic exploration, "entails the belated recovery or processing of the earliest forms of experience" (Phillips, 1994, p.16). I agree with Phillips that the psychoanalytic treatment of survivors of late onset trauma requires us to grapple with the fundamentals of self experience. On the surface, this does not appear to differ from the common psychoanalytic claim that a subjective experience of helplessness is the hallmark of a traumatic situation, reviving feelings of infantile distress. However, in directing our gaze to early integrating experiences that come together to form a core self, the experiences that ensure the integrity and continuity of self organization, I do not mean to imply that the trauma survivor is re-experiencing infantile helplessness.

Rather, I am emphasizing the notion that early integrating experiences inevitably involve the bodily states that underlie self experience.

Many contemporary psychoanalytic writers insist that maintaining the integrity and continuity of self organization is a superordinate aim for all people, independent of diagnostic category (Eagle, 1984; D. N. Stern, 1985; Modell, 1993; Lachmann 1996; Gedo, 1999). Indeed Modell continues, "the continuity of the self is preserved by virtue of the self's linkage with the homeostatic brain systems" (p. 48). The shattering and far reaching disruptive effect on the homeostatic brain system brought about by terror has long lasting neurological consequences as we have seen.

In line with the work of Thelen and Smith (1993, 1996), Damasio (1994, 1999), LeDoux (1996), Bucci (2001), and Edelman (2004) I am, then, advocating a different way of envisioning the effects of early development and the subsequent blow of adult onset trauma. Developmental experiences and the neural pathways that embody them are not an indelible imprint, as classical theory has posited, but a baseline for ongoing self experience. In the early years, traumatic experiences can be incorporated into dissociated self states. In adult life, however, physiologically and psychologically massive psychic trauma catastrophically disrupts the baseline sense of self that under normal circumstances would never be in doubt.

This is a long way from a metapsychology based on drives and fixed psychic structure, which previous generations of psychoanalysts had at their disposal when they attempted to understand the changes wrought by massive trauma. The question that faces clinicians today is how to translate this understanding of a more flexible and yet more fragile self into psychodynamic terms, into words that can bring understanding, that can address the subjective sense of collapse without positing essences or resorting to genetic interpretations.

Daniel Stern's (1985) empirical studies of infants focused on the acquisition of a core self achieved by the preverbal integration of the senses of agency, physical cohesion, continuity, and affectivity. These "invariants" or "islands of consistency," as Stern calls them, make possible, and in turn are elaborated by, intersubjective experience. Upon this autonomic psychic platform rests the verbal self, with its capacity to make and to derive meaning. Stern emphasizes that this core self is not a cognitive construct, not a hypothetical psychic structure, but an actual experiential integration. It is true that Stern's work has been criticized (Cushman, 1995, among others) and Stern himself has noted that his empirical self is one of several interpretations that can be drawn from his data. Nonetheless this particular construct of a bounded, cohesive, continuous, and agentic self does fit the subjective experience of most of us who live in the Western hemisphere.

As the psyche matures and self-regulation consolidates, the core self becomes the unarticulated and unformulated ground against which the figure of experience is projected. Normally completely taken for granted and operating out of awareness, like Bucci's (2001) subsymbolic systems or Damasio's (1994, 1999) neurological core self, it is "the primitive underbelly of experience" (Ogden, 1989, p. 83), like a heartbeat or regular breath. In trauma, this core self is catastrophically and chronically dysregulated not just neurologically, but psychically as well. At this autonomic level, physiological and psychological experience inform one another. Terror leading to catastrophic dissociation leaves a lasting biological impression with profound psychological reverberations. In the case of adult onset trauma, physiological, neurological, and biological explanations are far advanced, but the phenomenological consequences of these findings and their psychodynamic import have been less frequently explored.

I am proposing, then, that catastrophe disrupts the core self, quite literally fixing it in place, changing biology and psychic experience. The "bare autonomic faith in the body"—as Michaels (1996, p. 54) puts it so evocatively—is lost. In its defensive retreat into dissociation, the psyche has broken faith with the consistency and resilience of its core. It is as if the core self's psychological support systems, agency, continuity, cohesiveness and affect—all of which were temporarily disconnected by dissociation during the actual trauma—cannot be reconnected seamlessly. The self has lost the familiar ground on which it stood. It is an awareness that is never far from consciousness, that can come into sharp relief in response to external or internal cues, but often it is simply a hum in the background of experience, a knowledge of otherness, of the failure of the self and the self's ties, of the certainty of death. Indeed, this is Carla's experience. Having met her mortal self in the moment of dissociation, she has to continually remind herself that she is not dead. There is no longer a shifting between figure and ground. Death, her death, the death that already happened at the moment of trauma is figure, everything else fades into the background.

When our understanding of the unconscious includes unformulated, dissociated, and subsymbolic experience, when we allow for contingency, when we understand that meaning was reduced to the desperate need to survive, when our knowledge of the neurological and neurochemical alarm system leads to the realization that the influx of cortisone overwhelmed the ability to consolidate memories of the event in a comprehensive and subjectively meaningful way, clinicians can start to follow Donnel Stern's (2000) call to construct with a massively traumatized patient an understanding of what might have happened. With the fragments of experience that are remembered, whether those fragments are cognitive, kinesthetic, visual, auditory, or affective, it is possible to build a picture that starts to make sense of the way in which the self collapsed under the pressure of the experience.

In the next chapter, I take up each of the fundamentals of self-experience in turn, as they are disrupted by trauma, and I follow the impact of the loss of self-cohesion both in the moment of trauma and beyond. In Chapter 6, I trace the ways in which this catastrophic disruption poisons the survivor's object world, making an empathic analytic relationship difficult to establish. Chapter 7 demonstrates how the loss of symbolic function after a catastrophic event presents a particularly difficult challenge to psychoanalytic exchange and to self-reflection.

5

The Core Self in Crisis: Deconstructing Catastrophic Dissociation

A good theory will generate multiple, productive questions and conversations, not preemptive answers and categorization.

— J. Flax (1996, p. 589)

"What becomes disorganized," Kardiner (1969, p. 251) concluded his study of World War II combat veterans with battle fatigue, "is the whole series of action systems that carry out the intentions of the ego: cognitive, coordinative, executive (sensory motor) and autonomic." Kardiner's conclusion is prescient, for he appears to have anticipated advances in developmental and cognitive psychology and in the neurological sciences that only now reveal the intimate relationship between neurodynamics and psychodynamics when self regulation is taken as the focus of self experience. Each of the terrors that Jonah described and that I summarized at the beginning of the previous chapter—derealization, depersonalization, the loss of agency leading to a feeling of paralysis, the fear of physical fragmentation, the loss of affectivity and meaning, disruption of continuity and fear of annihilation—is a different facet of the catastrophic dissociative process as his core self literally came unraveled.

Eagle (1984) criticizes psychoanalytic thinkers for frequently conflating therapeutic and theoretical aims and contexts. Following a patient's narrative, constructing painstakingly an idea of what happened, and paying close attention to the intersubjective are therapeutic skills that any relational analyst strives for, but they do not explain the adult survivor's subjective experience. My goal in this chapter is to respect the necessary tension between theory and practice by following the epistemic model recommended by Protter (1988). Protter's incisive guide to ways of knowing in psychoanalysis suggests that a useful theory must address three epistemic modes concurrently: existential knowing, contextual knowing, and textual knowing. The patient's experience-near narrative and the interpersonal context in which it has been fashioned must be held together in the analyst's mind by an explanatory model to which the analyst will be referring and refining throughout the analytic process.

Existential knowing examines the patient's subjective or phenomenological state. In the case of late-onset trauma, it is particularly important to consider not just how the patient may be feeling during the session, but also to reconstruct, in minute detail, his subjective experience during the traumatic event. When patients permit themselves to recapitulate their traumatic experiences, their terror in the session can be almost as powerful as it was during the trauma; frequently they dissociate as they re-enter the scene that they have been trying to avoid. It is the analyst's job to enter that experience with her patient, however much resistance she may feel.

Second, Protter (1988) suggests that the context or intersubjective situation must be understood. Having to consider the patient's terror exposes the analyst to her own mortality, to her mortal self. The tension she experiences between the roles of voyeur and witness as she moves back and forth between these different positions—sometimes numb or excited but curiously impersonal, at other times immersing herself in the patient's experience—is the essence of the clinician's intersubjective predicament. It is in working towards and striking a balance between these two positions that the psychodynamic therapist will succeed in making herself available as a container of the patient's experience. This is the subject of Chapter 7.

The third and final strand of Protter's (1988) epistemic braid involves textual knowing. He emphasizes the necessity of developing a text that consists of an experience-near narrative for the patient that makes sense of her subjective experience of the trauma and its consequences, while the clinician develops a metanarrative as she attempts to rewrite the "primary story according to a more generalizable story from an alternative perspective" (p. 514).

The metanarrative proposed in this chapter is a parsimonious and generalizable model, a roadmap, if you will, that describes the dynamic consequences of trauma for the adult survivor. This model does not have recourse to developmental arrests, infantile trauma, or conflict, but suggests how adult onset trauma might undercut the very foundation on which a previously stable sense of self and self in relation to other was predicated, and why the psychic assault continues to reverberate through and to alter subsequent experience of self and other.

In the following, I review the impact of catastrophic dissociation on the motoric, sensory, affective, and cognitive systems as it is experienced psychologically at the moment of trauma, as it profoundly alters the subject's sense of self, and as a clinician might understand it dynamically. I deconstruct the phenomenology of catastrophic dissociation, examining its impact on each of the senses of the self, first through the words of survivors; this is Protter's (1988) existential knowing. Then through a psychodynamic lens, which is Protter's textual knowing. The subjective descriptions may appear to overlap, even though they are subtly different. It is this very redundancy that defeats the self's struggle to regain its equilibrium as each aspect of the collapsing core self is implicated by and implicates the rest.

In the language of nonlinear dynamic systems theory, catastrophic dissociation is an emergent, complex, and evolving process that arises in response to an environmental event and involves the interaction of the neurological, cognitive, psychological, and affective systems. Consistent with this argument, there is no single cause, but rather a complex neurological, cognitive, and affective response to the environmental event. It is further important to recognize that the process of catastrophic dissociation takes a different course with each individual but, at a certain critical tipping point, the subjective experience of having lost touch with a familiar self is similar for many survivors. In this way, I am attempting to capture the process by which an individual comes to experience radical and long-lasting discontinuity with his previous sense of self.

Too often, attempts to understand trauma are fitted or forced into schematic models; although the ideas that follow are presented systematically, they are not intended to describe a syndrome *per se*. My purpose is to suggest that the anticipation of annihilation—including as it does biological factors, neurological states of arousal, and the temporary relief provided by dissociation—assumes far-reaching consequences for the continuity of self-experience. Catastrophic experience in adulthood brings each aspect of the core self into question, shattering confidence in the invariants that previously formed and informed experience, jeopardizing the self that cannot, in fact, be separated from experience. Once the crisis is past, the conscious and unconscious impact of the experience, of the moment of surrender, as Krystal (1988) calls it, continues to live on in similar and increasingly alienating ways.

In examining the different facets of the core self to deconstruct the immediacy of the traumatic state and to trace how this experience translates into posttraumatic psychological sequelae, I reiterate that I am not suggesting a one-to-one correspondence between the traumatic state and earlier developmental stages. D. N. Stern (1985) warns against making analogous relationships between formative experience and later development: "Once formed each sense of self remains fully functioning and active throughout life. All continue to grow and coexist" (p. 11). In her discussion of subsymbolic systems, Bucci (2001) makes a similar point, emphasizing that it is not necessary to resort to infantilization in order to offer an explanatory hypothesis when these systems are disrupted.

In the literature on the long term psychological consequences of trauma, whether of childhood or adult onset, different authors believe that the traumatic reactions are driven by the disruption of fundamental aspects of psychic experience. To Krystal (1978, 1985, 1988), the sense of affectivity is compromised. To Reis (1993), it is time and the sense of continuity. To Pye (1995), it is agency and imagination as they interact with one another. To Slavin (1997), it is the relationship between agency and memory. To Grand (2000), it is agency and continuity. To Laub and Auerhahn (1989), the internal empathic other is lost; the survivor finds herself in a world devoid of benign objects. I contend that it is not one particular aspect of self-experience, but each of them as they interact with each other that fuels the reaction to catastrophic dissociation among adults. In the following pages, I summarize and synthesize these aspects of core nonverbal self-experience to demonstrate how intimately they are bound together and how their impact is experienced both during dissociation and beyond.

AGENCY

The worldview that supports the notion of personal agency could be called a birthright, the most reassuring legacy of the Enlightenment; it is a mainstay of psychoanalytic epistemology (Boulanger, 2002a; and as previously mentioned). Paradoxically, it seems, we do not question that we are the author of our actions until we have lost that conviction. This earliest and most fundamental invariant of core self experience (D. N. Stern, 1985; Fonagy et al., 2002) is first manifest, and a rudimentary impression of being the author of one's actions acquired, through motor behavior. Control over motor behavior is often lost during the moment of trauma. "I was frozen in place." "It was like a nightmare where you want to move but can't." These are common responses. Some survivors admit, with terrible shame, that in a state of terror they lost control of their bodily functions.

"I was paralyzed," Jonah told me, describing the belief that he had lost volition; that he had no control over his physical behavior. In this condition, he no longer experienced himself as a subject who could form and carry out intentions. Rather, he felt as if some external agent had taken control of his behavior. Speaking out of this frightening conviction, survivors say such things as "I felt like a puppet" and "I was on automatic pilot." A woman who was raped told me, "I found my hips moving. It was disgusting, but I couldn't stop. That's what he wanted."

Losing control to external agents, being at the mercy of another, shifts the lens through which the psyche focuses to the paranoid schizoid position. "Psychology without a subject" is how Ogden (1990, p. 45) describes the phenomenology of this psychic world. In this world, the self exists only as an object; the subject who makes choices and follows through on them is lost. Bettelheim, who on most occasions is not sympathetic to survivors of the Holocaust, describes his own reactions to being in a concentration camp: "I became convinced that those dreadful and degrading experiences were somehow not happening to me as a subject but only to me as an object" (reported in Des Pres, 1976, p. 81). Herman (1992) quotes a traumatized patient who described the experience of depersonalization in this way: "It wasn't like she was hitting me, it was like she was hitting someone else" (p. 98). The patient experienced herself as an insensate object.

A survivor of such experiences will often seek to reverse the involuntary loss of motor control as soon as possible. Timerman (2002), who was subjected to long periods of torture by the right wing regime in Argentina in the 1970s, describes a ritual he developed, making (and observing) almost imperceptible movements with his arm after each torture session as if to restore some sense of agency.

The very fact of dissociation represents an attack on agency—dissociation is not a choice; it is imposed by an overwhelmed psyche that is attempting to protect itself from further harm. "It is something that happens, that we do not or cannot control" (Slavin, 1997, p. 231). The loss of this most fundamental ability becomes generalized to the cognitive and emotional sphere. Once the immediate need for a psychological escape through dissociation no longer exists, the survivor finds that she cannot escape the neurologically generated intrusive memories and thoughts common to posttraumatic states. Although there may be some protection in the isolated world of the paranoid schizoid position, an ability to take cover briefly in the magic of splitting, the paranoid schizoid self as object is also chronically plagued by persecutory convictions. "Thoughts, feelings and perceptions are conceived of as constituting things in themselves" (Ogden, 1990, p. 27). Without an "I" to create and give meaning to experience, experience is driven by sensation. In this sensation-dominated world, the rapid cycling of state-dependent traumatic memories, prompted by a sound, a smell, an affect, a visual cue, a sudden turn in the weather, even a particular word, feel as if they are intruding, persecuting, unbidden, and uncontrollable. "The individual feels herself at the mercy of harrowing terrors, which she can only fend off by magical and tyrannical means," comments Pye (1995, p. 163), who also draws parallels between the paranoid schizoid position and the psychic world of the survivor.

Generating meaning, making sense of an experience or a sensation, is perhaps the most highly developed instance of personal agency. Traumatic memories often resist the survivor's need to make sense of them. Instead, assaulted by memory fragments and unidentifiable sensations, survivors find themselves further alienated from a formerly stable core self.

The case of Patrick illustrates how insidiously the sense of agency, undermined by a catastrophic event or series of events, becomes a loss that can extend far beyond the original trauma.

A much-decorated Vietnam veteran, Patrick was referred to me after he had been back from Vietnam for more than 20 years. In Vietnam, he crewed on helicopters flying into "hot" landing zones to evacuate the injured. Once, after his helicopter was destroyed and the pilot and crew chief killed, Patrick took command of the remaining men. Finding makeshift shelter in a deep, water-filled ditch, they remained hidden for 24 hours within yards of the Vietcong, never knowing when or whether their flimsy cover would be blown.

During the years after his return, Patrick worked as a policeman, moving up through the ranks to become captain of his precinct. As a soldier and a police officer, he was cited for many acts of heroism both in and out of the line of duty. A careful observer might have concluded that Patrick sought out dangerous situations to reenact and to master his posttraumatic anxiety. Experiments with those who have been exposed to traumatic circumstances reveal that endogenous opioids, activated during the stressful experience, function as analgesics, equivalent to eight milligrams of morphine. Since opioids reduce the perception of physical and psychological pain, paradoxically, they lead survivors to seek out further danger as a way of coping with anxiety (van der Kolk, McFarlane, and Weisaeth, 1996). Given the fact that Patrick's acts of heroism occurred in the line of duty, no one questioned his judgment and he was not consciously aware of any troubling symptoms. "I had no patience with that Vietnam Stress Syndrome stuff," he said. "I thought they were making it up. I thought they were lazy or cowards." But one night during a police raid, Patrick was wounded in his firing arm and trapped under fire in a dark apartment, suddenly unable to protect himself. Finally in a position where he could take no defensive action, he could not deny the annihilatory terror that had been fended off for so long. "I thought I heard helicopters overhead," he recalled. "I could hear Vietnamese being spoken around me, and I smelled the jungle. I was right there."

As we discussed the meaning of his vivid flashback, it became clear that Patrick had not had any sense of agency for many years. This man, who had shown not only courage but also ingenuity, drew no pride or confidence from the quick thinking that had kept him, and many others, alive. Patrick had come to believe that he was simply a puppet whose survival had nothing to do with the actions he took. "The man up there has plans for me," he would repeat, giving voice to the chronic helplessness he had felt since returning from Vietnam, where he had seen so many die senselessly. Patrick's attempts to make sense of his survival, to attribute it to God's will because his own sense of agency was so compromised, illustrates Caruth's (1996) point that it is not the incomprehensibility of near death, but the incomprehensibility of one's own survival, that give rise to posttraumatic repetition.

Patrick's belief that he owed his survival to God might be interpreted as grandiose or superstitious. But to Patrick, believing he had no control over his actions or their outcome and that his survival was in God's hands only increased his vulnerability. He no longer felt as if he was the agent of his actions; he no longer believed he could have intentions and follow through on them. This frightening loss of conviction in his own agency had been hidden for years behind a repetition compulsion that only confirmed to Patrick that he was a puppet in God's hands. Each time he survived another dangerous police operation, he failed to master the split-off affect experienced during trauma. He simply confirmed to himself that he had no agency because, once again, God had ordained that he should survive. The only way to end this Catch 22 would be accept his mortal self. These fears had remained unformulated until he began treatment, where he came to recognize his sense of chronic vulnerability. But Patrick was unwilling to do this, because in doing so he would have to accept his family's vulnerability as well. "Then I can't protect anyone," he would repeat each time we faced this particular hurdle together.

Like Patrick, the mother of a murdered child struggled to find a way to reclaim agency and restore the feeling that she was in charge of her destiny, trying to reason away how mortally vulnerable her family was. "If only I could believe that I was in some way responsible. If I had sent him out there to get something from the store, then I could believe that I can protect my other son. But I am helpless." Pitting logic against contingency is an attempt to deny the Real. When this denial doesn't work, the feeling of powerlessness contributes to the incidence of suicide among survivors. In the early years of her recovery from her near fatal rape, Brison (2002) writes that she believed that the only way to regain control over her life was to end it.

Slavin and Pollock (1997) and Reis (1993) point out that children who have been traumatized often deny the loss of agency. "They disbelieve themselves as victims" (Slavin and Pollock, 1997, p.574). This is a further distinction between survivors of childhood trauma and survivors of adult onset trauma. Many adults, like Patrick, find it impossible to deny the loss of agency. They remain transfixed by the fear of another catastrophe, knowing that, in the end, they will not win. Their intimate knowledge of mortality, the anticipation of nonbeing, has overwhelmed their ability to go on being. The catastrophe has shattered the comforting belief that reality is something about which they could safely have illusions (Winnicott, 1958). As I discussed above, it will be recalled that to Winnicott and Fairbairn, reality is something about which we must have illusions if we are to live without crippling anxiety.

PHYSICAL COHESION

The body, as the literal site of the self, "without which agency would have no place of residence" (D. N. Stern, 1985, p. 82), becomes paramount in arriving at a sense of core self as a separate unit. It would be tautological to suggest that nowhere is the dialogue between psyche and soma harder to hear as two separate voices than in the sense of physical cohesion. In this most fundamental realm, psyche and soma are one until they begin to articulate their separate positions. In the previous chapter, I reviewed the contributions of Bucci (2001), Damasio (1994, 1999), and LeDoux (1996) in establishing the intrinsic role that the neurological and subsymbolic systems play in maintaining a sense of core self. Psychologically, this is the world of the autistic contiguous position, "the barely perceptible background of sensory groundedness of all subsequent subjective states" (Ogden, 1989, p. 80). Here, experience is generated by touch and by signals from the body. And it is here that the first effect of trauma is registered, generating changes in the musculoskeletal system caused by neural and chemical signals, and particularly and more fundamentally in the viscera, registering danger well before reason sets in (Damasio, 1994). The body's familiar rhythms are interrupted by sustained terror. Autistic contiguous anxiety implies the impending disintegration of the sensory surface, the rhythm of safety.

In many cases, it is the corporality of the body that is most obviously vulnerable during trauma. Des Pres (1976) puts it this way: "In extremity everything depends on the body. None of us would wish to depend on something so puny, so frail and easily harmed as the human body. But for survivors there is nothing else" (p. 182). When the sense of physical cohesion is threatened during trauma, there is a fragmentation of bodily experience, leading to depersonalization, out-of-body experiences, and derealization.

Peter, abducted from outside a gay bar and beaten by a gang of thugs, described feeling as if he were hovering above a street lamp watching himself lying on the ground in a fetal position being kicked and punched. There was no pain; he was not registering the blows being landed on him. In fact, he had no sense of inhabiting his own body.

Similar dissociative episodes were described earlier, in discussing the loss of agency where a woman who was being beaten felt like an object. Peter realized that *he* was being beaten, but could not feel it. Without sensory feedback, the psychic conviction that one possesses a distinct integrated physical presence is lost. As the loss of agency reverberates through posttraumatic experience, so the sense of physical cohesion falls victim to a breakdown in the continuity of sensory feedback.

Previously a representational sculptor, Peter now finds himself (as he puts it, and note the passive voice here) fashioning distorted shard-like figures, as if he has lost faith in the body's coherence. Eventually, he admitted that the sight of his sculptures so distressed him, "They seem so broken, so powerless, so … unwhole," that he destroyed them and started again, determined to recapture his previous sense of coherence. Thus, in this private ritual, he was enacting and reenacting his own experience of being shattered.

Peter repeatedly acted out the unmentalized conviction that his self had been broken during the assault. Even though he could find no words for the feeling that he had been shattered not only in body but also psychologically, he demonstrated it symbolically and outside of himself by smashing his sculptures time and again. For other survivors, the body becomes the actual site in which memories that cannot be spoken, affects too powerful to be born, thoughts that cannot be thought and meanings too horrifying to contemplate are encrypted in apparently concrete symptoms. One young Chinese woman spent many months in detention seeking political asylum, increasingly withdrawn and mute except for periods when she would become agitated and insist to the prison doctors that she had a cancer growing in her uterus, although they could find no evidence of it. When asked by the attorney assigned to her why she was seeking asylum, she remembered only that she had fled her small village to escape a man who wanted to marry her. By the time she was incarcerated in the United States, more detailed memory of what had happened to her appeared to be inaccessible. With the help of an extraordinarily attuned and competent interpreter, who translated not only the very few words that she used to repeat her story, but also the painful stuttering that signified the absence of words that met my early attempts to understand the nature of her despair, it emerged that after being raped repeatedly, sometimes gang raped, and burned by her spurned suitor, she had been smuggled to safety by her terrified family, who had since disappeared. The memories lodged in her womb until they could finally safely be turned into words.

When psyche and soma are forced apart, their cohesion sacrificed to the need to survive psychically, the body insists on witnessing what the mind cannot bear. Witnessing another person's body being disfigured or dismembered has proved to be a singularly traumatic experience, often becoming the focus of posttraumatic memories and nightmares, particularly among combat veterans and rescue workers.

It is significant that even when there has been no physical injury, many survivors are preoccupied with their bodies. It is not the material body as the site of greatest vulnerability, but the psychic body, the body-in-mind, the host to agency, the interpreter of volition, the container of affect, that is subject to fragmentation and depersonalization when the psychic skin loses its reassuring and consolidating embrace, and the loss of psychosomatic collusion is most to be feared. Even as the psyche appears to come to its own rescue through depersonalization, as Peter experienced when he was being beaten up, separating itself out from the body, this breakdown in the continuity of sensory-dominated experience marks a violent disruption of self-experience with lasting consequences for the core self.

The skin as the literal divide between self and other, between inner and outer, does double duty as both psyche and soma. Anzieu (1985) describes the skin's pivotal role in structuring all of the other senses and in providing the earliest and most fundamental bonds with the outside world. As the nascent self is contained through the mother's handling of the body's surface, so the body becomes a psychic container, capable of establishing an interior object world inhabited by a benign object and capable of recognizing the separateness of others.

A key player in homeostatic regulation, the skin is represented in the brain's somatosensory complex. It is, in fact, the largest sense organ, and it is an obvious means to signify the body's boundary, because "it is an interface turned both to the organism's interior and to the environment" (Damasio, 1994, p. 230). Without a sense of inside and outside, pain and physical sensations cannot be located. The senses—sight, hearing, smell, touch, taste—are also located close to the surface or at the body's surface and they are readily imprinted with traumatic memories. These memories, divorced from cognition, are easily aroused after the trauma. Damasio (1994) describes how sensory input is coordinated with brain function: "signals from the outside are double, something you see or hear excites a special sense of sight or sound as a nonbody signal which also excites a body signal, hailing from a place in the skin where the special signal entered" (p. 231). Under normal conditions, in regular perception, the somatosensory and motor systems are engaged with the sensory system. When the senses become disengaged from perception, as can happen in dissociation, the disjuncture is shocking. Hearing voices and seeing people speaking is one of the earliest neuronal connections to be established as an attractor basin (Thelen and Smith, 1996, p.193). This most fundamental integration, this everyday fact that is taken for granted by those of us who can hear, can be undone in catastrophic dissociation. In Chapter 7, I describe the dreams of a patient in whom the senses became separated in this disorienting fashion. In Chapter 8, an apparent failure to have registered sound is revealed to be an instance of traumatically-induced deafness when the memory of the sounds the patient was hearing proved too horrifying to contemplate. Until the patient could safely remember the meaning of the sound without being further overwhelmed by its memory, she was haunted and disoriented by the "memory" of her temporary deafness.

The failure to register a sensation is not restricted to hearing, however. One man, who stood a few blocks from the World Trade Center with his video camera recording the destruction of the towers in considerable detail, failed to "see" the bodies jumping out of the upper floors while he was filming them. It was not until his attention was drawn to them by others, who were viewing his film, that he could actually see what was before his eyes. The sight had been too horrifying to allow into consciousness (M. M. Clark, 2005).

Many survivors become preoccupied with their skin, as if the breaking apart of the sense of physical cohesiveness and sensory feedback must be manifest on the body's surface. Kardiner (1969) notes that sensory skin disturbances were very common among World War II veterans. In the excruciating narrative poem *Fredy Neptune* (Murray, 1999), Fredy, who has witnessed Armenian women being burned to death, develops leprosy. The leprosy is a somatic metaphor both for the flesh he has watched burning and for the numbness that extends from the surface of his body to the depths of his psyche, collapsing the distinction between them.

With the loss of physical cohesion, the skin's psychic properties erode. The body can no longer contain agency, affect, or objects; the distinction between inner and outer collapses. Space and time cease to be dimensional; there is no escape from the immediacy of the trauma, and the fundamental bonds to a benign other are lost. Anzieu (1985) holds that cognitive functioning also falls victim to the disruption of physical cohesiveness; for thoughts to be thought, he argues, there must be a "certainty of continuity of contact with the supporting background object, which has, in fact, become a containing object" (p. 64). In Chapter 7, I describe in detail the loss of the capacity to think clearly as the senses unravel during trauma, and the necessity of finding a containing object in order to begin the process of restoring abstract thinking.

CONTINUITY

"Time is the brain's glue," writes Modell (2002, p. 22). Time is the psychological correlate of a neurophysiological substrate laid down in the earliest bonding between mother and child. Just as the environmental mother promotes the sense of physical cohesiveness with her touch, so, too, she instills a protosymbolic sense of time by the rhythm with which she rocks and soothes her infant, synchronizes affects, and times feedings to match the baby's needs. It is not time *per se* that the infant experiences, but the absence of time, what Winnicott (1965) refers to as going on being, which is punctuated by moments of arousal, discrete events that unfold to establish the anticipation of satisfaction or frustration. In identifying going on being with the consolidation of the true self, Winnicott (1965) emphasized the key role continuity plays in providing the context for a healthy psyche, time is most definitely the brain's glue. As physical cohesion represents the psychic envelope that contains the other senses of the core self and houses the benign internal object, so time is the "inner web of what we call psychical" (Loewald, 1980, p. 52).

Yet, as the research summarized in the previous chapter demonstrates, time is held hostage to the neurological functioning of traumatic memories and their psychic consequences. Through intrusive thoughts, dreams, and behavioral enactments, the past is an everlasting present and the present little more than a mirror held up to the past, foreclosing any view of the future.

The sense of continuity is doubly affected in trauma. During the immediate unthinkable anxiety, the body's familiar rhythms are interrupted by the rush of cortisol. Psychologically, temporal dissociation is frequent, a fugue state possible. "Time stood still;" "I felt as if things were happening in slow motion;" "I thought I'd gone into the fourth dimension," are expressions that survivors frequently use to describe the experience. Later, with the traumatic short-circuiting of normal integrating memory functions, time continues to stand still long after the event. "Time is gone," is how Jonah described the catastrophic loss of this fundamental aspect of self experience, meaning that there is no longer a past, present, and future for him, only the immediacy of the day he was assaulted. It has not become history; it is an everlasting and recursive present. This painful conviction once again parallels the paranoid schizoid mode of experience where there is no sense of history because "the present is projected backwards and forwards, creating a static, eternal, nonflective present" (Ogden, 1989, p. 62).

"One of the functions of the self is to reconfigure time, to juxtapose past and present experiences," Modell argues (1993, p. 161). A collapsed self can no longer perform this function, all that is left is a "meaningless now" (Loewald, 1989, p. 144). Mired in that meaningless now, the survivor is constantly reactive to a barrage of unintegrated eidetic and somatic memory fragments. Reis (1995) points out that reacting interrupts being, annihilating the continuous experience of consolidated subjectivity, foreclosing the individual's ability to remain conscious of his consciousness. "Thus," he argues, "a collapse of subjectivity results because it is only through a sense of temporality that there can 'be' a subject of subjectivity, a rhythm to one's being" (p. 229).

Reading the transcribed narratives of survivors' experiences during the terrorist attacks on the World Trade Center, Strozier (2005, personal communication) was struck by the fact that the accounts appeared to have been spoken in iambic pentameter; he offers many examples to support this observation. Meter, as anything basic to experience, begins in the self and has corporeal, physical, sensual, even sexual dimensions. "Our attachment to meter is deeply imbedded in those selfobject patterns, those central orienting images that constitute the nuclear self" (Strozier, personal communication, 6/25/2003). In reciting the story of what happened to him in a basic poetic meter, the survivor reestablishes ties to the fundamental rhythm of his unbroken self. As I discuss throughout this book and in detail in Chapter 8, few survivors come to treatment able to speak so fluently about their experience. Strozier's respondents were not seeking treatment; they had volunteered to describe their ordeal to social science researchers. However, this exciting insight into the rhythmic recitation of traumatic occurrences implies that as the narrator grows less inhibited by the terror of the memories and the fear that the account will exacerbate the trauma, increasing fluency may reestablish a bond to the essential rhythms of the pretraumatic core self. Then, as narrative proceeds, higher order functions cluster time into meaningful sequences.

Not only are the body's rhythms and an appreciation of historical time distorted by catastrophic dissociation, but this interruption has implications for the intersubjective as well. Tracing the body's fundamental rhythms to the earliest intersubjective experiences, Priel (1997) points out that the sense of time constitutes an emergent property of self–other differentiations. "The evolution of time is seen as a continuous process of construction of meaning in an intersubjective framework" (p. 413). Meaning is initially deduced from predictability that, in turn, relies on the caretaker's ability to time her interactions with her baby according to the baby's needs.

When continuity, as an invariant of self-experience, is traumatically disrupted, the consequences reverberate throughout the entire psychic system. Time is not only the brain's glue, but also the glue that holds the different senses of the core self together. The psychological sense of continuity is an organizing force mediating subjectivity, intersubjectivity, affectivity, and the ability to make sense of experience, all of which are compromised separately and together during a catastrophe and beyond.

AFFECTIVITY

Developmentally, affectivity is also shaped by temporal patterns, structured by the responsive presence of another, creating familiar internal states that provide consistency to the nascent core self. As time goes on, affects have the power to enliven experience or, if, they are too powerful, to withdraw and deaden it.

One of the few classical analysts to describe the potentially permanent consequences of adult onset trauma, Krystal (1988) believes that overwhelming affects are the final common path of traumatization leading to the subsequent disruption of self-experience. It is his thesis that, confronted with unavoidable danger, the affective state changes from anxiety (which is the signal of a perception of preventable danger) to helpless submission, or what he calls cataleptic passivity. Research (Damasio, 1994, 1999; and LeDoux, 1996; among others) shows that the terror of imminent annihilation cannot be distinguished from its complex biological correlates; terror cannot be teased apart from the somatic and neurophysiological arousal that accompanies it. Krystal (1978, 1985, 1988) pointed out long ago that this catatonoid state is a phylogenetically determined surrender pattern, which includes the loss of agency, physical cohesiveness and cognitive function as well as alexythymia, that is the failure to differentiate affects and to use them as signals. Further, he suggests, affect tolerance is impaired as a result of the trauma. "Certain affects have been rendered intolerable because they are experienced as 'traumatic screens,' inevitably linked to return of the trauma" (1988, p. 143). Somatic arousal and terror continually trigger one another in an exhausting feedback loop. Numbness becomes the survivor's only choice in managing the fearfully arousing state.

Speaking in a mechanical monotone, David, a combat veteran, summed up his sense of loss in this way: "I show no sad emotions ... I have no feelings. It's like there's nothing there. It's like half of your personality is gone because when you do a lot of killing and stuff like that, when you see a lot of death, you lose your feelings and your personality." Without familiar feelings to guide him, with traumatically disrupted internal patterns of arousal, and his failure to register subjective self states affectively, David has lost his sense of continuity, becoming unfamiliar to himself. The "I" who experienced a range of feelings is gone, and with it the sense of ownership of experience. No longer punctuated by affect, his life has become rote. He has, in effect, forfeited his subjectivity. Not only current experience, but memories are devoid of emotional impact.

It has been customary to argue that powerful affect triggers the dissociative response. Although affect is only one of the complex triggers of catastrophic dissociation, as I have been at pains to point out in this chapter, it is often here that the traumatized adult conscious registers her changed state. Survivors describe a range of affective responsivity during the moment itself. At the extreme end of this spectrum, nothing appears to register at all. "When time and space cease to exist and whole and parts become equivalent, infinite emotion ... renders the psyche inactive, it cannot be registered in consciousness. Catastrophic trauma is an absolute sudden absence" (Tarantelli, 2003, p. 919). This is Krystal's catanoid state. At the other end of the spectrum, the survivor recalls that he experienced a sense of danger, but it seemed strangely irrelevant. Henry (2004), a police captain and psychologist, offers a detailed account of his reactions as an experienced police officer who, on 9/11, participated in rescue and recovery efforts. He was aware of his fear but described it as "strangely disembodied" (p. 22). In this state he was able to work at Ground Zero throughout the day, but later found that what had seemed crystal clear at the time could not be assembled in his memory.

Once the immediate danger is past, some survivors continue to seek out danger, as if to reenact the traumatic circumstances that led to the collapse of the self. As I have already described, this triggers the paradoxically analgesic effects of increased serotonin in the survivor's brain. Deidre and her husband were referred to me by their eight-year-old son's therapist. It quickly emerged that Deidre's husband and son were frightened by the changes in her since the terrorist attacks in New York. On that day, Deidre had spent five hours walking home without her shoes that had been lost in the scramble to escape from the falling towers, not knowing whether her husband, who was a fireman, was still alive. Deidre had very little memory of that long walk except that, uncharacteristically, she found herself lighting candles in each church she passed. A previously devoted wife and mother, Deidre had taken up bungee jumping, paragliding, and other extreme sports. When I asked Deidre what it felt like to plunge off a bridge attached to a piece of elastic, she replied, "I don't feel anything. Maybe this way I can start to feel again."

It has been argued that repetition is an attempt to titrate and ultimately master the terror that was experienced during the initial trauma, thus restoring psychic equilibrium. However, it is important to distinguish between repetition in which there is an attempt to repeat an experience in order to assimilate it by turning passive experience into active, and the repetition compulsion following massive trauma, which does not bring relief but is instead an attempt to rekindle "the lost intensities of hope and fear," described by the English poet Edmund Blunden (Parsons, 1965, p. 176), a survivor of combat in World War I. In seeking out danger, the survivor is making a bid to push past the state of numbness common to so many survivors, of which David spoke so eloquently above. Numbness provides dubious protection from intolerable affect, for it alienates a survivor from all that is familiar to him.

Experiments performed by Damasio (1994, 1999) and his team of researchers add a further crucial dimension to the role that affect plays in the interacting with other aspects of the core self. His findings show that thought and feeling are inextricable neurophysiologically. At least two of the patients that I describe in the course of this chapter have noted a failure in memory under heightened affect; in Chapter 7 the difficulty in thinking clearly under these conditions is discussed in greater detail.

Losing the ability to experience feelings in a consistent fashion leads not only to a loss of subjectivity but this catastrophic loss has widespread interpersonal consequences. With the failure to register one's own feelings comes both the inability to share one's affective state with an other, and the failure to appreciate the other's affectivity, which is the basis of intersubjective experience lying at the heart of the capacity to feel related to others.

Coevolving and codetermined as they are, a threat to one aspect of the core self sets up profound reverberations for the whole. Van der Kolk, McFarlane, and Weisaeth (1996) refer to a cascade of biobehavioral changes occurring as a result of trauma, but psychically, as well as biologically, there is a domino effect when aspects of the self are traumatized. Realizing that she cannot alter the course of events, that contingency, not agency, is the rule, the survivor no longer feels herself to be a subject but an object, subject only to the whims of an unreliable and dangerous world. With threats from without and within, when the distinction between inner and outer no longer holds, the body-in-mind that houses this disenfranchised subject is not up to the task of containing agency, affects, or objects. The loss of interiority brings with it the loss of an internal object world and difficulties keeping thoughts in mind. The traumatic disruption of memory and internal patterns of arousal leads to unfamiliar feeling states that threaten the sense of continuity. The ruptured sense of time interrupts going on being, further compromising subjectivity and, thus, the possibility of intersubjectivity. With the loss of self as subject comes the loss of the self as interpreter and conveyor of meaning.

Although this account is by no means exhaustive, it is an attempt to capture the vortex in which the traumatized self is caught and to provide clinicians working with massively traumatized adults with a way of listening to their patients' experience and gathering evidence of the self's collapse. But the picture of the collapsed self is incomplete without recognizing the ways in which the core self is formed and informed by the social self. There are profound consequences for interpersonal relationships when the core self has collapsed. This is the subject of the next chapter.

6

The Relational Self in Crisis:
Further Deconstructing Catastrophic
Dissociation

It is the context of our thesis that psychic structure is relational and trauma is deconstructive.

— D. Laub and N. Auerhahn (1989, p. 398)

I turn once more to Kardiner (1969) to introduce this chapter, because his grasp of the all encompassing reach that is the hallmark of catastrophic dissociation is as sobering as it is accurate. "The posttraumatic state is the outcome of conflict in two areas," he wrote, "the relation of the subject to his own resources and his relatedness to the group" (p. 248). In the previous chapter, I described how each of the core self's resources can become compromised during catastrophic dissociation and thereafter. In this chapter, I consider the consequences of catastrophic dissociation for the survivor's relationship to her group, as Kardiner puts it. Many relational psychoanalysts believe that the failure of relational ties causes the posttraumatic reaction (Ferenczi, 1933; Bromberg, 1998; Coates, Rosenthal, and Schechter,

2003; among others). "Traumatic aloneness is what really renders the attack traumatic that is causing the psyche to crack" Ferenczi (1933, p. 193) concluded. The sense of profound isolation, the traumatic aloneness, which survivors of massive psychic trauma experience has three interdependent sources: the loss of the internal structuring ties that represent the internal object world, the loss of external social ties, and the imagined loss of membership in the human community. I consider each of them in turn.

Kulka (1997) captures the fundamental paradox of selfhood when he points out that "the *raison d'être* of the human being is not interrelating but the creation of experiences of significant selfhood—even if this goal can only be realized within the contextual cradle of relating with an other" (p. 186). It is no longer questioned that psychological development occurs within a relational matrix. Not only is the biological regulating system set in motion within that holding environment, but the sense of core self, of self versus other, of self as initiator, of self who experiences affect, and of self as a coherent whole moving through time is acquired relationally (D. N. Stern, 1985; Fonagy et al., 2002). Each aspect of the core self is learned in the contextual cradle of relating to another. Trauma shatters this state of relatedness with serious and lasting consequences not only for the relational self, but, as I described in the last chapter, the consequences also profoundly alter the survivor's experience of self.

Since Freud (1926) argued that infantile helplessness is at the root of traumatic reactions, in one way or another psychoanalysts have contended massive trauma returns those who face it to their earliest and most primitive experiences of being failed by another (Furst, 1967; Greenacre, 1967; Krystal, 1988; Phillips, 1994; Laub and Auerhahn, 1989), to feelings of anaclitic despair and the subsequent fear of fragmentation. Although I agree in principle with the phenomenology that earlier authors were attempting to convey, in keeping with my emphasis on process rather than structure, I seek to avoid language that locates the survivor in psychic infancy, equating catastrophe with an unpredictable mother. The earlier language implied that there is always a precedent in the survivor's internal world for the destruction wrought by trauma.

It is true that the covenant between the core self and its component parts is initially forged by the predictable and responsive presence of the mother as she regulates and helps structure experience. But Chodorow (1996) reminds us that subjective experience is a "continual process to be engaged intersubjectively without assuming that childhood causes, determines, or correlates with present functioning" (p. 47). In a recent statement, Laub and Lee (2003) reflect this change in emphasis from psychic structure to ongoing psychic process, which is very much in accord with the views presented here: "Our contention is that the same dynamics (decathexis of the maternal object and of the self) and a comparable phenomenology hold true not only for infantile symbolic maternal loss, but also for the traumatic loss of the good internal object at any age" (p. 441). Instead of attributing the destruction of the internal object world during massive psychic trauma to the disruption of the predictable internal mother with its potentially infantilizing and pathologizing connotation then, it is more accurate to say that as agency, cohesiveness, continuity and affectivity are challenged, inevitably the internal ties that initially served to bind the core self together and that remain necessary to its stability are also threatened.

Among self psychologists and relational psychoanalysts, there is an increasingly hopeful belief that facing a massive trauma with empathic others can inoculate one from experiencing the full range of traumatic symptoms (Kohut, 1984; Ornstein, 2001; Coates, Rosenthal, and Schechter, 2003; among others). In some circumstances the presence of others who offer recognition and encouragement would appear to mitigate the most pernicious effects of traumatic dissociation. In his analysis of Holocaust testimonies, Des Pres (1976) describes many instances of giving and receiving little acts of kindness and thoughtfulness that provided psychic comfort and kept object ties alive. In a moving tribute to the two friends who went through Auschwitz with him, Primo Levi (1958) describes the importance of maintaining these benign ties in order to counteract the malevolent effects of being a hated part object in the mind of the persecutor: "Part of our existence lies in the feelings of those near to us. This is why the experience of someone who has lived for days during which man was merely a thing in the eyes of man is non-human. We three were for the most part immune from it, and we owe each other mutual gratitude" (p. 172).

Anna Freud and Dorothy Burlingame studied two groups of children in war torn England. One group was evacuated from London and separated from their families and the danger of the blitz. A second group remained with their families, constantly exposed to the bombing. The authors' findings emphasized the importance of attachment during trauma. Those children who remained with their families under bombardment were less affected than those children who were evacuated and spent the war years in relative safety among strangers. In a book that addresses specifically the role of attachment in facing and recovering from the September 11th attacks, Coates, Rosenthal, and Schechter (2003) argue, "What defines trauma in the first place, what changes a challenge into stress and stress into a genuine trauma, may in part be derived from the fact that it is undergone alone" (p. 3).

Although I agree with Coates (2003) that the presence of attachment figures protects children from the worst consequences of a traumatic experience, adult experience is more equivocal. Separation, in itself, is traumatic for children. Children, whose reality is shaped by caretaking adults, can indeed be shielded from terror by responsible and responsive adults. Coates reports that in observing how children were reacting to the events around them, clinicians were able document that the children's attempts at comprehension and absorption were couched in terms provided by the family milieu. Anzieu-Premmereur (2002, 2003) reached a similar conclusion. She describes her work with children who escaped from the World Trade Center with their parents. She found sharp distinctions between those children who felt their parents were caring for them, those who were terrified by their parent's terror, and those who felt they had to step into the caretaking role themselves.

Unlike children who look to their caretakers for cues about their environment, adults have an immediate intellectual grasp of the danger of a life threatening situation and its potential consequences, often retreating from the sense of terror into catastrophic dissociation. This is the important distinction that Krystal (1988) made between adults and children faced with traumatic stressors (and, parenthetically, it is the first distinction that was ever drawn between the two). In the face of massive psychic trauma, he says, children are overwhelmed by intolerable affect. It could be speculated that this intolerable affect comes about because there are no familiar adults around, in which case separation itself becomes traumatic, as it did in the case of the refugee children in Freud and Burlingame's study. Alternatively, it could be argued that the children are made unbearably anxious by the unbearable anxiety of those who are caring for them. Krystal (1988) continues, "The adult form of psychic trauma comes to the fore with the development of ego functions and the ability to mobilize such defenses as denial, depersonalization, and derealization" (p.167).

Many survivors who count on the protective power of friendship during massive trauma experience the sudden death of these friends as the most significant loss of all, marking the beginning of catastrophic dissociation. This is found particularly among combat veterans, for whom the violent death of a comrade in arms is often recalled in repetitive and in-escapable graphic detail. If adults can keep a good object alive, even in fantasy, during a massive psychic trauma, the chances of surviving the state of catastrophic dissociation improve (Ornstein, 1986; Prince, 1998; Herman, 1992). But even Levi (quoted in Laub and Auerhahn, 1989), who, it will be recalled, attributed his survival to his friendships, finally concluded "in the end everyone is desperately and ferociously alone" (p. 49).

Depending on the nature of the trauma and circumstances surround-ing it, in the traumatic moment itself, the presence of other people can appear irrelevant as the desperate struggle to survive takes precedence. When the significance of external objects is suddenly voided, the internal object world becomes a void. Ferenczi (cited in Frankel, 1998) makes a similar point: "In the moment of trauma, the world of objects disappears partially or completely; everything becomes objectless sensation" (p. 47). Without interpersonal markers to metabolize and integrate the flow of experience, it becomes chaotic, unmediated impressions. Describing the consequences of the traumatic loss of the "internal structuring object map," Grotstein (1990, p. 281) conjures up the image of a black hole, "ex-perienced as spaceless, bottomless, timeless and yet, paradoxically con-densed, compact and immediate, yielding suffocation anxiety" into which the survivor feels pulled. Jonah drew into himself as he sought to survive the police assault through catastrophic dissociation. Dully aware that friends and neighbors were being attacked, he was not even con-scious at that moment that he could not protect them. But later he would become wracked with guilt about not having tried.

Bellinson (2002) has found that this particular kind of guilt, specific regrets for real life decisions—actions not taken, people not helped—plays a significant role in posttraumatic adjustment. She dis-tinguishes this from the generic survivor guilt described by Lifton (1967), who speculated that survivors need to justify their own survival in the face of the other's death through a process of identification with those who did not survive. This death-in-life once again recalls the para-noid schizoid landscape where the loss by projection of even bad inter-nal objects creates guilt at having destroyed them and terror at the state of objectlessness, leading to depersonalization. Prince (1998) makes a similar point, suggesting that survivor guilt may represent an attempt to maintain both personal continuity and ties to lost objects.

Massive trauma is not necessarily caused by an other's hatred and, although it is true that traumatic reactions caused in this way are often more toxic, natural disasters reveal perhaps more clearly how the loss of structuring ties can result in a bewildering unwillingness to engage in interpersonal relationships. Sociologist Kai Erikson (1976) interviewed surviving members of the community at Buffalo Creek after the collapse of a dam led to considerable loss of life and the destruction of both the physical and emotional community. Several years after the flood, one survivor told him, "I didn't want nobody around me. I didn't want nobody to speak to me or even to look at me. I wanted nobody even ten miles around me to call my name. I got like that. I just wanted to hit them and make them leave me alone" (p. 217). A second survivor spoke of his loss in the present tense: "I don't have the same attitude towards people that I had. It used to be that I cared for all people but not anymore. I just keep myself alive. That's the only thing I study about" (p. 217). Even though they were not the objects of another's hatred, these survivors had lost everything that was psychically familiar to them. With the collapse of the core self and the internal structuring ties comes the loss of desire to recognize or be recognized by another, and the loss of the possibility of belonging to a community of like minded people, robbing life of its meaning and leading to profound isolation.

More often than not, however, massive trauma occurs as a result of hatred and destructiveness. Under these circumstances, when we believe that we are seen as an object to be destroyed, to be eradicated, our own sense of self undergoes a profound change. "At our core," write Fonagy et al., (2002, p. 348) "is the representation of how we were seen." When past convictions and future certainties hang in the balance, when the core self is destabilized by the threat of annihilation, how we *were* seen is less relevant than how we *are* seen. I previously stated that the presence, even in fantasy, of others who perceive us as benign can partially mitigate the other's malevolence. In the absence of such benign others in actuality or in fantasy, or if the danger to the self is prolonged, the internal object world can no longer be sustained. How we were seen is less relevant than how we are perceived by the present destructive forces. Threat and harm endanger communion with another, making the internal object world vulnerable to the other's malevolence. Through projective identification, survivors of assault and genocide find themselves playing the role of anonymous part objects in an externalized version of the other's disordered psyche, trapped in the persecutor's unconscious, without recourse to a more benign or familiar internal object world of their own.

Living in an internal world populated by persecutory part objects that are projected out only to be experienced as redoubling their attack and, consequently, needing to be reintrojected in order to be controlled is the hallmark of the paranoid schizoid position. To Klein, this state of affairs is part of an inevitable immanent battle. Even if one takes the more benign view that infancy does not necessarily entail such nightmarish scenes, there is no question that the survivor of a catastrophe can find her internal world overwhelmed by paranoid schizoid phenomena. For the adult survivor who, prior to the catastrophe, experienced more frequently the relative security of ambivalence in the depressive position, it is highly disorienting to suddenly find herself in an impersonal world dominated by persecutory objects (Ogden, 1990). In this world, she has no subjectivity, no agency, and no sense of history; object use and mutuality suddenly seem beyond her reach, a vague memory of something lost, while others, who once felt important to her now feel like shadows with no substance of their own.

Ferenczi (1933) first identified the way in which the internal object world can be altered by purely exogenous causes. He maintained that when the benign internal object world is lost during trauma, the survivor will choose identification with the aggressor over the barrenness, isolation and meaninglessness of a world without objects. Identification, "should I say introjection of the aggressor" (p. 160), leads to an internal world dominated by oppressive forces. Ferenczi was specifically addressing the plight of children who were consistently betrayed by their caretakers. However, adults who are exposed to protracted terror at the hands of a malevolent other, who are held hostage or imprisoned, tortured, or become the objects of others' homicidal intent, will turn to identification with bad objects in a bid to make sense of meaningless experience. Rather than experience the cosmic isolation of an objectless world, the survivor assigns malignant meaning to the experience, arguing, "I must deserve this in some way," or "I am worthless." There are parallels here to the ways in which a child who is abused will come to believe that she deserves the abuse, sometime later entering into enactments in which she assumes the role of the aggressor. Bergmann and Jucovy (1982) describe a similar dynamic in survivors of the Holocaust, suggesting that they fall prey to sadistic fantasies and retaliatory wishes as a result of their exposure to brutality. Ornstein (1986, 2001) takes issue with this characterization, arguing that it unnecessarily pathologizes Holocaust survivors. In fact, as was described in the previous chapter, many adult survivors of massive psychic trauma have withdrawn from extreme emotions such as retaliatory fantasies and rage which, as Krystal (1978) puts it, become traumatic screens for dangerous affect states. The numbed and lifeless alexythymic state represents considerably less danger to the fragile emotional détente the survivor has achieved.

For some, the state of objectlessness proves too alienating. One young woman, who had been abandoned by her mother and repeatedly raped by her father until his institutionalization, found brief solace in an internal world that was devoid of good or bad objects. She described this state as, "Getting singular. I'm empty. There's nothing there." In this empty place, she was briefly invulnerable to the continuing internal attacks that identification with her father choreographed. But the sense of loneliness and her guilt over having destroyed her father, both in her internal world and in the external world, ultimately brought her back to the maelstrom of a disordered object world, where she sought out once again the kinds of relationships with which she was familiar.

With objectlessness comes meaninglessness; there is no internal other to guide expectations, no external other to understand the experience. The loss of the intersubjective means that inner experience cannot be shared. Or, as Felman and Laub (1992) put it, there is no longer "the other to which one could say 'thou' in the hope of being heard, of being recognized as a subject, of being answered" (p. 82). Tragically, this sense of loss is echoed in the outside world, where too often others are, indeed, reluctant to acknowledge the survivor's plight. Whether the survivor believes that her story is too horrific to share, or fears that she is making too much of the experience, or whether friends, family, and even clinicians have been unable to acknowledge the extent of the damage she has sustained, the survivor feels disenfranchised. The sense of belonging to and sharing in a community has been lost. This was Antigone's fate when she was banished from Thebes. "Cosmic loneliness" are the words D. N. Stern (1985) uses to describe the experience of life with no shared meaning.

How fragile is this self that is constituted relationally, can be undone by violence, and can be wounded again by communion with another. From this perspective, the relational self is both fundamentally connected and also fundamentally at risk. It is the clinician's task to be prepared, when others cannot bear to do so, to acknowledge the extent of the loss, to construct with the survivor a meaningful understanding of the collapsed self. The clinician must understand the extent of the damage that can be done by reality in the hope of being a good enough object who can safely be reintrojected. Shared understanding begins to chip away at the feeling of cosmic isolation. In this way, the process of rebuilding trust can begin.

Many short term therapies aimed at treating trauma offer prescriptions for recovery but fail to listen to the survivor's experience. In one successful and highly structured program in Israel, however, the emphasis is on joint experience and rebuilding a sense of community. In 20 weekly group sessions, lasting two and a half hours each, fourteen traumatized adults and three therapists focus on changing traumatically altered beliefs and affect with a combination of physical and group therapy. The exercises build confidence and restore a sense of agency. Over and above all, finding socially shared solutions that emphasize membership in the group lead group members to discover, with relief, that they are not alone (Boehm, 2004).

The therapeutic action of relational analysis is, by its very definition, located intersubjectively. This presents particular difficulty, because, as I have been demonstrating, catastrophes can uproot central aspects of self-experience, leading to questions about the viability of the self as subject and consequently undermining the very foundation of intersubjectivity. Langs (2004) cautions the relational analyst not to privilege the therapeutic relationship over real life experience outside of the treatment setting. This is an important caveat. Insisting prematurely on an examination of the patient's intersubjective experience, when the patient's internal object world has been so severely compromised by recent reality, denies the patient an opportunity to explore the experience of the collapsed self that should be foremost in the treatment. In the psychodynamic treatment of adult onset trauma, the clinician's task is to hold herself out as the other to whom the patient can, at first tentatively, relate, and to tolerate how irrelevant the patient may believe the entire process to be. The task is to tolerate a feeling of unrelatedness without analyzing it. In the early phases of working with an adult who has been severely traumatized as an adult, the work is not about the therapeutic relationship but about the survivor's disorientation.

This is the first of four clinical chapters, each of which addresses different aspects of working with survivors of adult onset trauma. Although each case has a crucial intersubjective element, in this first instance I describe a woman who had not sought treatment but had come against her will, with no belief that she could find relief from the deadness in which she was encased. Survivors who have traumatically lost the structuring ties to another, for whom the distinction between inside and out is no longer clear, who no longer have the internal conviction of the possibility of benign ties, who have no sense of their own subjectivity, enter treatment with little hope of recovery and little notion of what recovery means.

Ellen, a divorced woman in her early 40s, came reluctantly to my office, referred by the Employee Assistance Program (EAP) in the corporation where she worked as an administrative assistant. She had come to the attention of the EAP because her short temper and frequent absences were jeopardizing her job. I immediately felt uncomfortable and unwelcome in this slack-bodied woman's presence. The most remarkable thing about her appearance was the lack of anything to remark on. The clinic where I was working had the usual uninspired brown or beige anonymous furnishings, but it had never seemed more impersonal than when I was with Ellen. It felt to me as if she had cancelled herself out. I struggled to engage her, but she appeared indifferent to my questions, shrugging when I asked her how she felt about this inquiry. Beyond the need to comply with her EAP's directive so as to keep her job, she showed no interest in herself, no desire to engage or be engaged by the world and, in this instance, no wish to be engaged by me. I felt cancelled out as well. I did not feel comfortable confronting what seemed like resistance so early in the treatment because I was not sure Ellen had any incentive to stay in the treatment and I wanted to understand more about her emptiness. Occasionally, when pressed about something she felt I had already asked enough about, she would show a flash of irritation. But even that quickly subsided into—I would say avoidance, but it felt more like blankness. In my mind, I was tentatively formulating a diagnostic picture of terrible early deprivation, absent, maybe sadistic caretakers. I imagined the cumulative traumas of an emotionally impoverished household with depressed parents, the empty world of an only child with no one to mirror or model vitality. I was forming a hypothesis about this woman's character and the forces that had shaped it and wondering how I could intervene in the here and now.

From the EAP's referral form, I knew Ellen had been married. After a couple of sessions, I asked when she had gotten divorced. It seems odd to me now, in retrospect, that I asked when the marriage ended, as if the impersonal date was more important than details of the marriage itself. Perhaps it was because I had already sensed that time had only one dimension for Ellen and I wanted to introduce another dimension. As I was to discover, to Ellen dates on the calendar had no meaning anyway. Time had stopped for her. She answered my question in the only way she knew how to measure time: "After my daughter died."

Several years earlier, her eleven-year-old daughter's body had been found in an abandoned lot in the borough in which they lived. Ellen had not told the EAP counselor about her daughter's murder. She gave me no more than the outlines of the story I could have read in the newspaper. Her attitude was, in effect, "It's over. There's nothing you can do about it." And indeed, there was nothing I could do. I felt absolutely helpless. My immediate expression of shock and sympathy elicited only another blank stare.

I have deliberately chosen this case to begin these four clinical chapters because this is a patient who could have turned up in anyone's private practice or clinic caseload. The EAP director was not looking for a provider who was familiar with the consequences of massive psychic trauma because she knew nothing about Ellen's history. This awful event had thrust itself into Ellen's otherwise unremarkable life and, although it came to define her life, it was not something that she believed could be shared with other people. Sometimes survivors will not speak about what they have experienced because they are ashamed that they have not recovered. Sometimes, like Ellen, they are indifferent to the idea of recovery itself. Sensing how fragile is this self that was constituted relationally and undone by interpersonal violence, they know only too well the risks inherent in reestablishing any communion with others. In this chapter, in which I describe the crisis in object relations that follows adult onset trauma, Ellen is a powerful example of a survivor who was determined not to reconstitute relational ties.

Ellen did not feel as if she belonged to the human race: its concerns had no meaning to her; she believed her experience was beyond anyone's ability to understand. Her indifference to me and to the therapeutic process made her a particularly challenging, but not atypical, example of an adult who has survived massive psychic trauma. My job here was to establish myself as an other to whom she could relate, although this was not a goal she shared. I was shut out of her internal world just as she was shut out; there was no rage, no fear, no more grief, just deadness, and a resolute belief that it could not be otherwise.

After the session during which I learned about the murder, I was relieved to see my next patient. I felt released from the numbness that had seemed to encase both Ellen and me. By the end of the workday, my mind returned reluctantly to her. I found myself trying to fit her experience of the murder into the diagnostic picture I had already formed, trying to frame her reaction to this unimaginable loss in terms of the earlier pathology I had hypothesized. I had to remind myself that that had simply been my construct; with this new information all diagnostic bets were off. At the same time, I felt angry with Ellen. "It is intolerable not to impute some responsibility to the victim," writes Prince (1998, p. 51). "Surely she could have done something to move on with her life? She's been shut down for years," I argued with myself. What was I thinking? How could I be so harsh? At first, I thought I was reacting to the terrifying thought that I, too, could lose my only child, but behind this lay a possibly more frightening thought. Would surviving a catastrophe of this magnitude rob me of vitality and any shred of hope as it had Ellen? Could life cease to have any meaning to me too? "I died when she died" was Ellen's explanation for her complete lack of interest in herself. I was tempted to leave well enough alone and agree with her implicit suggestion that she had done what she could to deal with her loss. Ellen had opted for a life without community and a life without meaning. The possibility of exploring meanings paralyzed her. Did I have the right to bring her out of her self-imposed cold storage? But I had worked with survivors of massive psychic trauma long enough to know that I would be evading the work that had to be done.

At the suggestion of the District Attorney who was prosecuting her daughter's murderer, Ellen had gone to a victims' services group before the trial. In this time-limited work, she had been asked to talk about her feelings in front of a "bunch of strangers" as she put it. She had listened numbly as the parents of other murdered children described their losses; and she had been given a list of symptoms that were common in such circumstances. Here were formulaic explanations for her catastrophically altered perceptions and feeling states. The loss of her daughter and of all that was familiar to her had in no way been contextualized. Like Jonah, she had lost an irreplaceable part of herself, but, unlike Jonah, she believed that that part was her daughter. Without having worked toward an appreciation of the multifaceted meanings that the murder held for her, without having an opportunity to think through its impact on her, how that impact interacted with aspects of her own past, and how it came to be represented in and to shape her subsequent adjustment, the loss had become reified, the only reality in her life. It was a point of endless return. When she was at work or on the subway or sitting at home with the television droning in the background, her mind returned time and again to the day her daughter's body was found.

The following week, it was with dread that I returned to work with Ellen. I tried to find a way to reach her, but my most empathic analytic presence felt brutally intrusive; there was no internal object world with which to connect, and it felt as if there was no possibility of a space opening up in which such a world could be contained. Ellen barely acknowledged me. Session after session, for as much as I thought she could bear and as much as I knew I could bear, I returned to consider the moments from the time Ellen realized that her daughter was missing to the time when the child's body was found. Tracing the dissociative process, she spoke of her helplessness at the time, how nothing seemed real to her; nothing reached her, neither her neighbor's concern nor her husband's own grief had any relevance. Now she had arrived at this current stone-like state; it was as if she had simply stopped being.

Now I knew the "facts". Ellen had been slightly delayed returning from work; her husband had had to leave for his night shift; their daughter was to wait for her mother at the downstairs neighbor's apartment. When Ellen realized the child never got to the neighbor's house, she immediately "knew" something was terribly wrong; she called her husband and the police. At first I was mesmerized by the account, imagining the panic and despair, but when I started to push for more details, I felt trivial and trivialized. Before long, I found I was curiously bored. With some prompting, Ellen had recounted the facts, but there was a curious disconnect. It was as if she did not inhabit the narrative. She was not there. She seemed to be saying, "You can do nothing but witness. You are simply a passive observer. You are shut out of my inner life. I have no inner life, I am the sum of the horrors I have lived through." Indeed, I found that I could not get access to any inner life. The distinction between outside and inside had collapsed—not only to Ellen but also to me. In sessions, I was without reverie; I could not find a place inside myself where I could start to connect to what Ellen was reluctantly telling me. It was as if I had lost faith in the power of the analytic process, the faith that often carries me through rough spots. Instead, I felt like a voyeur, recording events but completely shut off from the subject of my observations, just as Ellen seemed shut off from me.

Many authors have written of the therapeutic power of constructing a narrative to describe what happened during trauma. Laub and Auerhahn (1989) emphasize the importance of "the process by which the narrator (the survivor) reclaims his position as witness: reconstitutes the "internal thou" and thus the possibility of a witness or a listener inside himself" (p. 85). Narrative reestablishes subjectivity (Wigren, 1999), reorders time (Reis, 1995), permits an exploration of disordered physical cohesiveness, and encourages the expression of previously intolerable affect. Noting, and in noting capturing the se-

quence between stimuli and intrusive memories begins the task of restoring agency (Pye, 1995; Slavin, 1997). Capturing somatic and eidetic
memories, and in capturing them bringing them into a linear sequence,
encourages the understanding of cause and effect rather than the helpless submission to apparently random memory fragments that could
previously be countered only by avoidance or by numbed submission.
Exploring somatic fantasies encourages the recognition that inside and
outside stand in juxtaposition to one another; that they are not as
porous as they appeared during the boundaryless moment of terror.

On the other hand, Grand (2000) wisely warns against an overly opti-
mistic belief in the power of narrative. And my experience with Ellen
certainly justified this reservation. In Chapter 8, I describe a case in
which the patient could not produce a spoken narrative. In her case, she
was afraid of the damage I would sustain if I really listened to what she
was telling me. She had to find a way of telling the narrative that would
do justice to her experience without doing her further harm and keep
me safe at the same time.

I have suggested that trauma's psychic fallout resembles the paranoid schizoid position. Ogden (1989, 1990) describes the cognitive
consequences implicit in this position. The loss of the self as subject
means that the self as interpreter of experience does not exist. The self
that distinguishes between words and what they stand for, between
symbol and symbolized, is no longer accessible when the psyche is engaged by the persecutory convictions of this position. In this concrete
world, perception and interpretation are one and the same. In this
concrete world, thought cannot be relied upon to provide a different
perspective.

In order for Ellen to reclaim the story she was telling me, not just as a
recitation of fact but as a story that had personal meaning to her, she
would have to give up the numbness and risk being flooded with feeling. She would have to reclaim agency, risk coming alive, and I had to
have the courage to believe I would not hurt her more by pushing for
more.

"I am not the same person I was," Ellen said wearily when I reflected
rather tentatively on what a hard time we were having talking to one
other. I asked her what was different about her. She looked at me wither-
ingly, but I persisted. Finally she answered, "I don't recognize the person I am. I don't like people no more. I don't believe in God. I don't
have happy thoughts like I did." When I asked her to tell me about the
person she had been, the first animated pictures started tentatively to

emerge—cooking fried chicken to take to church picnics on summer weekends; baking cookies with her daughter after school; going to the bowling alley with her husband on Saturday night; preparing for her daughter's first communion; gossiping with coworkers and neighbors. Loewald (1980) holds that "psychic time implies an active relation between the temporal modes of past, present and future"(p. 43). Maybe Ellen did not sense a future, but here was a past distinct from the interminable present of her daughter's death. She was starting to emerge from the place of psychic deadness where time has no dimensionality. But there were risks inherent in this movement.

In the moments after Ellen left my office at the end of this session, I found myself crying. I was astonished by my tears. I didn't expect them. I wasn't dwelling on the past session. My notes had been made, I was preparing for the next patient, and suddenly tears were running down my face. I realized that I was just as dissociated as Ellen was during our sessions. And I knew that the only way I could help her break through her dissociation was to break through my own.

A couple of weeks later, commenting on how many friends Ellen seemed to have had in the past, I asked whether she had any support in the community in which she lived now. She told me no one wanted to hear about her daughter's murder. "When I talk about it, it's like I'm not the same anymore; that's how they behave. It becomes a very individual experience. They become self-focused, like what would happen if it happened to them? You lose the connection to them. I feel very alone with it." I told her I could understand that, that I found it painful to listen to her, but that I knew the pain was greater for her than for me. "I don't feel it," she said. "I have no feelings any more." This exchange, where I felt I could interject myself and my own experience into our session, brought a shift in me. I no longer felt helpless or blank or paralyzed in horror; but instead I found I had tears in my eyes during the session—my affect had returned in her presence. Caruth (1996) describes the moment in *Hiroshima Mon Amour* when an unempathic slap made the heroine realize that she was alive. Although my remark hardly seemed unempathic, I knew that insisting that Ellen had feelings too felt like a brutal insistence on her separateness and on her humanity, a determination to pierce the dissociative armor with which she had shielded herself.

With the collapse of intersubjective space, the space necessary to communicate with another is foreclosed. Ellen had withdrawn into a closed world, convinced that she would find no one to listen to her. In fact, she was unable to distinguish between her own shut down self and the self of the other who seemed equally remote. This one-dimensional existence has a defensive advantage; being closed off protects one from the risks of emerging from the dissociated state into the world of feeling, with all its terrible meanings. The presence of another who strives to understand, even if she will never entirely succeed, redraws the boundaries between self and other.

With my heart in my mouth, I had opened up a space between us, I had reclaimed my own feelings and admitted them openly to her. I told her I believed that I had tears in my eyes for us both. She lashed out angrily. But there was a shift in her, too. Over time, she conceded that although she had been angry with me for talking about her pain, feeling the pain was better than the numbness, anger at me preferable to bitter indifference. It made her feel more human to know that she still had feelings. The perceiving, experiencing self—a self who could tolerate meaning and affect, who could measure time, reclaim agency and start to contain ties to good objects—had emerged from the paralysis of being wounded by reality.

In starting treatment with a patient who experienced catastrophic trauma in adulthood, I am often reminded of a sentence from Des Pres' (1976) work: "Never again will the survivor know the strength found in innocence" (p. 13). Innocence is a precarious strength, and an illusory one. Our goal in undertaking treatment with a survivor of adult onset trauma cannot be to restore innocence. But our willingness to become witnesses to the patient's experience unencumbered by a metapsychology that reduces that experience to prior pathology; to recreate, share, and expand an intersubjective field that has been rendered uninhabitable, is, in itself, enlivening and provides the basis for analytic work with these difficult conditions.

All psychoanalytic therapies rely on the patient's ability to symbolize, to reflect, and to make connections. In the classical psychoanalytic treatment of posttraumatic states, trauma is measured and analyzed solely according to the symbolic shape the traumatic event assumes in the patient's psyche. Whether one privileges a co-constructed narrative or searches for understanding in the symbolic significance of the experience, engaging in the process of meaning making with survivors presents particular difficulties. In the next chapter, I consider a further feature of catastrophic dissociation: the temporary and sometimes long lasting failure in symbolic functioning. This hallmark of the posttraumatic state presents an additional barrier to effective treatment.

In the chapter that follows, I take up, once again, the question of constructing a trauma narrative. In Chapter 9, I examine more of the ways in which analytic process can be subverted by the wish to remain innocent and to foster necessary illusions.

7

From Voyeur to Witness:
The Crisis in Symbolic Functioning
During Catastrophic Dissociation

It is in the nature of trauma to evade our knowing it.

— Laub and Lee (2003, p. 449)

During the war in Afghanistan, CNN interviewed a man whose wife had been killed by an American missile. "Now that I have no wife," he said, "I have no mind." Being confronted by a sudden catastrophic loss had destroyed this widower's mind, leaving him without the ability to think.

Whether massive trauma is experienced individually, such as a life threatening assault or torture; or in a group surviving terrorist attacks, combat, or near fatal accidents; or if it consists of witnessing acts of brutality and physical destruction, it is not unusual for those who have survived such terrors to feel that they have, in some frightening way, lost their minds. In this chapter, I examine this common, maybe even inevitable, response to being in, or close to, or hearing about, massive trauma. I suggest that it is frequently the case that clinicians who work in uᴄpth with survivors also find themselves struck thoughtless by the experience. In fact, I argue, experiencing an initial state of incoherence might be a necessary condition of the healing process when analysts work with this population. It is in our struggle to overcome this state and to become thinking professionals again that we can start to bear witness in the larger sense and in the small individual sense that we must every day with our patients. And it is through this work with the analyst's containing presence that the survivor ceases to be a mute observer to her own loss, starts to recapture her thinking self, and to become a witness to her own survival.

In earlier chapters, I have described the process by which the adult self collapses during massive trauma as the core self—the experience of agency, of affectivity, of physical cohesiveness and continuity—and the internal object world are challenged by catastrophic dissociation. The psychic implications of this collapse are many. Here I emphasize the role of the cognitive breakdown in catastrophic dissociation. This is the final aspect of Krystal's (1978) description of the catastrophically induced traumatic state. He writes that the catanoid state involves "the numbing of self reflective functions and the paralysis of all cognitive self preserving mental functions" (p. 113).

Although it is often the corporality of the body that is most obviously vulnerable during a catastrophe, it is not the material body, but the psychic body, the body-in-mind, the host to agency, the interpreter of volition, the container of affect, that fragments when the psychic skin no longer offers protection against assaults from the world. Anzieu (1985) points out that when the skin ego is compromised, when the psychic body has lost its ability to contain and to distinguish between inside and outside, there is no longer a place for thoughts to reside. Unspeakable terror—I mean the word unspeakable quite literally in this context—collapses the distinction between the external world and internal experience; it demeans meaning, subverts affect, and challenges representational capacity. In her description of the immediate psychic consequences of adult onset trauma, Tarantelli (2003) writes, "there is no longer an outside from which [a perception] came or an inside which can register it" (p. 919).

When the external world becomes a direct reflection of our most terrifying thoughts, feelings, fantasies, and nightmares, reality testing is beyond our reach and the survivor enters the world of psychic equivalence (Fonagy et al. 2002). Normally in psychic equivalence, mental contents appear to correspond to physical realities. Massive psychic trauma reverses the usual meaning of this term however; it is not that perception has been contaminated by unconscious fantasies, but rather that the psyche is overwhelmed by external horrors that find their equivalents in the unconscious. Nonetheless, the outcome is similar. In the state of psychic equivalence, thought and actuality have become one; the psychic space in which reflection can occur has been foreclosed; fantasy cannot be distinguished from reality; meanings are too threatening to entertain, and thinking and perception are replaced by "concrete mental entities that cannot be explored" (Caper, 1998, p. 145).

It was this phenomenon that initially struck Des Pres (1976) as he studied eyewitness accounts of the Nazi concentration camps. He referred to the literalness of life in extremity, meaning that people caught up in catastrophic circumstances become, and frequently remain, very concrete. Cognitively, catastrophic dissociation is characterized by a narrowing of perception and rigidity of mental processes; thoughts lose their elasticity in order to ward off annihilation anxiety and symbolic thinking is compromised. Describing the effect of external trauma on the mind, Tarantelli (2003) refers to a state of primary meaninglessness, an explosion "which renders the psyche inactive, [which] cannot be registered in consciousness" (p. 919).

Bion's theories about the constitutive role that thinking plays in structuring psychic experience make the following autobiographical account of the defenses he employed during combat in World War I particularly powerful. He describes how narrow and rigid his thinking became as he prepared for battle: "In desperation I stopped thinking about past or future: I began taking compass bearings of every object within my limited view. To my relief my fear began to ebb away. This scene was to be repeated over and over again in this new horrid shape throughout the war until at last it began to lose its horror by force of repetition" (1982, p. 201). About 90 years later, on September 11, 2001, a woman who worked high up in the second tower of the World Trade Center began to walk hurriedly downstairs with a friend after the first tower was hit, ignoring the loudspeaker announcing that the building was secure. On the 70th floor, her colleague went to enter an elevator that had just opened up. As she stepped into the elevator, the building rocked and the lights flickered. The second plane had found its target 15 floors above. Our heroine pulled her friend out of the elevator even as the doors were closing. They continued their descent in darkness as the building was filling with smoke. The stairwell was crowded with panicked people. All she remembers is obsessively counting up to 140 because she knew there were two flights per storey and she knew she last stopped on the 70th floor. Like Bion in the trenches in World War I, all she remembers of the experience is counting out the floors as she passed them. As Bion (1982) commented, "anything to hold at bay the dark and somber world of thought" (p. 286).

During catastrophes, when thoughts are free to roam associatively, the connections they make can lead to terrifying meanings and untenable anxiety. In the previously quoted passages, Bion makes clear how, by narrowing his perceptions and becoming obsessively focused on small details, he effectively destroyed potentially dangerous links between thoughts.

Henry (2004), a psychologist and police captain, gives us this invaluable first hand account of his experiences on 9/11 and his attempts to make sense of them afterwards. "I was completely convinced I could handle whatever I was called upon to do. I felt absolutely calm and composed, exhilarated, and even cheerful ... entirely focused with scarcely a bit of emotion" (p. 23). But, as he reviewed his experiences later, he found, "the images seem fragmented and disconnected, as they probably were, and as the symbolization process deteriorated they imparted little lasting meaning to the experience. ... When I tried to retrieve them or analyze them or consider them in light of new images and information, they seemed fragmented, incomplete, and unrelated" (p. 23).

Not only during the trauma but thereafter, links between memories and impressions that appeared so clear at the time are often destroyed to fend off annihilation anxiety that is proving literally unthinkable. In Chapter 4, neuropsychological research (van der Kolk et al., 1996; van der Kolk, 2002; LeDoux, 1996; Damasio, 1994, 1999) was summarized, providing evidence of the brain's failure to formulate thoughts efficiently under extreme stress. Damasio (1999) finds a consistent link between affect and cognition. In a state of unspeakable terror, when experience does not fit existing conceptual schema, in other words when it is experienced in the register of the Real, experience cannot be assimilated but is organized in memory on a sensorimotor or preoperational level, as unintegrated images, sounds, and sensations. Although he believed he was thinking efficiently and registering everything that was going on around him during the crisis, Henry (2004) subsequently discovered that dissociated terror undermined his thinking, leaving him with only scattered impressions of what had seemed at the time so clear. The flood of cortisol that is released during moments of sustained terror overwhelms the hippocampus, the function of which is to consolidate verbal memory. Simultaneously, unconscious emotional memories, the subsymbolic system, are facilitated, leading to a confusing disconnect between the affective and cognitive spheres. Consequently, cognitive memories are sparse, but sensory memories powerful and intrusive.

There is an impressive level of concordance between posttraumatic symptoms and recent neuropsychological findings, but it is important not to confuse the scientific facts with the survivor's subjective experience when thoughts become narrow, repetitive and concrete and when there doesn't seem to be a way of escaping from them or of using them productively.

Bion (1967) writes that "thinking is called into existence to cope with thoughts" (p. 111), but this is not the case in the state of psychic equivalence, when thoughts are exact replicas of terrifying external events. Thinking, in Bion's sense, requires that words are used symbolically, as signifiers, implying a distance between the experience of the word and what it signifies. Finding meaning depends on being able to make associations between different thoughts. Making meaning of an experience implies that the linked thoughts are resilient and flexible. Meanings multiply; they can withstand scrutiny, be inquired into, pulled this way and that. Meanings give rise to metaphors that yield new perspectives. Affects inhere in meaningful experiences and they too can withstand inquiry, varying and deepening as understanding grows.

Thinking and meaning are disrupted by the transgressive nature of trauma. One man who had watched people jumping out of the Twin Towers and the collapse of the towers and later recorded his narrative at the Columbia University Department of Oral History said, "My brain stops; it doesn't have the pathways to make meaning out of what I saw."

In previous chapters, I drew several parallels between the paranoid schizoid phase and the survivor's psychic state. When the psyche is in survival mode, the lens through which the world is perceived reverts to the concrete logic of the paranoid schizoid position. As Ogden (1990) has explored the far reaching consequences of this unreflective world, the self that acts as mediator between words and what they stand for, between symbols and symbolized, between immediate and mediated experience, is no longer accessible. In this state of unmediated experience, when the distinction between signifier and signified has collapsed, "states of mind become objective, metaphors tend to actualize, the word becomes flesh" (Des Pres, 1976, p. 174). In this state, perception and interpretation are one and the same, and thought cannot be relied upon to provide a different perspective. The loss of the self as interpreter of experience also implies that the self as maker and conveyer of meaning has been lost. Long after the trauma has ended, literalness and confusion can characterize conscious and unconscious attempts to recall and to understand fully and personally what happened.

At their worst, the chaotic somatic, visual, auditory and affective sensations that persecute survivors correspond to Bion's *beta* elements, raw sense impressions that cannot be linked to one another making them unavailable for reflection. Under benign conditions, *alpha* function turns these chaotic impressions into *alpha* elements that can be linked together and thought about, taking on emotional overtones and conveying meaning. Building on Bion's ideas, Caper (1998) introduces the notion of *antialpha* function that occurs when there has been a violent fusion of fantasies and perceptions, in short, in the state of psychic equivalence. In this state, Caper holds that thoughts cannot be born in mind but invade and deaden the mind instead.

When the distinction between signifier and signified has collapsed, words themselves *are* the experience. Heidi spoke English so fluently that I sometimes forgot it was not her mother tongue. During one session, she was recounting a dream: "I am driving a car, it's silver, I drift to the right, suddenly there is a huge...." She stumbled, was silent for a moment, then resumed, "valley, hole, cliff. The car drops down into the water." I asked her about her hesitation and the use of several similes rather than one word. "There's another word for it, I don't even like to say that word in German," she replied. "It feels like falling, I can't keep the experience and the word separate, it's like endless falling when I say it." Rather than being located safely in semantic space, the word Heidi was searching for and simultaneously avoiding is equivalent to the experience it evokes; the word has failed to enter the Symbolic register but resides instead in the Real.

At first, Jonah would break into a sweat whenever he tried to describe the near fatal assault he had survived several years earlier. "I can't cast a shadow over it," he said. I understood him to mean that he was being lived by the raw experience; he could not find words to cast that shadow, to distance himself from the immediacy of it, and thus place it—and himself—in the relative safety—and sanity—of the Symbolic realm. Or, to put this state of affairs in Bion's system: there was no *alpha* function to transform the *beta* elements, the raw sensory data, into *alpha* elements that could be thought about, linked together, integrated with affect and given meaning.

The endless and unproductive cycle of the survivor's fragmented thoughts and feelings is best captured in the repetitive dreams reported by survivors of massive psychic trauma. In the next several pages, I describe my work with one patient whose nightmares after the terrorist attacks in New York demonstrated the process of catastrophic dissociation and the concomitant loss and successive recovery of symbolic function.

Beth lived in an apartment in Battery Park City, a block away from the World Trade Center, facing towards the East River. On September 11, 2001, because she could not see the Twin Towers from her apartment, she didn't know of the attack although "a sound like a freight train coming into the living room" had briefly suggested something untoward was happening. But the sound stopped and—for a moment—everything seemed to return to normal. A few minutes later, her sister, calling from California in a panic, alerted her to the danger she was in; after which, trapped in her apartment, she watched what was happening less than a hundred yards away on television until the power was cut off. At one point, terrified screams from people she couldn't see made it clear that some new unseen disaster had struck. Then a black cloud spread across the window, forcing itself into her apartment. The outside world went dark as night and fell deathly silent. The first building had collapsed but she had no way of knowing. Beth remembers standing in her kitchen thinking, "this is the end of the world, I'm going to die here." She believed that she was being poisoned by the sticky, gritty cloud. She felt no fear, but she could not move. "It was strange," she said. "I was calm but I knew I was paralyzed." The unlinking of affect from a situation that clearly calls for terror, the failure to take action in the face of that danger, and the blithe way in which she registered her paralysis, are evidence of catastrophic dissociation at work.

Beth was eventually evacuated from downtown Manhattan by ferry. She spent the next two days alone in her weekend house on Long Island watching the endless feedback of the towers burning and falling on television. She remembers very little about those two days. At the insistence of a friend who recognized her uncharacteristic dysphoria and apparent indifference to those around her, she started treatment a month after 9/11. Every night in her half-sleep, she relived different aspects of the experiences she had survived. *"I am in my apartment on the telephone, the line goes dead. I am all alone in the world. I woke in a panic."* Or, *"I am in my apartment, I hear people screaming, everything starts to go black. I woke up in a panic."*

Beth's dreams are classic posttraumatic nightmares. They are the psyche's way of indicating that it is locked into the presymbolic mode of the paranoid schizoid position, where experience stands for itself. The unconscious has ground to a halt before the work of the Real and the creative dreamwork of condensation and displacement is unavailable. The psyche is involved in a desperate attempt to grasp the traumatic signifier, but repeatedly fails to bring the Real into the realm of the Symbolic. Ogden (2003) claims that repetitive posttraumatic night terrors such as these are not dreams at all: "If a person is unable to transform raw sensory data into unconscious elements of experience that can be stored and made accessible for linking, he is incapable of dreaming (which involves making linkages in the creation of dream thoughts)" (p. 18).

While Beth and I struggled to find words that would shelter her from the assaultive memories and dreams, she had a number of nightmares that traced the progressive recovery of symbolic thinking as sense impressions and affects started to come together and metaphors emerged from material that had previously proved too shattering to allow into consciousness. In the first dream

> I am in a hotel by the ocean. It is a beautiful day. I walk onto the balcony to get closer to the beach where people are sunbathing; they appear to be talking and laughing but, eerily, I can't hear them. Worse still, the sound of the waves crashing on the beach is not synchronized with actual breaking waves. I felt absolutely panicked when I woke up.

This dream captures the dissociative process at work; it demonstrates the breakdown in sensory feedback that often occurs during traumatic dissociation and that Beth had experienced first hand. It is a terrifying experience when sensory experience is not matched by perception, when the senses can no longer be relied on to distinguish between inside and outside, leading to the collapse of everything that was previously counted on. But, at the same time, this dream is *about* the phenomenon of dissociation; it is not a facsimile of the experience. There is a metaphor, a crude association to September 11: a beautiful day, a day that should be spent at the beach. And the beach itself becomes the setting for a further metaphor: the unsynchronized waves symbolize the breakdown in sensory feedback that Beth experienced during the terrorist attacks. Baffling emotional memories have been captured in images that begin the process of symbolization.

A few weeks later, Beth had a series of nightmares that further illustrated the disorienting and persecutory quality of the cognitive and affective breakdown that she experienced as she waited alone in her apartment for the world to end. In these dreams, Beth is sitting in a restaurant and a waiter delivers a letter to her; when she opens it she finds a sheet of paper covered with words and letters typed in different fonts pasted hodgepodge on the page. She can't make any sense of them. In each version of the dream she is overwhelmed by a different emotion—terror, disgust, joy, shame, relief. The feelings were far more powerful than anything she remembered experiencing in real life. What terrified her was not being able to understand these isolated words or to decipher their message. As she puts it, "There was no meaning," and therefore she could not understand how the overpowering affect was linked to the content of the letter. The series of meaningless letters and their accompanying affects provide a remarkable metaphor for the experience of catastrophic dissociation as I have outlined it. They capture both the intrusive and the aborted quality of thinking when, divorced from yet overpowered by split off affect, words lose their ability to connect together and so lose their meaning. The words represent *beta* elements: raw, disconnected, powerful and incomprehensible. But, these dreams were *metaphors.* They were not concrete repetitions of her experiences on 9/11, they did not even include concrete aspects of that day; symbols were being used that would eventually mediate, make sense of and finally help her integrate the experience. They indicated that Beth was no longer simply reciting the horrors she had endured, she was ready to think and to reflect on the experiences that she had endured and to consider some of the many meanings they held for her.

Beth had no immediate associations to these dreams; she was surprised and even frightened by their lasting power. Putting aside my normal practice, which would be to suggest that we wait to see what meaning we could attribute to them over the course of the next few sessions, I told Beth directly that I believed her dreams were related to her experience during the terrorist attacks and I described in as much detail as I could how they were capturing the dissociative process to which she had fallen prey. Beth was immediately reassured that the dreams were telling her she had not "gone crazy" on September 11 and curious to find out more about the ways in which her unconscious had found ways to protect her from terror but now left her fearful and confused. Davoine and Gaudillière (2004) also advocate immediate explication under these circumstances, "when the analyst gives the patient his word along with his words, he is actually returning to him what belongs to him" (p. 150). In his discussion of the difficulties of socially constructing traumatic experience, Moore (1999) suggests that interpretations that link previous constructions with consensual reality are critical when new material emerges.

UNMENTALIZED TRAUMATIC STATES
IN CLINICAL PRACTICE

There is a wonderfully apt line from T. S. Eliot's (1943) *Four Quartets:* "We had the experience but missed the meaning" (p. 39). Many of us who volunteered to work with survivors, families of those who had been killed, and relief workers, or listened to heart rending stories of loss, terror, and self doubt from employees in the companies we debriefed understood this quotation only too well. We had the experience but missed the meaning.

In the immediate aftermath of a disaster, everyone is reacting. Whether it is called crisis intervention, debriefing, or defusing, relief workers and mental health professionals can provide essential holding and concrete services. The tremendous advantage of properly trained mental health workers is that they know how to listen and how to be present without being intrusive. They imply that they can contain what survivors need to tell them without reacting, even though the toll is high. Hearing stories about horror and unbearable grief, relief workers may indeed, in all probability they will indeed, lose their own minds, later finding themselves prey to perseverating images and stories they have experienced second hand. Official and informal debriefing sessions with colleagues go a long way to helping process and detoxify what they have heard. But it is in a long-term therapeutic engagement that the opportunity to process and to contextualize, and therefore to make meaning of our patients' horrifying experiences, becomes the greatest challenge. It is a challenge on many levels, but most immediately frightening to a clinician who relies on her thought processes to reflect and to understand is the feeling that she cannot think, that she has lost her ability to reflect. Indeed, she feels quite dissociated herself, like a voyeur, as she listens to her patients describe their experiences. Thomas (2005) defines a voyeur as someone who witnesses a scene without being held to account. To put this another way, it could be said that the voyeur's subjectivity is dissociated; she gazes at an exciting scene, experiencing intense affect yet feeling simultaneously removed from the object of her attention. How do we move from the state of being struck thoughtless by what our patients who have survived a massive trauma tell us to the point where we can witness their ordeal and enable them to locate the trauma in ongoing experience. How do we enable them to become witnesses to their own experience? How do we move beyond "the professional numbing of the witnessing professional" as Lifton (1997) once put it? How do we become thinking and witnessing professionals again?

In the rest of this chapter, I explore the process between patient and analyst in the long term psychodynamic treatment of massive trauma that allows the patient to recover her symbolic functioning that collapsed along with the core self during the trauma. In this way, the self who can safely remember and make meaning of the experience is restored.

Josephs (2003) points out that when a patient is in the state of psychic equivalence, interpretive work is meaningless. When metaphors are no longer metaphors but actual events, when fantasy is unavailable as an escape from horror and reflection foreclosed, when words struggle to convey meaning teetering between being overwhelming or trivializing, how can the psychoanalytic clinician work?

I propose several answers to this question. In the previous chapter, I emphasized the difficulties inherent in, and importance of, building a therapeutic relationship with an adult survivor of adult onset trauma who is indifferent to the presence of others. In this chapter, I describe the process between survivor and clinician, the struggle to name and to contain the destructive elements of catastrophic dissociation. In the next chapter, I examine the importance of constructing a trauma narrative.

In treatment, through the process of projective identification there is an opportunity for the survivor's unbearable states of mind to be projected into the analyst in the hope that they will be transformed into something more bearable and returned. It is our job to contain and detoxify the terror, to make sense of the sensations, fragmented memories, and the overwhelming affect that appear to have incapacitated the thinking process. Fonagy et al. (2002) contend that moving a patient out of the state of psychic equivalence requires not merely empathy on the part of the analyst, but reflection. "Copying" the patient's internal state—that is, mirroring the patient's emotions correctly—is not sufficient. The analyst must go a step further, "offering a different, yet experientially appropriate re-presentation" (p. 289) of the events with which the patient is struggling to come to terms. In experiencing the analyst's mind as an external container that has not been destroyed by the unthinkable, a mind that can reflect on his experience without being deadened, the patient comes to identify with the analyst's reflective function. Bick adds that the external containing object is concretely experienced as skin "which, when incorporated gives rise to the fantasy of internal and external spaces" (quoted in Willoughby, 2001, p. 924), thus reversing the state of psychic equivalence.

However, the process is not an easy one for patient or analyst. I have had an experience in which a patient was attempting to get me to contain and transform something so awful, so absolutely unthinkable, that it took months to allow myself to know what was up. In Chapter 5, I introduced David, a veteran who described how half of his personality had gone since he became numb while he was in Vietnam. David went about his civil service job systematically and spoke eloquently about his loneliness and his paranoia. But when he began to recount certain experiences in Vietnam, he was almost giggly. His thinking became disorganized; his language deteriorated into neologisms; he was patronizing and dismissive toward me. Confused by these sudden shifts in mood and cognition, I would try to clarify what had just happened but I felt quite sluggish, somehow unable to get any traction in the face of his weaving and dodging, and I would start to feel foggy and withdraw. It took many approximate tellings and many occasions during which I felt totally out of touch with myself, with David, and with everything that had preceded this moment, for me to realize that my sluggishness was sign that I didn't want to understand what I was beginning to suspect. My mind had been invaded by David's thoughts that could not be thought, Bion's *beta* elements. David had been an enthusiastic member of a platoon that had raped, bayoneted, and burned its way through a South Vietnamese hamlet. David expelled the disordered contents of his mind in the hope that I would contain them and transform them into *alpha* elements, thoughts that we could share and render less paralyzing. My reluctance to have any knowledge of these atrocities, and so be even a passive witness to them, clearly contributed to my difficulty in allowing these wretched thoughts to take shape in my mind and, thus, help David start to metabolize them.

David's success in numbing himself almost entirely is an extreme example, but it serves a heuristic purpose. More often, survivors are "engaged in the struggle between finding meaning and experiencing numbing " (Prince, 1998, p. 47). In treatment, they speak of their experiences in language devoid of affect; first person pronouns frequently give way to third person accounts as the survivors demonstrate their discomfort in getting too close to the experience. Often, these are the patients who did not seek treatment after the event but thought they would grow out of their reactions. "After all," they argue, "time heals all wounds." When I come across these reluctant, lifeless accounts, I know them to be a defense against making meaning, against reliving and analyzing the ordeal in all its affective complexity and with all its cognitive implications. Others recount their stories endlessly and without relief, like the Ancient Mariner, and I feel like a captive audience, like Coleridge's (1797) wedding guest who "cannot chuse but hear" (p. 81). Endless repetition is another form of numbing. It has often been my experience that survivors who have been through grief counseling or trauma therapy but have not contextualized the experience, present in this way. They have arrived at a superficial understanding of the trauma that has, to quote Felman and Laub (1992), "canonized" the traumatic reaction, papering over affect and vitality and foreclosing deeper inquiry. In having their reactions identified as PTSD, these survivors feel, indeed they are led to believe, that everything has been taken care of, just as Ellen was when she sat in on a group for the parents of murdered children.

When patients who have survived massive trauma in the recent or the distant past first start to describe their experience to me, I often find that my mind literally scrambles as my thoughts try to get a hold on the horror I am hearing. Struggling to grasp the dimensions of what I am being told, or what is merely being hinted at, I am sometimes aware of a rush of disbelief and uncomfortable excitement. Frequently, I am mesmerized. I can't think clearly; my mind seems to be stuttering: "Did this really happen? Isn't she being a bit hysterical? Couldn't she have done something to protect herself? Maybe she brought it on herself in some way. This is terrible. It's the most dreadful thing I have ever had to listen to. How can she have survived? For God's sake, I can't even imagine what she's telling me. What would I have done? Wouldn't I just have fallen apart? I'm supposed to help her? Oh God, when will this session be over?" As I start to register my own absences and evasions, my shifting dissociative responses to the patient's material that is being forced into my mind, I make myself engage the dialectic between numbing and meaning. I have to struggle to get a hold of the survivor's experience, to experience the words emotionally even while I am thinking about them rationally, getting a glimpse of what it must have been like, starting to ask questions that help us evaluate and reevaluate the experience. This is what we must do if we are to construct a new meaning that moves beyond the survivor's collapsed self.

Mitrani (2001) summarizes the process by which the analyst becomes a container in the following passage: "The development of a space for keeping such horrors in mind comes about through a painfully gradual process, wherein the analyst's capacity—both to experience and to bear in mind such experiences—is itself encountered time and again by the patient and is eventually introjected" (p.1100). This painfully gradual process is a long way from the abreactive model that earlier analysts believed resolves the traumatic response.

Offering a more technical and somatically based interpretation of the phenomenon of projective identification, Bucci (2001) proposes a circular model of emotional communication between patient and clinician, in which the subsymbolic processes in each communicate with one another. "The analyst knows his own emotion by the activation of its affective core, by the sensations and visceral experiences he feels, by the actions he feels drawn to carry out" (p. 56). In this way "the analyst comes to know what he feels in multiple subsymbolic modalities before the symbolic meaning has been found or developed" (p. 58).

At first, not yet ready to imagine all the consequences to the survivor, not able to make use of my own thinking or theory to provide a third dimension, not able to use my own subjectivity or to imagine the patient's, I am simply a spectator, a voyeur passively watching a scene unfold before me. I am reminded of Bakhtin's (1981) criticism of the epic form in literature as static and inaccessible to personal experience, in contrast to the modern novel that invites engagement and is associated with "eternally living elements". To Bakhtin, the epic hero, like the survivor, is created during a period of turbulence. He is not a subject in his own right; he and his story are inseparable. The story is sacred, the audience listens reverently but cannot enter the narrative. I try to avoid imagining the tragic and immutable fate of the epic hero as I force myself to engage the dialectic between numbing and meaning and to introduce a new dimension of the survivor's experience. To quote Bakhtin once more, "One can't grope it, touch it, one cannot look at it from just any point of view; it is impossible to experience it, analyze it, take it apart, penetrate it to the core … impossible to change, to rethink, to revaluate it" (p. 20). And yet glimpsing, groping, penetrating and reevaluating the experience is what we must do if we are to construct a new meaning with the patient.

As I move painfully out of the two-dimensional role of voyeur, as my own dissociative episodes diminish, as the disorganizing *beta* elements are being transformed into *alpha* elements in my mind, I find my own subjectivity and start to locate my patient as a subject. The paralyzing experience of watching an epic move to its inexorable and tragic conclusion gives way to feelings and sensations that I can identify, and thoughts that start to reformulate what I am hearing. Reverie is possible. And the patient emerges from *her* position as a voyeur, as a mute observer to her own experience, a mere recorder of facts, to a place where she can reflect on her experience, rather than relive it each time she describes it. Questions can be asked. Connections can be made. New feelings emerge. A new point of view starts to take shape. Immediate experience is being mediated by reflection. The patient and I have moved out of two-dimensional space, out of the paranoid schizoid universe of binaries, where, without the mediation of the intersubjective, the only possibilities are one agent reacting to another or against another, where there is only doer and done to (Benjamin, 1998), victim and victimizer, now or never, where to act is to reenact traumatizing scenes. As I find my mind again, I dare to question without fearing that I will inflict further harm or trivialize the patient's experience in some way. Here is a middle term, a third position from which the patient and I can start to think and talk about her experience collaboratively.

When I am prepared to take responsibility for grasping the length, breadth, and depth of the patient's experience, and when the patient is able to experience me not simply as a spectator, but as someone with an independent center of subjectivity, as someone with a mind of her own, my contribution as witness can be of value. But now the patient must start to take responsibility for her own mind. Bion (as cited in Willoughby, 2001) puts the outcome of this process most succinctly: "the product of the container-contained relation is meaning" (p. 917). When the containing function has succeeded, when the *beta* elements have been successfully transformed by *alpha* function into thoughts that can be thought and shared, the patient is ready to reintroject them, to think for herself, so to speak, and to understand more fully what happened during the trauma.

It has become commonplace, particularly when abuse is involved, to speak of the analyst as witness to the patient's experience. Some regard the containing function itself as witnessing, for example, Poland (2000): "By witnessing I refer to an analyst's activity, that of 'getting' what the patient is saying without doing anything more active about it" (p. 21). I am emphasizing here that becoming a witness to a patient's traumatic experience, to her very survival, is a process, often a painful process, but the process is not sufficient unless the patient is also able to bear witness to her own experience. In the account of her ten-year recovery from a savage rape, Brison (2002) speaks of her search for a witness who was stable enough to bear witness. In fact, her entire book is testimony to the fact that it is she who eventually became the witness stable enough to bear witness to herself.

As I was writing this chapter, I asked Beth if I could use some of the work we had done together to illustrate the points that I was making, and I offered to show her what I had written. She was absolutely stunned. She said that she had no idea that her experience was worthy of note. It was my turn to be stunned. How had I failed to make it clear that I thought these experiences and dreams were significant? My question unleashed a flood of memories about events throughout her life to which her narcissistic mother and loving but severely alcoholic father had failed to respond: a nearly fatal accident on a sailboat at the age of 16, going to fetch her father from his office after a bender and arranging for the ambulance to take him to detox, finding her sister in the bathroom with her wrists slit, learning that her boyfriend had made a suicide attempt. I had heard many of them before but to Beth it was like talking about them for the first time. "All this really did happen to me didn't it?" It was not so much a question as a statement. Beth had become her own witness and in so doing she had also located a new sense of self as someone who could own and safely reflect on her experience.

I said at the beginning of this chapter that the analyst's initial state of incoherence might be a necessary condition of the healing process with patients who have survived massive psychic trauma. I was referring to the struggle I have just described. When we approach this work with survivors armed with overdetermined theories and formulae that explain away traumatic reactions, we are also armed against taking the patient's experience into ourselves and allowing our minds and our selves to be temporarily undone. Trying to force meaning on trauma prematurely demeans the survivor's experience; meaning must emerge from the process, it cannot be imposed.

A month after the series of letter dreams ended, Beth had another nightmare:

> It is sunrise or sunset on a beach. There are rocks on either side making it like a cove. It's an absolutely beautiful day, the ocean is a sparkling, a deep blue, the sky is clear. I am kneeling execution style with my hands

behind my back. I'm still alive but there are piles of bodies around me; everyone has been killed. The only sensation is that I have got to get up and run. I woke in absolute panic. But I also felt tremendous relief.

In this session, Beth recalled the short walk she had taken accompanied by emergency personnel from her apartment building to North Cove, from which she was evacuated by boat. "I know there were things along the path, but I don't remember what I saw exactly, so much dust; I know there were pictures in frames; I think there was a shoe…or something. It wasn't just litter; it was a reminder that there had been lives there." Until this nightmare, Beth had never conciously let her mind go beyond that reminder to the thousands of dead bodies lying buried and burned within a stone's throw of her home and her escape route. She said, "It's unimaginable, but I'm trying to think about it now." She, too, was ready to become a witness to the death of thousands and to the temporary collapse of her own mind. She was starting to acknowledge some of the meanings the experience held for her.

I quoted Eliot (1943) above, "We had the experience but missed the meaning." In the next line, that great modernist poet turned constructionist and continued his thought: "And approach to the meaning restores the experience in a different form" (p. 39). The meanings that we construct with our patients allow the *gap* in experience to *become* experience, and therefore to find its place in memory. These meanings will take different and constantly evolving forms. Ultimately, words will never be able to contain all the meanings and feelings that the catastrophic experience gave rise to; part will remain unknown and unknowable. However, our willingness to share the survivor's confusion before reclaiming our minds and so our subjectivity, before reclaiming some internal space for our own reverie, helps the survivor take her own mind as the object of her reflection. In this way, she will redraw the lines between internal space and the external world, to distinguish between thoughts and words and acts and perceptions. In the course of this process, analyst and patient move from the position of passive voyeur to that of active witness, paradoxically reclaiming agency even as they recognize how fragile this state can be.

8

The Ancient Mariner's Dilemma: Constructing A Trauma Narrative

One finds it in the midst of all this as hard to apply one's words as to endure one's thoughts. The war has used up words; they have weakened, they have deteriorated.

— Henry James (quoted in Sontag, 2003, p. 25)

A number of years ago, when I started writing about adult onset trauma, I came across the following comment in Paul Fussell's (2000) book, the *Great War and Modern Memory*. Describing the climax of a short story about World War I, he concludes, "This fiction provides a structure rather too artificial, but it is an example of the *necessity* of fiction in giving memorable testimony of fact" (p. 311, italics added). At the time I thought that was absolutely right; you can't talk about a traumatic experience head on, he is saying; if you really want to give the flavor of the experience, you have to make it up. I don't believe that this is true anymore because I have come to understand the conditions under which a vital trauma narrative comes together, which is the subject of this chapter.

Fussell's (2000) statement seemed true to me once because I was so familiar with the struggle that patients who had survived adult onset trauma would go through when I asked them to tell me about the terrible things that had happened to them and that had sometimes remained hidden for years: the murder of a child, watching a friend killed in combat, being brutally raped, and—more recently—escaping from the Twin Towers. Often the patient seemed quite dissociated as they recounted the details. More often than not, the narrative was what I have come to call safe or, more accurately, lifeless; it was unelaborated, not really addressed to the listener, to me; it was a rote description of "facts" but avoided any affective engagement on the part of the patient, and spared me too. If anything, I felt frustrated and a bit bored.

I call the opposite of a living narrative a lifeless narrative, rather than a dead narrative, because the latter implies that the narrative was once alive and at some point lost its liveliness. Most traumatic narratives, narratives spoken out of the state of catastrophic dissociation, are inevitably lifeless at first because the loss of symbolic function, as I described in detail in the last chapter, and the loss of subjectivity have overwhelmed the survivor's ability to participate in the process of meaningful narrative construction.

Finding a way to tell trauma is always a tricky business. Whether it is a memoir, a biography, or a narrative spoken to a therapist, finding the words to describe it, to relive it, to bear witness to it, and ultimately to make meaning of it, is no small feat. Sometimes words are too much, sounding shrill or mawkish; more often they are not enough, becoming numb and impersonal. Either way, meaning has been leeched out of them.

Des Pres (1976) and Krystal (1978), among others, comment on the surprising paucity of subjective reports of what it is like to live in a state of terror. Survivors prove elusive in treatment. Frequently they will resist referring to their traumatic experience, sometimes with the collusion of their analyst. As I have described in earlier chapters, catastrophic dissociation strips survivors of their subjectivity; leaving them without an "I" from which to speak of their experience and with little confidence that there is a benign other to whom they could speak if they would. First person accounts give way to the third person; memories are fragmented; the chronology jumbled for the passage of time has ceased to have any meaning. Sometimes the story is hard to follow with gaps reflecting memory's reluctance to reenter territory that may have caused the temporary—or not so temporary—collapse of the self. Accounts are curiously devoid of feeling, for catastrophic dissociation renders survivors intolerant of affect that may elicit fears of retraumatization. The Real resists being colonized by the symbolic, and attempts to subjugate these experiences, to bring them into psychoanalytic discourse without diminishing, or in some way denying the horror of what is frequently unspeakable, seem doomed to failure.

In Chapter 6, I summarized the benefits of encouraging a patient who has been traumatized in adult life to create a narrative that begins to undo the effects of catastrophic dissociation. I suggested, that under the right conditions, narrative can re-establish subjectivity, reorder time, permit an exploration of disordered physical cohesiveness, and restore a sense of agency. In this chapter, I distinguish between living and lifeless narratives, and I trace one patient's narrative, sparse and lifeless when she began treatment, as it came to life for both of us in a series of powerful sessions.

It should be understood that I am describing the construction of personal narratives as distinct from public narratives produced by the media, by politicians and religious leaders (Linenthal, 2001). These latter are what Langer (1991) calls "narratives of evasion", narratives that bypass the horror of the situation by grasping at reassuring story lines. Public narratives are constructed in the belief that the Real can be subdued by redemptive messages. As I write this paragraph, less than 24 hours after the full extent of the damage from Hurricane Katrina is becoming clear, one broadcaster, speaking to a former resident of New Orleans, wonders whether, in a few years, all this will be "just like dream. 'The scabs' will have fallen off and new skin will appear underneath." (National Public Radio, 08/31/2005). As if memory can be peeled off in layers and discarded.

In Chapter 4, I reviewed the ways in which social construction is challenged after massive psychic trauma. In the state of psychic equivalence, when the distinction between reality and fantasy no longer exists, when the psyche has been overwhelmed by the outside world that finds its equivalent in the imagination, the psychic space in which reflection can occur and construction can take place has been forfeited. As Moore (1999) summarizes these difficulties: "Potential reality overflows the capacity to construct it, and the result is not a reality created by one's experience, but a loss of one's capacity to participate in it at all" (p. 168).

Not only has the capacity to imagine, and so to construct, collapsed, but so has the distinction between self and other that is integral to social construction. Yet a living narrative is always dialogical. A living narrative intends a responsive subject, not necessarily the actual response of a subject to whom the narrative is addressed, or the physical presence of an other, but the possibility of a responsive subject who can engage what is being told. When the difference between subject and object has collapsed because of catastrophic dissociation, there is no subject to speak or to hear, no internal object to resonate, and no other to acknowledge or empathize. To create a living narrative, a narrator must imagine, and consequently desire, the presence of another, an object who is a subject in her own right, who listens and is free to have her own thoughts and reactions to what she is hearing. Narratives are lifeless when the narrator's object world does not contain, in Laub and Auerhahn's (1989) felicitous phrase, an "internal empathic other," and therefore the narrator has no anticipation of being heard.

The Rime of the Ancient Mariner, Coleridge's (1797) epic poem, provides a powerful illustration of a lifeless narrative. It will be recalled that Bakhtin (1981) contrasts the impersonal, tragic and static tone of the epic with an account written subjectively, in which there is a "continuing and unfinished present" (p. 30). It is that continuing and unfinished present that defines a living narrative. It is a narrative that can grow as thoughts, feelings, and meanings are free to explore and inform one another. In Coleridge's epic, the Ancient Mariner, who survived a horrifying voyage in which he witnessed the deaths of all aboard and feared for his own life, is now plagued by ghostly reminders of those dead men. He buttonholes one reluctant listener after another, compelled to tell his tale but fearing that no one wants to hear it. The wedding guest, who listens to the relentless details along with the reader of the poem, leaves "a sadder and a wiser man" (p. 105). But there is no sense of a relationship between the Ancient Mariner and the wedding guest; the Ancient Mariner simply moves on to seek out his next reluctant and impersonal audience. He does not so much seek engagement with a listener as an opportunity to repeat his story, seemingly indifferent to its impact. His audience is in a state of coerced mirroring in which "affective resonance is coercive, fixed solely by the affective state of the other, and eclipses any 'third'" (Muller, 1996, p.25). In the Ancient Mariner's recitation, as in other lifeless texts, the words are performed but there might as well be silence, for the words create a dead space in the listener that reflects the survivor's lifeless object world.

Throughout the course of this book, I have and shall take mental health professionals to task for their frequent failure to engage trauma narratives, for the many ways in which these narratives are evaded. Here

I focus on an additional difficulty: the fact that, in a state of catastrophic dissociation, the survivor fails to understand that her story *can* be engaged by another, and this failure can rapidly become a belief that no one wants to listen. It is true that, in attempting to tell their story, survivors sometimes find their words and affect expelled by the listener who experiences the words and affect as quite literally unbearable. Thus the audience, like the Ancient Mariner's wedding guest, leads the survivor to persist in telling lifeless narratives as a protection against the possibility of further rejection and disappointment. But lifeless narratives offer protection to the survivor, too, for they provide an escape from the dangers lurking in imagination and memory. Obscuring meaning or holding back associations through the rote repetition of a few facts, the survivor seeks to avoid feelings of helplessness and terror. In effect, the survivor is afraid that the story *will* be engaged by the other and so necessitate her own engagement in bringing the narrative to life. Some survivors are additionally concerned that their narrative will damage the other, not that the other cannot listen but that the other will become corrupted or will be destroyed by what they hear (see also Hirsch, 2003).

Before establishing themselves as empathic listeners to survivors, clinicians must establish themselves as listeners who can break through the traumatic aloneness that descended during catastrophic dissociation. Emphasizing the relational turn to the intersubjective third, Ogden (1997) refers to a necessary collision between analyst and patient where language is used to communicate and bring the other back into the psychic picture, rebuilding the link between self and other, thus reminding the patient that there is the possibility of a responsive audience. There are no formulae for effecting this link: the type, depth, and length of the trauma interact with personality, with environmental supplies, that is, with the availability of someone to speak with immediately after surviving a catastrophe, with the degree of safety in speaking with someone, with their receptivity, with the length of time since the trauma, and with a host of other variables. Ellen, whose daughter had been murdered and whose treatment is described in Chapter 6, could no longer ignore me when I asserted my presence by speaking about my own feelings and insisting that hers had to be different from my own. I compared this to the unempathic slap in *Hiroshima Mon Amour* (Caruth, 1996), as I reclaimed my subjectivity and established myself as someone, different from her, who did want to know about her experience. In Chapter 7, I described the process through which I came to contain Beth's split off affect and fragmented impressions of her experiences. I described how I reflected on those experiences out loud and fed them back to her in a way that enabled us both to construct a narrative about her internal experience on the day she was evacuated from Ground Zero.

In a step beyond containment, Eshel (2004) describes "I-dentification:" a profound and inclusive aspect of containing that "incorporates yet transcends projective identification" (p. 326). For some survivors, this profound sharing, where separateness is temporarily suspended, is the only safe way in which a living narrative can be told. I interviewed one young woman, a survivor of the Rwandan genocide, only once in the Immigration and Naturalization jail where she was awaiting a hearing on her request for political asylum. Celeste seemed to understand only too well the difference between living and lifeless narratives and how much the former demanded of both participants. At first she repeated, almost verbatim, an account of her experiences in Rwanda that I had read in her court papers. She was informative, efficient, and unscathed; I had to know more if I was to present a convincing psychological case for her to the INS judge. I asked her if we could go over the account again, speaking about some of her feelings. "Do you mean in detail?" she asked, looking at me very closely, as if to evaluate my ability to go there with her. When I responded that I was prepared to listen to anything she had to say, she spoke fluently and powerfully. As she spoke, the tension between joining and observing—the tightrope that clinicians walk in every session—disappeared for me; to borrow another of Eshel's expressions, "at one ment" (p. 239), I became one with Celeste. My own boundaries were temporarily suspended as I absorbed terror, disgust, humiliation, pain, and grief that were to haunt me for several weeks. In subsequent correspondence with Celeste, I came to understand that knowing that I could experience all this and survive, knowing that I was a separate person who had voluntarily stepped into her experience, began the process of reanimating her object world and reduced her sense of having been rendered untouchable by her rapists.

At the other extreme, Poland (2000) emphasizes the necessity of a completely separate listener: "It mattered to my patient that I serve as an other, someone she could see as hearing and grasping the anguish she was going through and who recognized the crucial import of her inner struggle … it was important to her that I see her as a separate real person" (p. 18).

The negotiation between analyst and patient from object to subject, from container to witness, from being one to establishing separate subjectivities, are all aspects of the same treatment process as the therapeutic couple moves towards constructing a living narrative in which, to paraphrase Kardiner (1969), many of the fragments of catastrophic dissociation are reunited and the "patient is able to re-establish the conviction that he did not die and was not disintegrated by the experience itself but by the fear of annihilation" (p. 254).

I suggested in the last chapter that when the analyst can, herself, fulfill the role of witness, she serves as a transitional witness until the patient can become a witness to her own experience. However, for some survivors the task of constructing a narrative is complicated by the need to formally bear witness to others' suffering. Those who have survived when others have died often feel a moral imperative to bear witness to those deaths. Yet, the act of bearing witness exerts a tyrannical hold on the teller, who forfeits everything in becoming identified with the struggle to survive and to remember those who did not. Rather than offering personal details with which others can identify, this witness has no personality of her own, as if the burden of bearing witness to others' suffering has beaten the self into a further retreat.

Jill was one such case. She had escaped from her apartment at Ground Zero with her infant son, Daniel. A professional woman who had ended an extended analysis several years earlier, Jill briefly returned to her analyst after the terrorist attacks. From her account of this session, her analyst appeared unable to imagine what had happened to her, or even to acknowledge that her experience had been substantially different from his own as he sat in his uptown office and followed the unfolding events on television. After a perfunctory "that must have been scary," he spoke about his relief that his children had not been in New York on 9/11. Jill left chastened and disillusioned; her fear was confirmed that those who had not been immediately involved in the attack, no one outside Strozier's first zone, would be able to understand how changed she felt. In the account of his experiences after the terrorist attacks, police psychologist Henry (2004) had a similar feeling; he describes his wish to get back to "the Zero where things made more sense" (p. 55) and his rage at a world that could not acknowledge his different reality.

Jill felt completely alone, unrecognizable to herself as she struggled to appear unchanged to others. A course of Eye Movement Desensitization and Reprocessing (EMDR) did reduce some of her intrusive visual memories, but did little for her sense of disenfranchisement and feelings of depression. By the time she was referred to me, on the second anniversary of the terrorist attacks, she was ashamed of her continued focus on the event when everyone else appeared to have moved on. She spoke to no one about these feelings but lived in a state of alertness to the possibility of repetition and despair over the impossibility of regaining her previously buoyant sense of self.

I have chosen Jill's narrative for several reasons. Most important, I believe that it traces the progressive elaboration of associations and affect as the narrative becomes animated by our mutual interest. Jill admitted, after we began the process of trying to construct a more meaningful account, that at the beginning I was not there. "When I talk, I am not relating to you," she said. And her narrative showed it; she was just going through the motions. The fact that this narrative had to be written down for Jill to feel safe enough to fully engage it obviously does not mean that all trauma narratives have to be written, but the fact that it was written down allows the reader to follow its progression exactly as Jill and I did.

Normally, an exceptionally articulate woman—as I have come to discover—for over a year, when I could get Jill to speak of something other than everyday concerns, she repeated the same lifeless story that she had told me in our first sessions. She repeated it almost verbatim with similarly numbed affect, staring off to my left, never making eye contact.

Jill was acutely attuned to me from the first moment she stepped into my office, checking to see whether I would be able to hear what she had to say, whether I would be interested in it, whether I would burden her with my own experience, worrying that I was too close in age to her, or not sufficiently experienced to be of any help. If my mouth was dry or if I appeared tired she was solicitous, but privately wondered whether I was taking medication for depression or whether I was up to the task of working with her. In the end, she held back because she was very worried about sharing any of these thoughts with another person and so contaminating them. It is intrinsic to Jill's sense of self with other, of the other's inevitable frailty (or duplicity), so characteristic of her to focus on the other's state of mind and health to the exclusion of her own, that she could not speak her experiences out loud, nor could she let them go. She could not risk distorting them in any way that would not do justice to what she had experienced and to those who had died, to whom she felt responsible. Commenting on the burden of being an accurate witness, Brison (2002) reported that keeping the "true" story of her rape straight in order to reproduce it at trial was deadening and took conscious effort (p.107). Thus, Jill consciously held on to her unchanging story, afraid to give it up and afraid to engage it too deeply.

After 16 months of treatment, Jill remained paralyzed by what had happened to her on September 11, 2001, now almost three and a half years earlier, yet she dismissed my attempts to get her to explore the experience further. Finally, I resorted to a technique that has been used in the short-term treatment of trauma (see Pennebaker, 1993; Park and Blumberg, 2002; Peri, 2004; among others). I suggested to Jill that she could dictate her story to me and that I would write it down and transcribe it; then, the following week, we could review together what she had said and see if she wanted to add anything further. It was clear that Jill would not have been able to write the narrative herself. In her catastrophically dissociated state, the words themselves were too dangerous and did not provide enough distance from the experience. Jill needed to more fully recapture symbolic function, to be able to safely reflect on the meaning of the words she spoke before she could use them to construct a narrative herself. In her mind, dictating the words to me and having them recorded on paper introduced a third, impersonal medium, removing me from the interpersonal field and offering us both shelter from the immediacy of the experience.

It was then that I discovered that, in some ways, Jill and I had been working at cross-purposes; she wanted to make sure that she told her story as she had witnessed it. I wanted to encourage her to bring more of herself into it, to reconnect with and recollect aspects of herself that had been overwhelmed or split off during her four hour ordeal. The narrative that Jill dictated and that I recorded became, in effect, the therapeutic third, an intersubjective endeavor that I had been unable to accomplish during the earlier phase of treatment, given her fear of retraumatization, of traumatizing me, and of losing her witnessing connection to those to whom she felt responsible. Reading the written text added an entirely new dimension to the story that she had been repeating and to which I had been trying to bring more texture for over a year. It offered Jill a way of getting the memories outside her—as she put it—without losing or distorting them. It offered us both something outside of her on which we could safely focus. After she had read the completed manuscript, as it is presented here, with all the associations added, Jill said:

> It's like reading someone's story that is exactly like mine. I have separated from the experience and someone else has had it; someone else understands. I am split reading the story; it's like it's from someone else. It's as if you [GB] had written it yourself. I don't need to relive the image of the guy jumping any more. It's become important for me to know that

other people will see the story somehow; I think there is a certain way people never got a part of the story; it had no significance for them. This makes it more human; I have this need for people to know about it.

I now present two sections of Jill's original narrative with the flatness, contradictions, and repetitions intact, and then re-present the narrative interspersed with the associations, and further associations to those associations, that built up with each successive reading, so that the reader will be able to follow the increasingly layered meanings and affect that emerged as the written narrative that Jill and I constructed grew full of life even as she was describing death.

I didn't hear the first plane going in. I was in my bedroom with an indirect view of the World Trade Center out of the window on the left. Daniel was on the bed. My mother-in-law left a message. I don't remember hearing any noise. I wasn't particularly scared but then it was like the second plane lowered itself down, but I don't remember hearing any noise. It was in slow motion. No markings on the plane, just grey. I thought it was from a foreign country. Now I realize it was moving so fast I couldn't see any markings, but I thought it was moving slowly. Watching the crunching. Watched the plane come from the south tower into the north tower and it disappeared. I don't know where it went, it disappeared. Then I thought there would be more planes. "We are being attacked." I was on the 23rd floor and thinking they would hit us.

I said, "I have to go, I have to get him out of here." I started talking out loud to myself. I told Daniel "You have to get up." I threw clothes on his bed and pulled on my own clothes. No stockings. Talking to myself in the second person, "You need your big bag, wallet, keys. Put him in his carriage in his wet diaper." I didn't look out the window again. I wound the dogs' leashes around the handles of his carriage and went into the hallway. No one was there. I was worried about my neighbors. I rang their bells on the way to the elevator. There are seven apartments.

I said to my neighbor Frank, "Please don't stay here." I was clearly anxious. I said, "I think we should leave, get away from these buildings, there may be more planes coming, the tower may fall." He said, "Do you want me to go down with you?" We may have rung other people's bells. I don't know whether they came to the door. They said, "We're staying." At the elevator we waited and waited. Daniel was really quiet. Frank was so tall. I kept saying I was scared. He said, "So am I" and we hugged each other. It was so comforting, it is the most I have ever been comforted by a person touching me since my mother held me after a nightmare, I was enveloped by him, it felt so much safer.

There were two ways out, the courtyard and the back way out facing the water. The doorman said, "You have to exit to the back of the buildings facing the water." People in the lobby were wandering around, not knowing where to go. I think part of the fuselage had gone into one of the buildings, there was a fire, the lobby felt silent.

I was looking for someone to help, for guidance, a police officer, someone to help with the responsibility that I had for the baby and the dogs. It was becoming clearer and clearer that I was alone.

I went out the back, there were twenty or thirty people in little groups huddling looking up, holding dogs, people didn't look terrified, like they thought it was just a really bad fire. I didn't think anyone was feeling the same level of fear that I was feeling. I couldn't swallow. A woman gave me a frozen bottle of water. No one commented on the fact that I had the baby. People were milling around, waiting for something, talking and looking up, they weren't moving, just standing around. That bothered me. I felt we should be getting out of there. It wasn't right just to be standing there, I thought if the tower topples over it will kill us. It will fall all the way into the river.

In response to one of the very few questions I asked, Jill spoke of her conviction that she and her child were about to be killed. She then described how she moved on alone, at one point trying to protect her son from seeing a badly burned man being evacuated in a cart. She continued:

The thing that bothers me still is that there was no sound. The only auditory thing I remember is a woman shouting, "Oh my God, they're jumping out" and "Oh my God, the tower is coming down." I wasn't far from the chapel and the marina and someone screamed, "O my God, they're jumping out." And I looked round and saw the man in the business suit, like a bird trying to fly. I left there when two or three were jumping together. Then the voice started again, "Don't look back, just keep on." I don't know if I said it out loud. It was successful only for a short time. I had gotten almost to Stuyvesant, on the sidewalk, I think they had blocked off the sidewalk by the river. All I remember is total terror and helplessness.

This account, as it stands, took Jill several weeks to complete. The experience of telling it caused her so much distress that in each session we would spend time before she started to talk and after she had spoken reflecting on the experience of describing these events to me, how vivid they remained in her mind's eye, and whether this exercise would be of any help to her. When I had typed up her account, it took us many more weeks to review what she had said. Each week we returned to the original manuscript with the previous week's additions. I now repeat the original text with Jill's additional associations.

> I didn't hear the first plane going in. I was in my bedroom with an indirect view of the World Trade Center out of the window on the left. Daniel was on the bed. My mother-in-law left a message.

The reader will note how factual this first account is. Devoid of affect, it is simply a description of what she registered perceptually. On rereading this introductory paragraph, Jill started to interject some of the feelings she experienced as she looked at the fire, and to remember more of the chronology of those first few moments of awareness of the tremendous danger she was in.

> My mother-in-law said, "Turn on the TV. Look out the window." I thought "Holy Shit, what could have happened out there? It's a terrible fire out the windows." Maybe it was 10 minutes later I got a call and I took it and it was Daniel's babysitter and she told me a plane had gone into the World Trade Center.

The original account continued:

> I wasn't particularly scared but then it was like the second plane lowered itself down but I don't remember any noise. It was in slow motion. No markings on the plane, just grey. I thought it was from a foreign country. Now I realize it was moving so fast that I couldn't see any markings, but I thought it was moving slowly. Watching the crunching. Watched the plane come from the south tower into the north tower and it disappeared. I don't know where it went, it disappeared. Than I thought there would be more planes, "We are being attacked." I was on the 23rd floor and thinking they would hit us.

On rereading this paragraph, Jill was able to reflect more fully on the experience of watching and subsequently describing her close-up view of the plane going into the tower.

> It's so visual, no one ever talks about it, watching the plane go from one to another, like watching a bullet from one body going into another. It's incredible it didn't take the top of the tower off.

Between us, Jill and I were beginning to find a way of allowing her narrative to grow without the words posing an immediate threat. She found that she no longer had to follow the story to its conclusion but could stop and reflect on her own experience and behavior. "It's like freezing a frame in a movie. You can leave off and pick it up again when you want to," she said. The ordeal was becoming something that had existed in the past, which could be returned to at will like a regular memory rather than continually asserting itself over the present moment.

The next paragraph, added on rereading the previous addition, is an even more striking example of the evolving meaning of this part of the experience as Jill explained what the bullet metaphor meant to her:

> This reminds me of how the people down there experienced the towers. They enveloped us and protected us and cast their shadow over us. We would see them when we were outside with our dogs and coffee. We watched them, watching the sun reflected in the windows. They were like these big parents holding us. They were very large and powerful, guarding the life of our neighborhood. Symbolically this is why it's like a bullet going from one body to another, these two parental figures, it was amazing how much they could take and wondering how much more they could take. When they went down it was like the death of everybody in there, the death of the buildings. They were parents, they cast a gold protective shadow.

It had taken three readings of her original narrative and over a year of treatment for Jill to frame this part of her escape so poignantly. In this neighborhood, in which she had chosen to raise her family, she had felt, possibly for the first time since she was a teenager, absolutely safe and protected from harm. There is, of course, a temptation to further analyze the meaning of the parental towers, for this woman who had been so terribly failed by her own parents. Had I done so, I would have run the risk of reducing her experience on 9/11 to a reflection of her childhood sorrows, but her horror went so far beyond that. Frawley-O'Dea (2003) reports a case in which, after many weeks of listening to a patient whose husband was a firefighter, talking about coping strategies during and since the terrorist attacks, she attempted to draw parallels between her patient's experiences as a child exposed to an uncle who sexually abused her, and her husband being sent into danger at Ground Zero. The patient "let me have it in no uncertain terms. She felt that I was devaluing the present day, very good, very normal, very real reasons for her concern about her husband's safety," Frawley-O'Dea (p. 79) concludes. I repeat Des Pres' (1976) statement that "attempts to interpret the survivor's experience—to see it in terms other than its own—have done more harm than good" (p. 157). "When death itself is the determinant," he concludes, "then behavior has no meaning at all in a symbolic or psychological sense" (p. 155). When her narrative was almost concluded, Jill herself said, "There is no experience that matches this. Where you think to yourself, I can't, I won't ever get beyond this." This, then, is a strong recommendation when working with survivors of massive psychic trauma to listen and not to interpret, to join the patient without imposing understanding borrowed from what Des Pres calls the realm of civilization.

I now return to Jill's original narrative after seeing the plane going into the second tower. Once again, this first account is utterly factual yet conveys the immediacy of the experience; rather than summarizing her thoughts or conversations, she conveys them in the present tense as an internal dialogue, as if they are actually taking place.

> I said, "I have to go I have to get him out of here." I started talking out loud to myself.

"The voice was impersonal," she reflected as she reread this account.

> I told Daniel, "You have to get up." I threw clothes on his bed and pulled on my own clothes. No stockings. I was talking to myself in the second person, "You need your big bag, wallet, keys. Put him in his carriage in his wet diaper." I didn't look out of the window again. I wound the dogs' leashes around the handles of his carriage and went into the hallway. No one was there. I was worried about my neighbors. I rang their bells on the way to the elevator. There were seven apartments.

> I said to my neighbor Frank, "Please don't stay here." I was clearly anxious. I said, "I think we should leave, get away from these buildings, there may be other planes coming, the tower may fall."

On rereading this section, Jill stressed that she was always afraid that the towers would fall. "That was my concern that it would fall over."

> He said, "Do you want me to go down with you?" We may have rung other people's bells. At the elevator we waited and waited. Daniel was really quiet. Frank was so tall. I kept saying I was scared. He said, "So am I" and we hugged each other. It was so comforting, it is the most I have ever been comforted by a person touching me since my mother held me after a nightmare, I was enveloped by him, it felt so much safer. The elevator opened, it was completely packed. People seemed excited rather than terrified, not realizing that this could be the end of the world.

As Jill continued her original narrative, it is striking how alone she felt during her ordeal, as if no one grasped the danger except her. This traumatic aloneness became a constant theme during her escape and permeated every aspect of her life thereafter. By the time she reread the manuscript for the first time, however, she had achieved a more empathic perspective on her neighbors' apparent excitement. "It was nervous excitement," she concluded.

On reaching the lobby her original narrative continues,

> There were two ways out, the courtyard and the back way out facing the water. The doorman said, "You have to exit to the back of the buildings facing the water." People in the lobby were wandering around, not knowing where to go. I think part of the fuselage had gone into one of the buildings, there was a fire, the lobby felt silent.

Rereading this passage, Jill can reflect further on her motivations as she stood in the silent lobby.

> The silence was remarkable. I was looking for someone to take control, to say "You have to go this way." People were aimless like in a psych ward. I saw the back yard of the buildings, people in little groups talking, everybody looking up.

On her second rereading, the meanings deepen further to incorporate her sense even then of how changed she will become as a result of this experience.

> The world and reality as you have always known it had suddenly changed, that's an amazing emotional experience. "Things will never be the same," I kept thinking. "The world will never be the same, my world, the world." I knew we would never be safe again, there in my backyard I knew we would never have the fantasy of invulnerability, that was when I was first aware of it.

Rereading the narrative once again, she paused to say, "Even now I don't let myself go to the feeling of it. But there is something disengaging about having it outside of me. I don't have to remember all the details because they are written down." The original narrative continued,

> I was looking for someone to help, for guidance, a police officer, someone to help with the responsibility that I had for the baby and the dogs. It was becoming clearer and clearer that I was alone. I went out back, there were twenty or thirty people in little groups huddling looking up, holding dogs, people didn't look terrified, like they thought it was just a really bad fire. I didn't think anyone was feeling the same level of fear that I was feeling. I couldn't swallow. A woman gave me a frozen bottle of water. No one commented on the fact that I had the baby. People were milling around, waiting for something, talking and looking up, they weren't moving, just standing around. That bothered me. I felt we should be getting out of there. It wasn't right just to be standing there, I thought if the tower topples over it will kill us. It will fall all the way into the river.

Again, as she reread this part of the narrative, Jill commented on her sense of isolation.

> What seemed very difficult to me was that I seemed different from all of them, the experience I was having was different from anyone there. I couldn't walk over to anyone to get comfort, they weren't moving. They didn't seem to feel they were in imminent danger. I was in disbelief that no one tried to include me. That Bob, who owned the pet shop, he just said, "We're over here if you need something." It made no sense to me that they were standing around doing nothing. I was in conflict.

> I feel stupid saying it but I kept thinking, "If I didn't have the baby and the dogs I would go over and help. People must need help over there." No one seemed to be helping the people in the tower.

The belief that she should have found a way of offering help to other people became a constant source of remorse for Jill. As Bellinson (2002), whose work I described in Chapter 6, suggests, Jill's decision, however necessary, not to offer help to others and instead to save herself and her baby complicates her recovery. Jill senses that her disenfranchisement and the alienation from her previously socially concerned self will not yield until she has had the opportunity to undo what amounted to a necessary abandonment of others in need. She does not recognize herself in the young woman who fled from danger rather than facing up to it.

> I didn't hear any ambulances. It was like a white out, like we used to have in Massachusetts in the winter, you couldn't see anything. The air was full with papers, you could put out your hand and grab papers. People were walking through them. As the windows exploded or imploded there would be more papers, an explosion and a stream of paper. There was inertia watching these people stuck standing around talking, and I am thinking, "Come on we should leave, come on let's go!" I thought the tower would come down on us. And my other concern was that there were more planes. People were saying there were five of them and they had only counted three, I didn't know if there were any in New York, and here they were standing around holding their dogs, talking. I stood there maybe ten minutes and I wanted to see if any of the restaurants had opened, maybe I could get some water, I needed it so desperately. This woman gave me this bottle of frozen water and I tried to give it back and she said, "Keep it." Once I got that, that little knowledge that someone gave a shit, I could leave. I put together this plan, we would stay as close to the river as possible and walk north. There were more and more papers coming out. It was 9:15 already.

There is a long pause in the narrative, then Jill continued:

I was seeing myself leave and beginning a journey, I was trying to remember if I was talking to myself out loud in the courtyard, it almost feels like I said out loud, "Just go!" I was remembering thinking it. Then my life took this journey and it's never been the same. It was the end of my home.

Reading this portion of her narrative yet again, Jill repeated, "I have been homeless ever since that day." Erikson (1976) details the particularly complex symptoms to which those who have survived massive psychic trauma and also lost their homes and communities are subject. Jill has become homeless. She has given up her home that was contaminated both by the dust and by the memories of what she saw there, the ugly smoking stack of twisted steel and concrete; but she is also emotionally homeless, unable to settle into a recognizable self state. She was still ruled by the memories of escaping her home and of what happened next, troubled by the specific loss of auditory memory. She alternated between worrying about this missing part of her experience and chalking it up to her much stronger visual memory. As Jill's original narrative resumes near Stuyvesant High School, she said again:

The thing that bothers me still is that there was no sound. The only auditory thing I remember is a woman shouting, "Oh my God they're jumping out" and "Oh my God the tower is coming down." I wasn't far from the chapel and the marina and someone screamed, "O my God, they're jumping out." And I looked round and saw the man in the business suit, like a bird trying to fly. I left there when two or three were jumping together. Then the voice started again, "Don't look back, just keep on." I don't know if I said it out loud. It was successful only for a short time. I had gotten almost to Stuyvesant, on the sidewalk, I think they had blocked off the sidewalk by the river. All I remember is total terror and helplessness.

The following week, in her associations to this portion of the written text, Jill came to understand why she had dissociated the sounds of that day.

I don't recall any noise. In *Fahrenheit 9/11* it was unbearable. I don't know whether I was blocking it or whether I heard it for the first time when I saw that film. It became intolerable listening. [She paused.] Now I have just remembered this, I remember hearing loud sounds and I remember trying to identify what it was. Someone said that "that's the sound of the bodies hitting the ground." I was in total denial. Individual sounds of something hitting, a dull thud, no metal. I squinted my eyes so that I couldn't distinguish between the bodies and a hunk of the building. If you squinted it just looked like black things falling. Once it was clear, after I watched four people jump off, I knew I didn't want to see any more.

A few weeks later Jill added further to this reconstituted memory:

The bodies exploded when they hit the ground and that was the sound that we heard. The only sound I remember clearly was car alarms. I remember thinking why didn't I hear fire engines, police, maybe I could only hear my own voice. I remember I didn't look back, right before the tower came down a ton of people jumped. I was haunted by the man in the suit jumping out from the south tower. The man in the suit with his arms outstretched trying to fly. I saw him over and over again. I feel more distant from the visuals, there is less emotional intensity.

With more distance from the immediacy of this memory, Jill added two comments to the story of the jumping man who had remained alive in her memory for over three years.

He jumped because anything was better than to be burned to death, death is better for him to make the final act in his own control. I started to squint so that they would look like pieces of paper, there were pieces of building falling, I did that right after I saw the people holding hands. There were hundreds of them jumping, so many. Watching him jump out, it was surreal, it was weird, he came down slowly, it looked like he caught some wind, that's why it reminded me of a bird. Every time I think of his arms outstretched in his suit with his arms out, his body horizontal to the ground … I hadn't yet squinted my eyes so I really saw him. It's impossible to know how to process something like that. When people were jumping out I didn't think of them hitting, I just knew they were going to die, I just knew it was a jump into death. But I saw that man over and over and over. I must have seen that man jump hundreds and hundreds of times. Later I became obsessed with finding out who he belonged to, who he was. I wanted to tell his family that he made a choice, that he wasn't burned to death. I never told any one about that obsession.

Like so many survivors of adult onset trauma, Jill appeared to have resumed her everyday life within a few months of the terrorist attacks. She found a new apartment in a different neighborhood, continued to hold down a demanding job, to raise her children, to struggle with her husband, and to meet friends and colleagues. But she remained silent about the topic that was foremost in her mind: her preoccupation with what she had been through and the extent to which she felt changed, alienated from herself and distanced from others.

Most survivors of adult onset trauma do not need to produce a written account of their experiences when they find a clinician who recognizes their catastrophic dissociation. Nonetheless, following Jill's written narrative permits a systematic exploration of the process by which traumatic memories are constructed and the dynamics of that process. As I transcribed Jill's account, I demonstrated my capacity to contain her memories without distorting or minimizing them. Understanding that I was not damaged—that I could record what she was saying, process it and hand it back to her, in this case quite literally verbatim—allowed Jill to feel sufficiently held that she could reflect further on what she had said. Over time the text, that at first had been recited to no one—"You are not there," she had said—became my story—"It's as if you had written it yourself," she said—from which she felt detached enough that she could even smile at a turn of phrase. When it was sufficiently comprehensive and detoxified, the narrative became her story again, to which she could return when she wanted, not when traumatic memory demanded. Our ability to reflect on the process of narrative construction itself, what it was like to part with the story, to be able to entrust it to another, to get it back in the same form yet subtly changed by the mere process of transmission, emphasizes the necessity of closely following manifest content in the construction of a trauma narrative. The text became a transitional object, neither hers nor mine, both inside and outside at the same time, constantly open to reflection and change.

This chapter amounts to a plea for psychoanalysts working with adults who have survived catastrophic trauma to privilege narrative. Narrative is transfigured memory that, in its turn, if it is a living narrative, further transfigures memory. The importance lies not in the memory itself but in the power to gather all the disparate impressions into a coherent whole, and in the rigorously intersubjective experience necessary to this process. In privileging narrative, we privilege the successive unfolding of increasingly complex experience. To privilege narrative is to understand that to relate a traumatic memory (or any memory) is to construct the memory, to formulate experience that has previously remained unformulated (D. B. Stern, 1997). That is, experience that may have been brought in bits and pieces into the margins of consciousness, only to be banished before it reached the level of coherent thought. In the stark case of trauma, this unformulated experience has frequently made its presence felt in somatic symptoms, in repetitive dreams and in intrusive imagery to which associations are scant. In an act of insubordination against the Real, we believe that to the extent that the patient's collapsed self can be reanimated, this will happen in the presence of an other who encourages her patient to cast her verbal, affective, and associational net more and more widely. Thus, urging her to capture and, in so doing, to formulate a more personal understanding of the dissociated fragments that were spun off during the traumatic experience and lodged in distressing symptoms. We do not believe that this process reveals the truth, *per se,* indeed, we do not believe that there is *a* truth to be discovered, but we do hope to help the patient construct a living narrative that does justice to her experience.

A living narrative is always an open text. The Medieval scholar, Sylvia Tomasch (2004), defines Palinodic discourse as discourse that is addressed to a lack. Texts, and I would add narratives, are always, inevitably, incomplete. It is the continued construction of those narratives, week after week, month after month, that is the essence of a psychoanalytic process. In working with survivors of adult onset trauma, we discover that this process is complicated by the wish to capture something that will always remain partly elusive. In this way, we continue our Palinodic discourse with the patient, addressing the gap between experience and the further attempts to find meaning in it. Our act of insurbordination against the Real can never entirely subdue the Real, but it does oppose the forces of the Real, the gaps and evasions necessitated by horror, with a subjective voice that continues to question and to strive for understanding.

9

The Strength Found in Innocence: Resistance to Working Psychodynamically with Survivors of Adult Onset Trauma

We are, I believe, incapable of both maintaining our sanity and genuinely experiencing our own mortality.

— T. Ogden (1997, p. 18)

After the cases described in the last three chapters, it will be clear that these are troubling conditions to face clinically, and, perhaps, particularly challenging to the psychoanalytically trained clinician. If this book does no more than convince the reader that trauma in adult life shakes the very foundation of a formerly solid core self, I have accomplished an important goal. In acknowledging this fact, the clinician is also acknowledging her own vulnerability to both catastrophe and to the loss of a familiar self that she always may have taken for granted. In this chapter, I review the many guises that resistance to facing this unsettling truth can take in both survivors and the clinicians from whom they seek help.

The day after the terrorist attacks in New York, several of my patients offered to give up their sessions so that I could volunteer to work with survivors and relief workers. I was touched by their suggestions but I wondered what lay behind this sudden altruism. Thinking back to the hours immediately after the attack, when I walked downtown to the Red Cross Headquarters as wave upon wave of blank faced, weary people dragged themselves uptown, I remembered my grim determination. I remembered how relieved I felt to be doing something, taking some kind of action. Instead of staying home with my family, desperately trying get news of our friend and neighbor, Betty, who had just that week jubilantly started a new job in a company whose offices were high up in the World Trade Center; instead of watching the endless television reruns of those previously unimaginable scenes, I chose to get busy and push aside the feelings of disbelief and helplessness. But by the following morning, tempting as it was to remain in the thick of things, I knew I must volunteer on my own time and resist my patients' suggestions to skip their sessions. Rather than the temporary relief of "doing something," I would join my patients and listen to their shock, their fears, their uncertainty and vulnerability, feelings that very much reflected my own.

My first session that day was with Noam, who began by reiterating his belief that he shouldn't be with me, that I should be out there helping people who really needed it. Five years earlier, Noam had barely survived an accident in which his father was horribly disfigured and killed in front of him. Before beginning treatment, Noam had been living a marginal life, unable to plan a future, withdrawn from friends and family, skating gingerly on the thin ice of a life constructed to avoid anything that would trigger memories of the freak accident. And now here was another instance of random violence taking not one, but thousands of lives.

When I did not reply to Noam's comment that I should be volunteering at Ground Zero rather than seeing my regular patients on this first day after the terrorist attacks, there was a silence. I asked him to tell me what was on his mind. He burst out, "The ability to take people's lives impresses me. It's an erotic rush, like a bloodlust." But he quickly became deflated,

> I can't get there, at least I can't stay with it. I know what happens after all the killing ends. I don't want this knowledge. It's unbearable. I don't want to accept that it just happened, that there's nothing you can do to stop it or to protect yourself. It makes me feel like a girl. Other people

don't know about these dangers; they keep trying to blame someone, find a way to make it alright; they don't understand it will never be alright again.

Hearing Noam's words, I was reminded once again of Des Pres' (1976) haunting phrase, "never again will the survivor know the strength found in innocence" (p. 256). Noam's innocence had been forfeited when he gazed at his father's mutilated body slumped on the car seat beside him. At that moment, he looked his own mortality in the face.

In general, as I have discussed in previous chapters, psychoanalytic literature has paid scant attention to death anxiety; indeed, Freud maintained that the unconscious is incapable of representing its own death, claiming instead that the fear of mortality is analogous to the fear of object loss, loss of the object's love, castration anxiety, and censure from the superego (Freud, 1926). Others have commented on this oversight, suggesting that Klein's concept of annihilation anxiety provides a more fitting template for the terror experienced during massive psychic trauma. Hoffman (1998) argues that, over time, cognitive structures develop to encompass the idea of death. He suggests that there is a dialectic between the sense of being and the anticipation of nonbeing; one is figure, the other ground. Clinicians who work with survivors of massive psychic trauma know that the anticipation of imminent destruction or witnessing the destruction of another collapses this dialectic between being and nonbeing. Rather than acknowledging that they have survived, survivors often react to the experience of having dissociated in the face of massive trauma as if they have not survived. Death becomes the figure in a landscape devoid of life.

Noam had intimate knowledge of this landscape; he knew only too well how contingency could smash into a previously ordered life, changing it beyond recognition. By urging me to work with those who had been immediately affected by the terrorist attacks, he was hoping to avoid a session in which the feelings of terror and emptiness, that could get stirred up by any reminder of the accident in which his father was killed, would inevitably come to the fore. He wanted to imagine me taking some action for both of us, doing something "on his time" that provisionally would have rendered us both less helpless. If I had accepted Noam's offer, I would have given in to my wish to feel effective and to temporarily quell the fears that kept me awake that first night after the terrorist attacks, alert to the sounds of planes overhead, making endless escape plans to meet any contingency. In my sessions with patients after the terrorist attacks, I knew I would often have to face these fears head on. This would be the case both with those patients who, like me, had not been directly harmed but whose sense of a safe and predictable world had been shaken, and with those patients who had survived the attacks in person.

Noam's reluctance to come to treatment, my temptation to avoid the session, neither of us wishing to dwell on our sense of vulnerability, contained in microcosm many of the elements that make working psychodynamically with survivors so difficult. Whether they have survived terror attacks in groups or torture individually, whether it has been an accident, a natural disaster, or intentional violence, whether the destruction was to the self or to a loved one, as in Noam's case, treatment must involve both patient and clinician immersing themselves in the landscape of death.

In working with the survivors of massive psychic trauma, the psychoanalytic clinician often meets with considerable resistance from her patient. Technically, the term resistance is reserved for those words and actions that impede the expression of unconscious material. Survivors are resistant to reliving the traumatic experience; they would prefer to avoid recalling the moments of total helplessness when the self ceased to be familiar and dependable but collapsed in the face of threatened annihilation. And for every form of resistance that the survivor can summon, the clinician has to struggle against her own resistance, the fear of recognizing her own vulnerability to psychic trauma, of meeting her mortal self in her patient's experience. Patient and clinician alike are reluctant to engage in the disorienting task of opening themselves up respectively to reliving or bearing witness to terror.

Catastrophic trauma is corrosive. It corrodes the survivor's sense of self, her relationships with other people, and her ability to think. It sets her apart from those who are still privileged to draw their strength from innocence. Clinicians find that working with patients whose selves have collapsed under the weight of massive psychic trauma is disorienting. This work can rob them of their psychodynamic perspective, leading them to question their usual tools. Trauma can excite, horrify, frighten, numb, or push clinicians into an uncharacteristic helping mode.

In this chapter, I describe several guises in which resistance can appear. And I point out the ways in which clinicians may, themselves, be resistant to undertaking this difficult work. Some of these resistances are, in effect, built into the very practice of psychoanalysis, taking the form of theory and technique. Some are unconsciously motivated. Others are born of the conscious conviction, found among survivors and those who want to help them, that the patient has already suffered enough, that talking about it will do more harm than good. There is considerable overlap among these forms of resistance; my purpose in attempting to separate them is to impress upon the reader how easy it is to lose our analytic footing when we are confronted by the insidious nature of catastrophic trauma.

CLASSIC PARADIGMS

Reisner (2003b) contends that "the authority of theory is an attempt to align the analyst's therapeutic ego with a greater, more authoritative ego—the theoretical ego—presumably freed from the distortions of any individual ego processes" (p. 271). I would add that psychoanalysts most often have had recourse to this theoretical ego when their individual egos are most challenged. In Chapter 3, I reviewed the difficulties that classical psychoanalysis encounters in attempting to account for the consequences of adult onset trauma. This failure is intrinsic to traditional psychoanalytic metapsychology, which is constructed against the notion of contingency, offering its followers shelter in the fold of psychoanalytic omnipotence. I suggested that this fold protects the clinician from having to imagine the terrors that the patient has survived or from imagining that such a fate could befall her.

In one striking example of the classical psychoanalytic failure to attend to adult onset trauma, Freedman (1978) describes the case of his patient, P., who sought treatment because of his compulsion to masturbate under the sheet in the barber's chair while he was being shaved. After an early childhood, during which he was exposed to scenes of considerable brutality—such as watching animals slaughtered and witnessing the difficult and bloody birth of a sister—in the rural Polish village in which he was raised, P. was later singled out as a Jew and teased for having been circumcised by the Christian pupils in the school to which his ambitious father sent him. This material clearly provided fertile ground for classical interpretations about castration anxiety. However, when he was a young adult, P.'s parents and extended family were murdered by the Nazis. For a period of time, P. himself was confined to the Warsaw Ghetto, which he left each evening to enter the town of Warsaw, passing as a Christian in order to obtain provisions to sustain those who were incarcerated with him. In this heroic nightly endeavor, P. "felt safe as long as his penis was not exposed (p. 760)." Eventually, he was captured and placed in a concentration camp.

In his elegant and complex interpretation of P.'s compulsion, Freedman (1978) lists many causes contributing to his castration anxiety: the violence he witnessed as a little boy, the humiliation he suffered in his Christian school, his relationship with his stern father and depressed mother. Freedman uses the words trauma and traumatic several times in the course of this article, but never once in relation to the Holocaust. At no time does he speculate about the impact of P.'s Holocaust experience, the possible enactment of his fear of exposure as a circumcised Jew while he was masquerading as Christian in Warsaw. Of the several analysts whose enthusiastic commentaries accompany this case, only Blum (1978) speculates about the contribution of P.'s experience in the Holocaust to his compulsive behavior.

Although this paper could be dismissed as out of date, it serves a heuristic purpose in pointing out the striking lacunae that can develop when a confining theory is too closely adhered to; or when, under stress, the analyst's therapeutic ego becomes aligned with the more authoritative theoretical ego, to reiterate Reisner's (2003b) point. As important, if not more so, the paper demonstrates P.'s apparent indifference to his experience in the Holocaust. In the course of this book, there have been many opportunities to point out the difficulties that survivors of adult onset trauma demonstrate in acknowledging the psychological damage that they have sustained as a result of their experience. It is as if acknowledging this fact admits to further helplessness. Without a clinician who can make the connection between a patient's symptoms and real life terror, what has frequently been the most powerful and private experience in the patient's life is further negated.

Those analysts who attempt to retrofit catastrophic events into the existing theoretical framework often leave patients feeling blamed and misunderstood. Prince (1998) agrees that many classical interpretations, what he calls psychohistorical myths, were designed to protect the analyst from the trauma of bearing witness to the unsettling and long lasting effects of trauma. Describing her experience working after the terrorist attacks, Frawley-O'Dea (2003) concludes, "It can be stablilizing for us to work on our own and our patients' traumatic responses as metaphor rather than unwaveringly stare in the face of current dangers and uncertainties" (p. 77).

Consider a more recent example of a psychoanalyst's appeal to the "authority of the past" (Chodorow, 1996) when confronted with catastrophic trauma. Seeley (2005b) reports that one self-identified psycho-analyst explained to her, "Helping patients injured by 9/11 was exactly like helping them with any other difficulty, in that it involved analyzing their internal conflicts and asking, 'Why are they hurt? What *really* is it pulling up? What is it *really* about, and what are they *really* saying?'" (p. 25, italics in original). Whatever explanation this analyst eventually settled on was an attempt to turn uncertainty and fear into immediately recognizable emotions. These are desperate bids to normalize a traumatic situation and make it one in which psychic reality, rather than the Real, figures; one in which contingency played no part. It is an attempt to make it a situation with which the analyst is more familiar.

Mills (1998) maintains that "Theory entails deep moral judgment" (p. 167). Consciously and unconsciously, survivors can and do feel judged by the clinician's choice to take refuge in inadequate theoretical formulations, to sidestep the decentering experience of working with massive psychic trauma in adult life.

PROFESSIONAL CENSURE

There are many reasons to cling to old paradigms. I suggested that they offer the clinician the reassuring shelter of familiar ideas and prevent the unsettling examination of external events. But peer pressure to construct the world through the lens of drives and fantasies is also a powerful motivating force. Arlow (1984) puts the classic psychoanalytic argument succinctly: "What constitutes trauma is not inherent in the actual event, but rather in the individual's response to a disorganizing, disruptive combination of impulse and fears integrated into a set of unconscious fantasies" (p. 533). Des Pres (1976) is at his most indignant in criticizing psychoanalysts who have sought to view survivors' preoccupations as if they were the result of unsettling unconscious fantasies rather than a reaction to terrifying and uncontrollable external events. He proposes instead, "We cannot know, we have no way of knowing what provokes a survivor's behavior unless we accept at face value the contents of her story" (p. 13). Throughout this book, I have urged psychoanalytic therapists working with survivors to listen and not to interpret, to join the patient without imposing an understanding borrowed from the world where terrorist attacks, torture, rape, industrial accidents, and hurricanes are the stuff of nightmares, not of waking lives.

Yet, as we saw in the previous section, in many places where psychoanalysis is practiced, Arlow's (1984) view continues to be the coin of the realm. "This isn't really psychoanalysis!" is a statement that many analysts dread hearing when they work with survivors. Davies and Frawley (1994) and Wigren (1999) wrote of their fearful anticipation of this kind of response from fellow analysts as they began to treat survivors of childhood sexual abuse. Kogan (2004) describes how paying attention to her patient's external reality threatened her identity as an analyst. When she was able to acknowledge her patient's fear, he gratefully accepted her support: "Until now Jacob had perceived me as representing a persecutory internal reality that seemed to him irrelevant in a period of danger" (p. 747). Like Kogan, I find myself struggling with my own identity as a psychoanalyst with every survivor with whom I work and with every paper that I write on this topic. Even as a relational analyst with more freedom to take external reality into account, I fear that my emphasis on how the patient's reality was altered during and since the trauma would be considered an evasion of the reality between us. I have to remind myself that until that external reality has been credited, the survivor of an adult onset trauma frequently enters discussions about the therapeutic relationship only to placate her therapist. To the patient, such discussions often appear irrelevant.

FELLOW SUFFERERS

There is a common belief among survivors that the only person who can understand their plight is another survivor. For two years or more, Jill (discussed in Chapter 8) felt that she could only be comfortable around people who had been at Ground Zero during the terrorist attacks or immediately thereafter. Similarly, Henry (2004) writes of his conviction that only another cop who was with him on September 11 would understand how he was feeling. Stolorow (1999) quotes a traumatized patient who insisted that the world is divided into normals and traumatized, and argued that "there is no possibility for a *normal* to ever grasp the experience of a traumatized one" (p. 465, italics added). In part, this belief comes about when friends and relatives indicate implicitly, if not explicitly, that they cannot bear to listen to the survivor's story. In part, it can be attributed to short term treatment models that attempt to normalize posttraumatic symptoms and suggest ways of countering them, leaving survivors feeling alone and misunderstood. And in some part, it is the legacy of psychoanalytic clinicians' failure to engage external realities, and their survivor patients who have found their therapists remote or out of touch. Nonetheless, I take issue with Stolorow's patient's. When survivors turn to self-help groups or work exclusively with one another, this practice can perpetuate the isolation the trauma survivor experiences, creating a survivors' "ghetto" (Kadushin, 1986). In this ghetto, survivors help other survivors, emphasizing the frequently unformulated belief that a survivor's alien and alienated mortal self cannot be integrated into the rest of the world, reinforcing her conviction that she is, indeed, not normal.

Reporting on work undertaken after the terrorist attacks on New York City, Coates, Rosenthal and Schechter (2003) argued to the contrary that that when the therapist has actually shared the trauma "this facilitates greater emotional clarity" (p. 13). It could be argued that this greater emotional clarity would ensure that the therapist cannot deny the patient's traumatic reality, and is more disposed to focus on it, but this is not always the case. It should be noted that Coates was referring to analysts in New York City who were only too aware of the terrorist attacks, but most of them had not been forced to flee the actual conflagration. Analysts who have experienced life threatening trauma themselves are sometimes no more prepared—and often less prepared—to relive the details of another's trauma than those who have not experienced massive trauma directly. Mitrani (2003) found repeatedly that the "coincidence of vulnerability" between a therapist and her patients who have experienced similar traumas may impede a full psychodynamic exploration.

One explanation for this phenomenon is found in Fonagy et al.'s (2002) developmental studies. Survivor clinicians who have experienced massive trauma firsthand and have not had the opportunity to work through their own catastrophic dissociation may have difficulty offering understanding while simultaneously conveying their firm belief that the patient has, in fact, survived. Fonagy et al. (2002) emphasize the necessity for parents to be in a "pretend" mode when their children have been frightened or hurt. On the one hand, these parents must match their children's fear; they show empathy but at the same time they are clear in their own minds that the child can surmount this particular crisis. Parents, and by extension clinicians, who have been unable to work through their own terror may convey instead their own unassuaged and unassuagable despair, leaving the child, and by extension patient, in a state of psychic equivalence.

Eshel (2004) discovered that not having experienced feelings of profound loss in her own life, the absence of this coincidence of vulnerability, was an advantage in her work with a profoundly damaged patient. She was able to contain and detoxify the overwhelming feelings that her patient had dissociated, but that she, Eshel, had not previously encountered.

CONTAMINATION

In the state of psychic equivalence, when catastrophic dissociation has led to the collapse of boundaries between inside and outside, and between self and other, some survivors fear that speaking about how and what they survived will in some way harm the other. In effect, they agree with Stolorow's (1999) patient, believing they should not expose a nonsurvivor to their own trauma. Feeling that the other will be contaminated by the disorienting realities they have to tell, they carefully edit their stories, ostensibly to spare the clinician; yet in so doing they also spare themselves.

Patrick, the police officer whose paralyzing helplessness was discussed in Chapter 5, came to treatment 20 years after he had returned from Vietnam. After a long period of apparent high functioning, a violent encounter during an arrest left him phobic about leaving home and suddenly assaulted by memories of the men who had died in combat with him many years earlier. He entered treatment complaining of problems with his children and sudden uncharacteristic rages. Since his return from Vietnam, his whole life had been organized to deny the impact of some of his experiences there, but the facts of Vietnam were with him every day:

> I knew I was different when I got back; I didn't have the same feelings any longer, but I didn't want to be like one of those guys who sat around complaining all the time. I figured I was just getting older. My Dad was in World War II; he was like this, too.

I liked this man. In his company, I felt safe and appreciated. I looked forward to seeing him. But I felt uneasy; even while I was engaged by his presence, I feared that I was not engaging him. I knew that there was something superficial about our work. We spoke of his worries about his children, the fear that he could not protect them from harm. He complained of sudden impotence but wanted to ascribe it to being over 40. I felt seduced into not dwelling deeply on his experiences in Vietnam. When the topic did come up, I felt two-dimensional and dissatisfied. I longed to get back to talking about his kids' problems in school, his wife's dissatisfaction, engaging his shy humor, the tough guy persona to whom I related so easily. I wanted to get back to the place where he would engage me in the present. But I knew that there was more work to be done; his stories about Vietnam seemed to be just that—stories. They were curiously devoid of personal meaning. They had no staying power; they were lifeless. When I work effectively with survivors, I can run the events that they are describing in my mind like a film, or a dream that I have told myself in order to remember it, allowing meaning and affect to emerge from the structure of the narrative. Outside my sessions with Patrick, I was startled to realize that I wasn't clear what I had heard. "Did he tell me this or did I imagine it?" Like the untold dream, I could not be sure. It was as if in the telling he was saying to me, "Let's agree not to remember this." I was responding to the pull to join him in dissociating his experience in Vietnam.

It was only by dint of very specific questioning, returning time and again to a particular scene, asking for thoughts, feelings, sensations, impressions, and actions, that I was able to persuade Patrick to fully describe and relive the dissociated and, consequently, unformulated experience he had been protecting us both from. "I don't think you want to hear this, doc," he said when he realized that we had circled back to a particular hamlet in South Vietnam where he had watched an ARVN put a bullet through the head of a young woman suspected of being Viet Cong. "People shouldn't have to listen to things like this unless they saw it, too." I persisted as carefully as I could, trying to imagine and—this time—finding that I could imagine only too well his horror, his impotence, and his self-doubt. Where was he physically in relation to her when this murder took place? Could he see the expression on her face or hear the sound of her voice? What did the gun sound like? Had he known this young woman? Could he have intervened? What happened next? Who took charge of her body? What kind of life did he imagine she had had? Could he imagine her with a boyfriend, with children, with parents? Demonstrating that I was prepared to work with him to construct details that had been deliberately left vague for years, enabling him to bring the scattered impressions, fantasies about her, and unbearable sense of helplessness into a whole went a long way to helping us understand the constant acts of heroism that Patrick had performed since his return from Vietnam.

During World War II, Kardiner (1969) wrote, "It took seven months of distressing labor and enormous suffering on the part of the patient to reunite these events in their proper sequence and ultimately to enable him to envisage the experience in its totality and to tolerate it." (p. 254). When Kardiner wrote these words, he was implicitly suggesting that abreaction is not sufficient. Based on the work of Breuer and Freud (1895), abreaction holds that, in evoking painful or troubling memories and linking them with their affective component, the survivor will experience relief. Kardiner was arguing that the goal of treatment is not to re-construct the truth, but to facilitate the construction of a narrative that contains all the scattered physiological, affective, and unmentalized impressions whose unconscious expression subverted the patient's attempts to rejoin the world of the living. It is only when a clinician is alert to a survivor's possible wish to preserve her from knowing such ugly truths that she can urge the patient to construct a trauma narrative.

VICARIOUS TRAUMATIZATION

It is easy to lose our analytic footing when there is a possibility that we can be traumatized by the material we listen to; it is often the case that we fail to emerge as the witness who is stable enough to bear witness, to quote Brison (2002). Serving as a container for the terror, helplessness and sometimes disgust of the traumatic scene can be disorganizing.

In the previous section on the fear of contamination, I considered the difficulties that can arise when the patient is aware of how permeable boundaries become after massive psychic trauma and fears contaminating the therapist with her own experience. This section will focus on the difficulties that occur when the therapist does, indeed, become vicariously traumatized, when the clinician's inner experience has been altered as a result of her work with a survivor (see also Saakvitne, 2002; among others).

Shatan (1973) originally identified the process by which clinicians who work with survivors can manifest posttraumatic symptoms themselves. Flooded by the patient's material, they experience intrusive ideation, become hypervigilant and develop startle reactions, or alternatively they grow withdrawn and preoccupied. On occasion, finding themselves unable to digest portions of their patients' horrifying experiences, these clinicians pass them on to colleagues in the guise of peer supervision or professional presentations, repeating the assault that they themselves have experienced. Thomas (2004) suggests that these traumatized clinicians are using their patients' stories, often in self-aggrandizing ways, as if they were talismans to protect them against further victimization.

The following case material demonstrates the clinician's ongoing struggle against vicarious traumatization. As I listened to Beth, whose case I previously discussed in Chapter 7, recounting the details of being trapped alone in her apartment a stone's throw from the World Trade Center, fearing that she would be suffocated by poisonous gas, her affect was quite flat, despite the tears that fell silently and continuously. I found myself almost unable to stay in the room with her. She spoke as if she were reciting a lesson, words that she had repeated to several people before she got to my office, yet I could feel the hairs on the back of my neck starting to rise. I was aware that I was feeling all the confusion and terror she endured that day and, on this day, the task felt too much for me. I wanted to break into her narrative with something that would reassure me, if not her, that she was still in one piece, that there was hope for her. It was as if I was experiencing feelings where she appeared to have none, asking (at first silently) questions where details were missing, in my mind's eye visualizing scenes she appeared to have overlooked, and I felt overwhelmed. When I left those early sessions, my affect was flat; I felt exhausted and withdrawn.

Caper (1998) elaborates upon the difficulty of becoming a container, a witness who is stable enough to bear witness, arguing that the success of projective identification depends not only on the state of mind of the projector but also on the object's state of mind. In urgent and aggressive projective identification, "one may evoke an unbearable state of mind in the object in the (unconscious) hope it will be transformed into something more bearable then returned" (p. 142). "Truly unbearable states of mind cannot be encompassed (borne) by the mind, i.e. thought about, doubted or tested because they encompass, invade and deaden the mind instead" (p. 145). When thoughts prove unthinkable, sometimes the analyst recoils consciously from the task; at other times the experience is so disturbing that she might feel as if she has lost her own mind. This phenomenon is explored in detail in Chapter 7 in the course of my discussion of the loss of symbolic function after massive psychic trauma. In this chapter, my emphasis is on the analyst's often unconscious attempts to avoid a joint exploration of the survivor's phenomenological state. Offering premature consolation or genetic interpretations are ways of sidestepping the work that has to be done. Alternatively, passively recording what is being said without working to give it shape—as I believe I did early on with Patrick, when I could not allow the appalling execution scene that he needed to tell me to cohere in my mind—is an indication not merely of avoidance, but also of the fact that Patrick's deadening states of mind had invaded my own mind. And I had to struggle not to let this happen with Beth.

As I listened to Beth, I reviewed the predicament she was in: how alienated she was from anyone who had not experienced the terrorist attack, how she felt like a broken puppet just going through each day in rote fashion with no will and no feelings, how the clock seemed to have stopped at 8:52 A.M. on September 11. Even her dreams, classic posttraumatic nightmares, remained stuck on that day. I reminded myself that my clock had not stopped. I may have been flooded by the thoughts and feelings that she couldn't bear to experience, but this session would end. With this realization, I moved beyond the state of vicarious traumatization. I was able to join Beth empathically. And, simultaneously, I was able to convey to her that time can be parsed into past, present, and future. The material could be titrated, put aside, returned to in future sessions. By ending the session on time, I was, in effect, creating a past. Referring to the time we would have to talk about this further in a couple of days, I was emphasizing the possibility of a future. Beth responded to this implied sense of a future and further containment by starting to dream more creatively about her escape from Ground Zero and all the personal meanings it had for her.

For those who work with survivors, experiencing vicarious traumatization is inevitable at some point. Hirsch (2003) makes explicit the other side of this vulnerability, the advantage of vicarious traumatization. "It is assumed among psychoanalysts that we work most effectively when our emotional boundaries are most thin, when we can optimally feel the feelings of our patients while also being highly attuned to our own raw affective states" (p. 669).

NOT KNOWING

Freud (1920) introduced the notion of the death instinct in order to explain the repetitive nightmares and intrusive thoughts that plagued combat veterans after World War I. These frightening and uncontrollable thoughts, he argued, represent "the most universal endeavor of all living substance, namely to return to the quiescence of the inorganic world" (p. 33). Many analysts have difficulty with this particular construct, but Laub and Lee (2003) do see evidence of the death drive at work in massive psychic trauma. However, they argue this evidence is found less in the intrusive symptoms than in the destructive and silencing force of trauma. The difficulty of keeping thoughts and memories of massive trauma in mind is a common phenomenon and proves particularly problematic in the treatment of posttraumatic states.

In the immediate aftermath of a disaster, the mental health community, relief workers, and survivors are alert to the possibility that they or their patients will be experiencing symptoms of acute stress. As the months and years pass, expectations change. It will have become clear throughout the course of this book that survivors do not always come to treatment in the knowledge that some of their symptoms can be traced to their survival. Failing to recognize this connection is an indication of the destructive and silencing force of trauma. To observe the avoidance of situations that may call the disaster to mind, to note the mind's proclivity to obliterate traumatic experience, and to recognize our own inexperience as mental health professionals in acknowledging the long reach of adult onset trauma is to see the Real at work.

Trauma precludes its knowing, but this should not preclude its telling. There is frequently an active, persistent and violent refusal to fully know what happened, to give shape to the experience, and thus to acknowledge its impact. For many survivors, this takes the form of speaking only reluctantly or in passing about the catastrophe that they have survived, believing that they should have "gotten over it long ago." Freedman's (1978) patient, P., who submitted to an exploration of his childhood horrors without apparently insisting on equal time for his experiences during the Holocaust, is an example of this denial. For some, the destruction of associative links is so successful that they are unaware that this overwhelming event continues to shape their being in the world and their experience of themselves and others. Even as they strain to be a part of things, they remain disenfranchised by their brush with annihilation.

Reisner (2003a) describes a provocative young woman he saw in intensive psychoanalytic treatment who led him on a witch-hunt into her relatively uneventful childhood. It was only after several years' treatment and unremitting posttraumatic symptoms that it became clear to her analyst that she had been seriously traumatized not in her childhood, but in her 20s as a member of violent a cult. The fact that this episode had never once been touched upon in the course of several years' treatment is a testament to the power of the Real to keep salient material out of the Symbolic register.

When Jill began treatment two years after the terrorist attacks, on the one hand, she acknowledged that her life had never been the same since the attacks; but on the other hand, she tried to dismiss the significance of the experience. A psychologically-minded patient, Jill insisted on drawing parallels between escaping from Ground Zero with her baby in his stroller and a painful time in her adolescence when she had accompanied her very depressed mother on a difficult trek around their neighborhood. There were parallels to be drawn, but Jill later discovered that she was relying on these similarities in order to leave blank the most frightening aspects of her escape from Ground Zero for which there was no equivalent in her early life and which she dreaded exploring with me.

RETRAUMATIZATION

Perhaps the most insidious resistance to working psychodynamically with a survivor of adult onset trauma is inspired in the analyst by her sympathetic reaction to the patient's fear of retraumatization. When confronted with the level of deadness and despair that some survivors project, or others' insistence that they should be restored to the way they were before the trauma, it is difficult to approach this work with anything but paralyzing caution. Not only does the analyst fear being traumatized herself, but fear of hurting the patient more than she has already been hurt is a very strong factor in resisting analytic enquiry.

Psychodynamic clinicians working with survivors of childhood trauma are familiar with the ways in which the original trauma is reenacted in the therapeutic relationship as patient and therapist unwittingly and alternately lay claim to the roles of victim, perpetrator, and onlooker. This is what I encountered in my work with Roberta, described in Chapter 2. In working with survivors of adult onset trauma, a similar dynamic can be found. The clinician who encourages the patient to relive moments of the trauma can be experienced as a heartless perpetrator. The patient who floods her analyst with details of the scene can feel herself to be an aggressor, or may be experienced that way by the analyst. The therapist who fails to bring instant relief can be seen as an indifferent bystander. Avoidance of this inevitable struggle by being prematurely reassuring or paying more attention to the symptoms than the survivor's internal experience subverts the analytic process. These are common countertransferential pitfalls, all of which threaten to retraumatize the survivor.

Offering false reassurance is a sure sign that the clinician is reluctant to listen to the patient. Langer (1991) provides the transcript of an oral history interview with a Holocaust survivor in which the interviewer repeatedly tells the narrator that she survived because she was plucky. The survivor left the interview feeling as if her experience in the camps was incomprehensible to the interviewer. By turning the survivor into a heroine, the interviewer demonstrated her shortsighted wish to protect the narrator from the traumatizing force of her feelings. But instead, she was conveying to the narrator that she was not prepared to listen to the most troubling and humiliating aspects of survivor's experience.

A further indication of the clinician's avoidance is apparent when the clinician relies on her own intellectual defenses to fend off the patient's affect, obsessively insisting on collecting details and, in so doing, flooding the patient and often forcing her to retreat from therapeutic engagement.

In an article that finds parallels between the clinician's personality style and common countertransferential reactions in treating survivors of adult onset trauma, Hirsch (2003) writes

> Some of us may be too frightened by our own terrors and imply to patients that they contain theirs, not to penetrate our own vulnerable boundaries. Or if our terror is explicit, we may evoke feelings in patients who have adaptively put away their raw affects. [p. 669]

It is clear that in this inevitable symbolic replay of the traumatic encounter, the clinician's struggle is often between overempathy, overidentification, or flight!

It is impossible to fully engage traumatic material without being challenged in your very being to react, and it is important for the clinician to continually monitor her own reactions. There is always countertransference in working with trauma, and there is always the danger of confusing clinical intervention with these personal reactions. In fact, the real question each clinician must constantly ask herself is which personal reaction will be therapeutic. Knowing this is, I believe, the essence of containment and the opposite of dissociation to which we inevitably fall prey at some point in the course of this work. Tutte (2004) also emphasizes the "deep emotional commitment" that the treatment of massive psychic trauma demands. "This is not intended to demean important concepts such as neutrality and abstinence, but rather to attempt to rethink and relocate them in a new context of technique" (p. 915). Once the clinician is able to reformulate what she is being told, to question, to fill in, to imagine for herself without fearing that she will do further damage by trying to escape or to reassure, or by becoming obsessively focused on details that the survivor is not ready to face, the painful reenactment can come to an end. The clinician's ability to have an independent reverie about the patient's experience (Ogden, 1997) introduces a third dimension into the analytic session, one that breaks the enactment deadlock where the only possibilities are one agent reacting to another or against another, where there is only doer and done to (Benjamin, 1998), victim and victimizer, indifferent or overexcited onlooker and confused survivor. When the patient is able to experience the clinician as someone who can grasp her experiences without flinching and without flooding or being flooded, she has found someone who is stable enough to bear witness.

I began this book by stating that psychodynamically trained clinicians bring to this difficult work with adult survivors of massive trauma a unique ability to treat the whole person, not just the symptoms of trauma but the inner experience of deadness and alienation that terror often creates. Without a witness and words to capture this experience, the survivor remains fearful and confused. The sense of being alone and isolated—a consequence of the trauma—is confirmed rather than repaired by the treatment. But this work exacts a high price from the clinician. "The strength found in innocence," the title of this chapter, is intentionally ironic, for the analyst, too, must give up any pretense of innocence. She must be prepared face her own mortality, the fear of which often lies at the heart of her resistance to working with massive psychic trauma.

10

The Psychological Politics
of Catastrophe: Local, Personal,
and Professional

The real behavior of survivors often goes unobserved because it is covert and undramatic, not at all in accord with our expectations of heroism.

— Terrence Des Pres (1976, p. 154)

Outside the town hall in Santa Fe, New Mexico, a roughly fashioned adobe monolith commemorates the massacre of a local Native American tribe. It is some ten feet tall; stuck into the four foot plinth on which the monolith rests are fragments of everyday life: children's plastic toys; a sock; a toothbrush; a tattered teddy bear; chipped plates and cracked cups; a family photograph behind broken glass, the frame partly obscured by sandstone. The shocking poignancy of these familiar little objects scattered in and by the enormity of the memorial conveys, at a glance, a meaning that words alone must struggle to contain. How does one simultaneously describe the personal losses and the vastness of such an event? How does one fit one's understanding of the individual survivor into the larger picture of the catastrophe without losing sight of that individual's own struggles, without objectifying them in some way? How does one keep the individual's plight in mind without submitting to the mind-numbing enormity of a catastrophe? There is always a tension between an individual survivor's need for recognition, understanding and engagement on the one hand, and society's need to map trends, to categorize, to plan for, and to provide social programs on the other. These needs are at odds with one another. Too often, the general obscures the particular. As psychoanalytic clinicians, we turn our attention to the particular, to the socks and combs and discarded toys, the evidence of disrupted lives. Our practice concerns the individual. We cannot and should not work from the position of the general; but in the case of adult onset trauma, more than other psychological condition, there is often pressure to do so.

In this final chapter, I turn my attention briefly to the commemorative adobe monolith. I consider some of the general issues that concern and obscure adult onset trauma before I return to the individual. Unlike most matters with which psychoanalytic clinicians concern themselves—the private hurts, everyday confusion, disappointments, and dissatisfaction—adult onset trauma very often invites the public gaze and thrusts those clinicians who would treat survivors into an unaccustomed forum. More often than not, the events that give rise to adult onset trauma become a matter of public record. Inevitably, such events draw attention and commentary and attempts to regulate how they will be perceived through the media and through politicians who use them as political capital. Inevitably, too, these attempts at regulation will impact memories of the event and expectations about how the event should be experienced. These expectations hold true both for the survivors who have been immediately impacted by the event, but also for those who would treat them.

Just as they destabilize those who fall victim to them, catastrophes also destabilize bystanders. These distant witnesses are often many times removed from the immediacy of the disaster. They find themselves alternately enthralled and repelled by what they see represented in the media or hear from immediate survivors. Horror has a pornography of its own. The need for mastery compels fascination; terror at the ultimate futility of pitting oneself against contingency fuels repulsion. Finally, indifference (Clark, 2005) becomes the most adaptive position. In previous chapters, I have explored the way in which clinicians who would work effectively with adult onset trauma struggle between these two poles, between the "fascination of the abomination" and the "powerless disgust," to quote the passage from Conrad (1902, p. 7) with which I began this book. I have described the struggle to stand on a middle ground and to engage the individual terror directly and without flinching; and I have demonstrated how often indifference, in the form of theory or technique, becomes the preferred position.

The politics of catastrophe and the dangers of these destabilizing forces also find expression in the contradictory history and reception of the diagnosis of Posttraumatic Stress Disorder. The act of diagnosing or of being diagnosed thrusts any individual into the public arena. When adult onset trauma occurs individually or in a group, when individuals face almost certain death and seek refuge in catastrophic dissociation, they are subject to the diagnosis of Posttraumatic Stress Disorder and thus they enter public discourse. I stated at the outset that this book is not about Posttraumatic Stress Disorder; but inasmuch as it concerns itself with responses to terror and the legacy of that terror, it will inevitably be seen as part of that literature.

The diagnosis has fallen victim to trauma's capacity to enthrall and to repel. It contributes to the tension between the imperative to acknowledge and the danger of indifference into which fascination and disgust inevitably sink. Attempts to capture and categorize reactions to terror seem doomed to failure, for too often they trivialize rather than do justice to these reactions.

The diagnosis itself is the legacy of political action taken in the 1970s by Vietnam veterans, by women's groups, and by Holocaust survivors who believed that their particular plight—as combat veterans; as survivors of rape, battery, and incest; and as individuals who experienced the Shoah first hand—was not represented in the diagnostic choices that were then available. It is a bitter irony that in its mandate to represent these disenfranchised groups, the diagnosis has become a caricature of what those who originally lobbied for its inclusion in DSM III (APA, 1980) had intended. Industries have sprung up around the cluster of symptoms labeled PTSD, inevitably shaping, obscuring, and denying an individual survivor's reactions. Statistically determined cut off points are necessarily established by epidemiologists seeking to determine the incidence or prevalence of PTSD in a certain population. Protracted arguments about which symptoms do or do not belong in the diagnosis take place each time DSM is revised, as if an individual survivor's experience can be represented or changed by the inclusion of a particular symptom. The question of whether predisposing factors play any part in developing PTSD is constantly debated. These epistemological questions have considerable political implications that can shape how an individual's experience is understood by mental health professionals and by the public at large. However, the individual experience itself does not change even if the public's perception does. The political stakes are high. Government funding for treatment after a disaster is often contingent on meeting criteria for the diagnosis. Insurance coverage for mental health is always contingent on meeting these criteria. What percentage of the population is said to be psychologically affected by a particular catastrophe is determined by arbitrary cut off points, as if those who do not meet criteria have escaped unscathed. Private compensation packages are debated in court, as expert witnesses vie with one another about the appropriate label for a survivor's symptoms. Decisions about how to characterize and treat the negative reactions experienced by troops in combat depend on the availability of mental health services and what is considered a psychological reaction or a "normal response." Whether to label troops cowards or acknowledge their psychological reactions to combat depends on the particular stage a war is in.[1] When a survivor steps onto or is placed on this contested stage, her individual reactions are easily obscured by its contentious history.

For some, the diagnosis does serve an important role, offering relief to survivors who had not previously understood that their symptoms form part of a recognizable reaction to an extraordinary event. It becomes a reference point in a world where categories have suddenly collapsed. Too often, though, the diagnosis marks the end of an inquiry, rather than the beginning of treatment. With overuse, misuse, and even correct use, the very words Posttraumatic Stress Disorder have become a cliché, a form of avoidance or denial for many mental

---

[1]*N.Y. Times*, 12/30/2003. Jeffrey Gittleman reported that a "battle hardened" Green Beret, who showed all the symptoms of PTSD and had to be returned to the United States after seeing an Iraqi cut in half by machine gun fire, was about to be put on trial for cowardice. This action was clearly taken to discourage other troops from seeking discharge on psychological grounds.

N.Y. Times, 11/26/2005. Benedict Carey reported that for those returning from Iraq, "whether their difficulties are ultimately diagnosed as mental illness may depend on the mental health services available" (p. A8).

Washington Post, 12/27/2005. Shankar Vedantam reports that, with the spiraling costs of PTSD treatment for war veterans in general, at an internal Department of Veterans Affairs meeting in Philadelphia, the department was reviewing the scope of PTSD criteria and the validity of screening techniques. This process could have profound implications for diagnosing returning soldiers, leading to many returnees who might otherwise have qualified for treatment being turned away.

health professionals. When details of the trauma itself, and of its consequences, have been categorized and fixed in place, the response to terror is reduced to a formula. Rather than encouraging understanding of
the experience, it is forced into recognizable and socially prescribed
categories that discourage further investigation. In the very act of being labeled, the subject located by this diagnosis has ceased to be a subject, becoming instead an object of curiosity or a statistic. In her great
pacifist essay *The Iliad or the Poem of Force*, Simone Weil (1940) writes
that violence turns anyone subjected to it into a thing. Regrettably, the
diagnosis that was created to acknowledge reactions to violence com-
pounds the objectifying forces of violence.

   In an argument that locates the politics of Posttraumatic Stress Disorder within the larger political arena, Seeley (2005a) and Pakman (2004)
suggest that the frequency with which the diagnosis is made sidesteps
society's need to trace issues of violence to their source in the fabric of
society. Seeley insists that a government that places the responsibility
for treating traumatic sequelae in clinics and individual consulting
rooms evades the final responsibility for having created the conditions
under which terrorist attacks and violence occur in the first place.
Rather than privatizing the experience with a diagnosis, Seeley counsels
political action.

   With the relational turn, psychoanalysts have become increasingly political and increasingly aware of a century's failure to provide for many
survivors of the harsh realities of life within our theory and our practice.
Our discourse is becoming more inclusive of these underserved populations, be they minorities (Altman, 1995), the poor (Cushman, 1995;
Layton, 2005), immigrants (Perez Foster, Moskowitz, and Javier, 1996;
Boulanger, 2004) homosexuals (Butler, 1990), or women (Benjamin,
1988). It is important to recognize that many members of these groups
are also more vulnerable to violence and more likely to have faced destructive situations in which they feared for their lives than those who
have traditionally sought out psychoanalysis or psychoanalytic psychotherapy. On a concrete level, the urban poor are exposed to more violence, and more of them are minorities. Some have fled persecution in
order to find sanctuary in America, only to live with constant reminders of
the violence that they have fled. Women are frequently the targets of life
threatening violence because they have in some way transgressed personal, family or group norms. Erikson (1994) demonstrates how the
poor are more likely to live in the path of natural disasters or in neighbor-
hoods where they are exposed to environmental malfeasance. Whether

they are African Americans in the 9th ward of New Orleans, whose homes and lives were disproportionately lost during the hurricanes of 2005; or mining families in Buffalo Creek living in the path of an industrial accident; or Native Americans whose community is threatened by a toxic spill, these populations are often silenced by shame and confusion at the failure of the world to acknowledge their experience. Now that psychodynamic clinicians have turned their attention to these underserved people, it is important to bear in mind that if these confrontations with catastrophe and violence are not also directly addressed in treatment, they can take a psychic toll that lasts a lifetime. As psychoanalysts increasingly appoint themselves spokespeople for those who have not been well served by the mental health profession as a whole, and by psychoanalysis in particular, it is incumbent on us as clinicians to develop an awareness of the insidious and corrosive impact that violence and terror have on adults, just as they do on children. Independent of other psychodynamic matters, and recognizing how frequently the survivor is indifferent to his own survival, if clinicians do not undertake the work of restoring the collapsed self, of enabling those who finally find treatment to pick up the threads of their lives and to weave themselves back into the fabric of society, we are ensuring that the legacy of adult onset trauma will be visited on future generations. Time and again, those who are alert to trauma's psychic toll find that their gaze is directed to its relentless spiral through sociopolitical movements, across temporal barriers, transmitted from one generation to the next, and always already embodied and enacted on a personal level. See also Apprey (1998), Grand (2000), Davoine and Gaudillière (2004), among others.

Political action of the sort that Seeley (2005a) advocates, addressed to those who overtly or covertly encourage the spread of violence and ignore the conditions of poverty and anomie under which it is more likely to occur, does not preclude individual work with those who are its victims.

Our particular psychological discipline has taught us the danger of evading what lies beneath the surface, knowing that finding a cognitive rationale—or, I should add, a metapsychological rationale—for the reaction to horror does nothing to heal that reaction, but it does increase dissociation both on an individual and on a societal level which, in a painfully familiar feedback loop, further blunts our capacity to sustain an understanding of horror. I have argued that psychoanalysis is less practiced at looking beneath the surface when it comes to adult onset trauma. Psychoanalytic theory has provided a very narrow range of interpretations for the sense of destruction found there.

This book is an attempt to address, very specifically, how psychoanalytically trained clinicians might think about and work with survivors of adult onset trauma. For the most part, this work will occur when the symptoms have become chronic. There are many reasons why survivors do not seek immediate treatment or do not get the kind of treatment they need.

Society at large has expectations about the recovery from catastrophic violence. Politicians' and media's mandate to spin the news and to shape public perception emphasizes uplifting conclusions and simple dichotomies: good guy, bad guy, evil villain, surviving hero. A survivor who does not feel heroic has a difficult time finding a place for his self-doubts in this discourse. In a startling glimpse at how in-depth work with survivors is viewed by the public at large, Linenthal (2001) describes those narratives that I have called living narratives as *toxic* narratives. According to Linenthal, toxic narratives are personal narratives that deal with the ongoing pain of survivors, narratives that seek to portray the full impact and horror of the event. He points, instead, to preferred redemptive narratives that emphasize religious and political messages. These socially meaningful but often personally empty narratives are the ones that survivors are expected to tell themselves and others.

On an individual level, survivors themselves are often afraid of seeking the kind of treatment that will require reliving horrifying events. Ashamed not to have been able to withstand the assault, not to have "bounced back," these survivors remain silent about their catastrophically altered sense of reality. They believe that their experience has cast them outside society's walls. Sometimes they have sought treatment, but the treatment modality has been too superficial.

Throughout this book, I have been addressing the importance of long-term psychodynamic work with survivors but, as many clinicians found after 9/11, the immediate needs after a trauma are pressing (Coates, Rosenthal, and Schechter, 2003; Danieli, Dingman and Zellner 2005; Knafo, 2004). Appropriate treatment at the right time can obviate the need for later treatment.

In the months after 9/11, Seeley (2005b) conducted a field study of psychotherapists who had responded to the emergent conditions. Although many psychiatrists, psychologists, and social workers made important spontaneous contributions to the welfare of survivors and their families, Seeley's report is an indictment of an undisciplined mental health profession thrusting its help willy nilly, failing to understand the context and the culture in which they were so determined to operate, all the while admitting that they did not know what appropriate help was. One respondent reported that "he and his colleagues had gone from one location to another on September 11, frantically searching for people to help" (p. 283). Another said, "I can't dig I have a bad back…But I can talk to people, I can try to help them. I can cheer them up. I can help them cry. I can hold their hands" (p. 283). Many were frustrated that their particular skills appeared irrelevant at that moment.

Based reports she had read about the blitz in London in World War II, Fromm-Reichman (1946) urged mental health professionals to step out of their accustomed roles and to simply offer physical and moral comfort to survivors. It is immediately apparent that, by taking this low-key approach, the professionals were facilitating a connection to empathic others and preventing traumatic dissociation from getting a stranglehold on the personality. With the same goal in mind, half a century after the London blitz, the Israeli psychologist Berger (2004), who has faced too many emergent situations, points out that the survivors' immediate needs are not psychological but informational; clinicians should be prepared to abandon their traditional role and to meet practical needs where possible. They should act as liaison between survivors and their families, offering humane empathic support, and providing them with a sense of safety and security.

With varying levels of success, several short-term and time-limited treatments have been developed to deal with the aftermath of catastrophes. In the United States, most immediate post trauma treatment models are currently based on Critical Incident Stress Debriefing (CISD; J. T. Mitchell and Everly, 1995). Originally, CISD was developed specifically to treat the survivors of accidents in the workplace and first responders who had witnessed or experienced serious injury or death. The treatment begins either at or near the scene of the accident, ideally in a group meeting in which a trained professional or facilitator encourages "some ventilation of feelings and reactions" (p. 37) in order to gauge who may be at risk for developing an acute stress reaction. At this preliminary meeting, checklists of symptoms are made available to all group members. J. T. Mitchell and Everly suggest that this initial defusing meeting be mandated.

The formal CISD meeting, held within 48 hours of the incident, and taking three to five hours to complete, has four distinct phases. There is a fact-finding phase, in which participants take turns describing who they are and what they experienced. This is followed by the "feeling phase", during which participants are asked to describe how they felt during the catastrophic event itself and their feelings at the current moment. During this phase, information about unusual symptoms and behavior is solicited, on the basis of which the facilitator is able to teach the group "something about stress response syndromes" (p. 38). The emphasis throughout the entire procedure is on normalizing symptoms, steadfastly maintaining that reactions to stress are to be expected in the immediate aftermath of a disaster. In the final phases, support and reassurance are offered and the group is encouraged to mobilize resources. Referrals for further treatment are made if they are deemed appropriate. A follow up meeting may be necessary several weeks later. Mitchell and Everly's own research has shown that this intervention has optimal results if it is undertaken within 24–48 hours of a disaster. Its effectiveness decreases as the length of time between the catastrophic incident and CISD grows; by six weeks the effectiveness is minimal.

There is considerable debate about how effective are such short term solutions to massive psychic trauma; whether they interfere with coping skills and the natural process of recovery from trauma (Cochrane Library, 2001; Herbert et al., 2001; Moran, 2003; Berger, 2004). Recently, The Cochrane Library (2006) concluded that single session individual debriefings do not reduce psychological distress nor do they prevent onset of Posttraumatic Stress Disorder at a later date. Whether survivors are hurt or hindered by CISD would appear to depend on several factors, including but not limited to whether or not these sessions are mandated. Forcing survivors to relive their experience against their will is never therapeutic, nor will it encourage them to seek treatment when they are ready to do so. The facilitator's personal experience with the trauma itself and professional experience and level of comfort in listening to extremely traumatic material are important considerations. There is no question that if it is handled sensitively, with a practiced ear for those who are close to being flooded or who are being avoidant, an initial debriefing of the event can begin the process of integrating the traumatic experience. Putting words to recently dissociated experience can determine whether a particular survivor will require further professional help.

To make CISD the entire process, or the foundation for a therapeutic process, is short sighted but consistent with the goals of insurance companies and government-funded disaster programs that regulate not only to whom but also how and for how long postdisaster treatment may be dispensed. It is unfortunate that the United States' national disaster service infrastructure is in the hands of administrators who believe that a four-hour mental health training is sufficient before crisis counselors can be put to work. The crisis counselors accredited by FEMA require no mental health training beyond this four-hour specialization. Because this is the only way to make services uniformly available, these counselors are trained to work from a manual. "One intervention fits all," as Silverman (2004), a psychoanalytically trained clinician who underwent the FEMA training, puts it. Many of these posttrauma protocols emphasize behavioral exercises to combat the effects of surviving a catastrophe, and, as in the CISD treatments on which they are based, counselors hand out checklists of anticipated symptoms and behaviors to counter them. There is a descent into concreteness and meaninglessness, an avoidance of any interiority or personal reflection.

Bellinson (2004) and Silverman (2004), both psychoanalytically treated clinicians, described their experiences treating survivors of 9/11 under the auspices of various government regulated programs where they were expected to correct the problem mechanically, in time-limited work, using checklists. The entire enterprise is designed to "minimize painful affect by reframing it in such a way that the effected person starts to lack conviction and credibility in their own dysphoric feelings" (Silverman, 2004).

Among the several short-term treatments currently being developed in Israel, the work of Berger (2004) and his colleagues at the Israel Center for the Victims of War and Terror, shows promise in addressing and alleviating the immediate symptoms of trauma before they become chronic. The Traumatic Memory Restructuring model is an early intervention that differs from those treatments based on CISD in several critical dimensions. Survivors are screened to gauge their suitability for the intended treatment, and each treatment is timed and matched to the individual survivor's ability to tolerate it. The proposed model offers a set of principles to guide clinicians in restructuring survivors' traumatic memories, rather than the manualized procedures adopted by some disaster counseling programs in the United States.

Trained clinicians provide a holding environment and prepare survivors by teaching coping skills, such as relaxation techniques and imagery exercises, before asking them to describe their experience during the traumatic event. While the survivor is speaking, the clinician monitors bodily changes in order to enhance the survivor's somatosensory awareness, which is understood to be a precursor of emotional and cognitive processing. Once the traumatic memory has been related, the clinician reframes troubling cognitions, such as feelings of guilt about not having done more to help others, and repeats the traumatic narrative back to the patient. At the end of treatment, the patient is encouraged to write an account of her ordeal and to read it to others.

This short-term model, set in motion within one to eight weeks of a traumatic event, is based on the neurological findings summarized in Chapter 4 of this book. It is designed to provide an integrative multimodal approach that "facilitates simultaneous processing of traumatic memories on somatic, emotional and cognitive levels during the first weeks and months following a traumatic event" (Berger, 2004, p. 22).

In a preliminary outcome study, Berger (2004) found that over two-thirds of the survivors of suicide bombings, who began treatment within one to eight weeks of a traumatic event, made a significant recovery from the symptoms of acute stress and were no longer considered at risk to develop long term reactions.

Eye Movement Desensitization and Reprocessing (EMDR; Shapiro, 1995), like other exposure therapies (for example, systematic desensitization, *in vivo* desensitization, or flooding), is often pressed into service as a short-term treatment after a traumatic event. In EMDR, the survivors are asked to select the image that is most indicative of the traumatic event and to describe how they would like to think and feel about the event in the future. "Once traumatic material is activated, the patient watches the therapist's fingers or a mechanical device move, usually laterally; this effort causes the patient's eyes to move. The eye movements seem to push along the processing of the memory of the traumatic event" (Paulsen, 1995, p. 33). Although the underlying mechanism for this treatment's success is not understood, it is suggested that EMDR protocol "elicits hypothesized traumatic neural networks and facilitates emotional processing of the contents of these neural networks" (p. 32). Embedding any of these exposure therapies in a more comprehensive treatment avoids many of the pitfalls of short-term therapies. Wachtel (2002) reports considerable success in using EMDR in conjunction with psychodynamic therapy.

Many of these short-term treatments are based on the principle of abreaction. Research (for example, Keane, 1995) has shown this to be an effective treatment in the short term with acute reactions when undigested intrusive memories are often the most overwhelming symptoms. At best, and this is the outcome to be desired, short-term treatments reduce symptoms and, if they take place sufficiently close to the time of the trauma and address the symptoms of catastrophic dissociation, they reduce the likelihood that the traumatic reaction will become chronic. The longer survivors wait to seek treatment, the more convinced they become that they have suffered irreparable damage, and the more their psychic disenfranchisement becomes a reality.

With or without immediate intervention, epidemiological studies have found that about one-quarter to one-third of those exposed to massive trauma develop long-term psychological reactions. However, epidemiological studies are constrained by diagnostic practice. Many survivors of adult onset trauma, who will eventually develop symptoms, do not immediately meet criteria. Sometimes, there is a latency period of as much as twenty years (Archibald and Long, 1968; Moran, 2003; for example). Patrick, the Vietnam veteran described in Chapters 5 and 9, would not have met criteria on his return from Vietnam. Five, ten, even fifteen years later, he would have denied that he was experiencing any reactions to having been in combat. His symptoms became adaptive, earning him a reputation as a hero. The very private belief, that he had no control over his life and no way of protecting his family, was too terrifying to consider. He kept testing it in increasingly dangerous situations, as his relationships with his wife and children grew more and more strained.

I am not prepared to suggest that no one survives a massive psychic trauma unscathed, but I am arguing that epidemiological studies and diagnostic criteria do not capture individual experience. And here I return to the dilemma that I described at the opening of this chapter, the necessity of not being blinded by the larger picture of a catastrophic trauma, of not losing sight of the painful evidence of individually disrupted lives. This is the psychoanalytic clinician's role. This book has explored issues inherent in the long-term treatment of adult onset trauma on the assumption that many survivors enter treatment once the traumatic reaction has become chronic.

I have argued that, in working with the survivors of adult onset trauma, rigorous attention to the patient's experience must take precedence over any preexisting theory of mind. Invoking early conflict, developmental arrests, or childhood trauma as an explanation for the alienation of adult onset trauma is tantamount to blaming the victim, which is a political position. It should not be a psychoanalytic one.

In his address at the 44th International Psychoanalytic Congress in 2005, Vinar rejected the "lineal development which mechanically subordinates current experiences to infantile neurosis. Extreme experiences, as in the case of war and torture, are able to shape and reconfigure the existing organization of the psyche" (p. 323). But this opinion is not shared by many in the psychoanalytic community. After the terrorist attacks in New York City, Stimmel (2003) argued eloquently for a more traditional approach. "We are in more danger of trivializing the painful magnitude of September 11 if we insist on treating it as a thing apart. … The seductive pull of egocentric attachment to trauma makes it a perfect magnet for resistance such that more prosaic passion and pain are given less of a chance to be worked through" (p. 26). Most of the time, our work as psychoanalytic clinicians is with the more prosaic passions and pains; it is with the small endurances of everyday life that can overwhelm and defeat a sense of liveliness. Adult onset trauma takes us into a different arena, out of the quotidian into the custody of horror. There are occasions when a patient lays claim to extremes of experience but, in fact, was not faced with death. This is, of course, a matter for more traditional psychoanalytic understanding. But when an adult has faced the random indifference of nature or been confronted with the terror of immediate annihilation at the hands of a familiar or unfamiliar aggressor, it is not a question of "either/or" but of "both/and." There must be room in our work for both the quotidian and, when and if it is present, for the immensity of horror, and within the immensity of horror for the individual context. If the painful magnitude of adult onset trauma is not treated as a thing apart, as this is so very clearly the survivor's experience of it, we are in danger of kicking over the traces of the trauma, taking that swift terror of death and burying it in the mundane, confusing it with the little indignities of everyday life.

In Chapter 1, I described some of the reasons why psychodynamic treatment is necessary with survivors whose reactions to a catastrophe have become chronic, impoverishing the internal object world and consequently impacting relationships, constricting thought and affect, taking the meaning out of work and leisure, collapsing the self and obliterating the sense of belonging. I pointed out that there is always a relationship between the survivor's dynamics, the psychological impact of the traumatic event itself, the psychological consequences and meaning that event assumes, and current symptoms. To overlook any of these variables and their interaction with one another is to fail the patient. The trauma must be contextualized. If it is given short shrift, the patient feels misunderstood and blamed, her ordeal minimized. On the other hand, if the trauma is emphasized but its psychic consequences are not considered and understood in and of themselves, the patient continues to be

overwhelmed by aspects of internal experience that have not been articulated and that, therefore, remain inchoate and incomprehensible. A
further complication arises when survivors have had a treatment that focuses in depth on their traumatic experience but has failed to integrate
the experience into their ongoing lives. In these cases, survivors become professional survivors, chronic witnesses whose repeated
references to their traumatic experience amount to little more than
self-righteous bids for attention and for special treatment.

I have argued for close consideration of the trauma narrative but that is
not enough. In his deconstruction of the narratives given by Holocaust
survivors, Langer (1991) writes, "Oral Holocaust testimonies are doomed
on one level to remain disrupted narratives. ... Instead of leading to further chapters in the autobiography of the witnesses, they exhaust themselves in the telling" (p. xi). This is where psychodynamic treatment is of
vital importance. We must ensure that the survivors we treat, who share
their narratives with us, do not exhaust themselves in the telling. We must
take our work with the survivor beyond the trauma, filling in the subsequent and previous chapters in the patients' autobiographies to which
Langer refers. In the description of my work with Patrick, Ellen, Beth, and
Jill, I focused particularly on the way that I worked with them to understand how they had responded to the terrifying circumstances they had
survived, and on the way in which catastrophic dissociation had left them
alienated and confused. This work would have remained incomplete if I
had not incorporated their traumatic histories into a broader understanding of their lives and personalities.

Bernstein (2000) suggests that the goal of psychoanalytic treatment is
to assist "the analysand in making the past a living present held within a
bearable yet unpredictable future" (p. 347). This is never more accurate
than when the present of an adult onset trauma has rendered the
pretraumatic past inaccessible and a future without the trauma unimaginable. To construct, to elicit that construction, to change, and to grow,
psychodynamic treatment with survivors of adult onset trauma is not
about memorializing the trauma; it is about acknowledging it fully and
moving on. My goal is to enable the patient to live her life in spite of the
trauma, not to be lived by the trauma. Earlier I described my dilemma as
I wondered how to help Jonah search for the soul he believed that he
had lost as the victim of an act of unprovoked violence. Mills (1998)
holds that the dialectic between past and present is the essence of the
soul. Reestablishing that dialectic restores the soul and that, as
Bernstein points out, is also the essence of psychoanalytic treatment.

This is a book about the consequences of violence and narrowly missing violent death or witnessing it but not, in fact, escaping it. In this examination of the phenomenology of horror, I have insisted that the wounds inflicted by reality in adult life become psychic reality and lead to the collapse of the self. This does not happen in every lifetime, but psychoanalytic clinicians must always be alert to the evidence of a self that has collapsed under the weight of terror. I am a stranger in this world, and, if I am lucky, I shall remain a stranger. In these uncertain times, though, I have less certainty that I shall. I travel through this world with those who are less fortunate, who know intimately the world between two deaths. I have tried to convey their experience as I understand it. In so doing, I hope I have done justice to the trust that they placed in me.

References

Adams-Silvan, A., & Silvan, M. (1990), A dream is the fulfillment of a wish: traumatic dream, repetition compulsion, and the pleasure principle. *Internat. J. Psychoanal.*, 71:513–522

Alpert, J. (1995), *Sexual Abuse Recalled: Treating Trauma in the Era of the Recovered Memory Debate*. Northvale, NJ: Aronson.

Altman, N.(1995), *The Analyst in the Inner City*. Hillsdale, NJ: The Analytic Press

American Psychiatric Association. (1954), *Diagnostic and Statistical Manual of Mental Disorders*, Washington: APA Press.

_____. (1968), *Diagnostic and Statistical Manual of Mental Disorders (2nd edition)*, Washington: APA Press.

_____. (1980), *Diagnostic and Statistical Manual of Mental Disorders (3rd edition)*, Washington: APA Press.

_____. (1987), *Diagnostic and Statistical Manual of Mental Disorders (4th edition)*, Washington: APA Press.

_____. (1994), *Diagnostic and Statistical Manual of Mental Disorders (5th edition)*, Washington: APA Press.

Anzieu, D. (1985), *The Skin Ego*. New Haven, CT: Yale University Press.

Anzieu-Premmereur, C. (2002), Après le 11 Septembre à New York: Des enfants. *Champ Psychosomatique*, Paris 2002, 28:55–68.

Anzieu-Premmereur, C. (2003), Après le 11 Septembre 2001 à New York. Unpublished manuscript.

Appelfeld, A. (1994), *The Story of A Life: A Memoir*. New York: Schocken.

Apprey, M. (1998). Reinventing the self in the face of fascism and transgenerational hatred in African-American communities. *Mind and Interaction*, 9:21-48.

Archibald, H. C., & Long, D. M. (1968), Persistent stress after combat: A twenty year follow-up. *Archives of General Psychiatry*, 119:317–322.

Arlow, J. (1984), The concept of psychic reality and related problems. *J. Amer. Psychoanal Assn*, 33: 521–535.

Bachant, J., & Richards, A. (1993), Review essay: Relational concepts in psychoanalysis. *Psychoanal. Dial.*, 3:431–446.

Bakhtin, M. (1981), *The Dialogic Imagination*. Austen, TX: University of Texas Press.

Baranger, M., Baranger, W., & Mom, J. (1988), Infantile psychic trauma from us to Freud. *Int. J. Psycho-Anal*, 69:113–128.

Barratt, B. (1997), Boundaries and intimacies: Notes on the performance and reperformance of "The Law" in psychoanalysis and elsewhere. Presented at a meeting of the International Federation of Psychoanalytic Educators, April, Ann Arbor, MI.

Becker, E. (1973), *The Denial of Death*. New York: Free Press.

Bellinson, J. (2002), One way to understand trauma: with regret. Presented at the William Alanson White Sex Abuse Service, June, New York City.

_____. (2004), Fish on a bicycle: Psychoanalysis in trauma recovery after 9/11. Presented at Division 39 of the American Psychological Association, April, New York City.

Benjamin, J. (1988), *The Bonds of Love*. New York: Pantheon.

_____. (1998), *The shadow of the other: Intersubjectivity and gender in psychoanalysis*. New York: Routledge.

Berger, R. (2004), Early interventions with victims of terrorism. In: *Living With Terror, Working With Trauma: A Clinician's Handbook*, ed. D. Knafo. New York, Aronson, pp. 150–164.

Berger, P., & Luckmann, T. (1966), *The Social Construction of Reality*. New York: Doubleday.

Bergmann, M., & Jucovy, M. (1982), *Generations of the Holocaust*. New York: Basic Books.

Bernstein, J. (2000), Making a memorial place: The photography of Shimon Attie. *Psychoanal. Dial.*, 10:347–370.

Bion, W. R. (1967), *Second Thoughts*. Northwood, NJ: Jason Aronson.

_____. (1982)., *The Long Weekend, 1897–1917*. Abingdon, U.K.: Fleetwood.

Birsted-Breen, D. (2003), Time and apres coup. *Internat. J. Psycho-Anal.*, 84:1501–1516.

Blum, H. (1978), Psychoanalytic study of an unusual perversion—discussion. *J. Amer. Psychoanal. Assn.*, 26:785–792.

_____. (1986), The conception of the reconstruction of trauma. In: *The Reconstruction of Trauma*, ed A. Rothstein. Madison, CT: International Universities Press, pp. 7–27.

_____. (2003), Psychic trauma and traumatic object loss. *J. Amer. Psychoanal. Assn.*, 51:415–431.

Blunden, E. (1965), 1916 seen from 1921. In: *Men Who March Away*, ed I.M. Parsons. London: Chatto and Windus, pp. 176.

Boehm, E, (2004), A Community Response to Terrorist Attacks in Israel. Presented at Columbia University, July, New York City.

Bonano, G. (2004), Loss, trauma, and human resilience: How we underestimated the human capacity to thrive after extremely aversive events. *American Psychologist*, 59:1, 20–28.

Bonomi, C. (1999), Flight to sanity: Jones's allegation of Ferenczi's mental deterioration reconsidered. *Int. J. Psycho-Anal.*, 80:507–542.

Boulanger, G. (1985), Posttraumatic Stress Disorder: An old problem with a new name. In: *Stress and Recovery in Vietnam Veterans*, eds S. Sonnenberg, A. Blank, & J. Talbott. Washington, DC: American Psychiatric Press, pp. 13–30.

_____. (1986), Predisposition to Posttraumatic Stress Disorder. In: *The Vietnam Veteran Redefined: Fact and Fiction*, ed. G Boulanger & C. Kadushin, C. Hillsdale, NJ: Lawrence Erlbaum Associates, Inc., pp. 37–50.

_____. (1990), A state of anarchy and a call to arms: The research and treatment of Posttraumatic Stress Disorder. *J. Contemp. Psychotherapy*, 20:5–16.

_____. (2002a), The cost of survival: Psychoanalysis and adult onset trauma, *Contemp. Psychoanal.*, 38:17–44.

_____. (2004), Lot's wife, Cary Grant, and the American dream: Psychoanalysis with emigrants. *Contemp. Psychoanal.*, 40:353–372.

_____ & C. Kadushin, eds. (1986), *The Vietnam Veteran Redefined: Fact and Fiction.* Hillsdale, NJ: Lawrence Erlbaum Associates, Inc.

Brenner, C. (1986), Discussion. In: *The Reconstruction of Trauma: Its Significance in Clinical Work*, ed. R. A. Rothstein. Madison, CT: International Universities Press, pp. 195–204.

Breger, L. (2000), *Freud: Darkness in the Midst of Vision.* New York: Wiley.

Breuer, J., & Freud, S. (1895), Studies on hysteria. *Standard Edition, 2.* London: Hogarth Press.

Brison, S. (2002), *Aftermath: Violence and the Remaking of a Self.* Princeton, NJ: Princeton University Press.

Bromberg, P. (1993), Shadow and substance. *Psychoanal. Psychol.*, 10:147–168.

_____. (1998), *Standing in the Spaces: Essays On Clinical Process, Trauma and Dissociation.* Hillsdale, NJ: The Analytic Press.

Bromet, E., A. Sonnega, & R. Kessler. (1998), Risk factors for DSMIII–R Posttraumatic Stress Disorder: Findings from the national comorbidity survey. *Am. J. Epidemiol.*, 147:353–361.

Bucci, W. (2001), Pathways of emotional communication. *Psychoanal Inq.*, 21:40–70.

Butler, J. (1990), *Gender Trouble.* New York, Routledge.

Cabaniss, D., N. Forand, & S. Roose. (2003), Conducting analysis after September 11: Implications for psychoanalytic technique. *J. Amer. Psychoanal. Assn.*, 52:714–734.

Caper, R. (1998), A theory of the container. In: *A Kleinian View of Self and Object*, ed. E. B. Spillius. London, U. K. ST: New Library of Psychoanalysis, pp. 135–155.

Card, J. (1983), *Lives After Vietnam: The Personal Impact of Military Service.* Lexington, KY: Heath.

Carey, B. (2005, November 26). The Struggle to Gauge A War's Psychological Cost. *The New York Times.*

Caruth, C. (1996), *Unclaimed Experience: Trauma, Narrative and History.* Baltimore, MD: Johns Hopkins University Press

Chodorow, N. (1996), Reflections on the authority of the past in psychoanalytic thinking. *Psychoanal. Quart.*, 65:32–51.

Churchill, W. (1955). Speech before the House of Commons, London, UK.

Coleridge, S. (1797/1998). The Rime of the Ancient Mariner *in The Portable Coleridge* (pp. 80–105). I. A. Richards, Ed. New York: Viking.

Clark, M. M. (2005), Echoes in the search for meaning in stories of catastrophe: The struggle between conscious and unconscious mourning in oral history accounts of September 11, 2001. Presentation given at Division 39 of the American Psychological Association Conference, April, New York.

Clark, M. M. (2006) Holocaust Video Testimony, Oral History, an Narrative Medicine: The Struggle against Indifference. *Literature and Medicine* 24: 266–282

Clark, R. (1980), *Freud: The Man and the Cause.* New York: Random House.

Coates, S. W., J. L. Rosenthal, & D. S. Schechter, eds. (2003), *September 11th: Trauma and Human Bonds.* Hillsdale, NJ: The Analytic Press.

Cohen, J. (1980), Structural consequences of psychic trauma: A new look at beyond the pleasure principle. *Int. J. Psycho-Anal.*, 61:421–432.

_____. (1985), Trauma and repression. *Psychoanal. Inq.*, 5:163–190.

Cooper, A. (1986), Toward a limited definition of psychic trauma. In: *The Reconstruction of Trauma: Its Significance in Clinical Work*, ed. A. Rothstein. Madison: International Universities Press, pp. 41–58.

Conrad, J. (1902), *Heart of Darkness*. New York: The Modern Library, 1999.

Cushman, P. (1995), *Constructing the Self, Constructing America*. Reading, Ma: Addison Wesley.

Damasio, A. (1994), *Descartes' Error: Emotion, Reason, and the Human Brain*. New York: Avon Books.

_____. (1999), *The Feeling of What Happens: Body and Emotion in the Making of Consciousness*. New York: Harcourt.

Danieli, Y., R. Dingman, & X. Zellner, J. eds. (2005), *On the Ground After September 11*. New York: Haworth.

Davies, J. (1997), Dissociation, repression, and reality testing in the countertransference. In *Memories of Sexual Betrayal*, ed. R. Gartner. Northvale, NJ: Aronson, pp. 45–75.

_____, & Frawley, M. (1994), *Treating the Adult Survivor of Childhood Sexual Abuse*. New York: Basic Books.

Davoine, F., & J.-M. Gaudillière. (2004), *History Beyond Trauma*. New York: Other Press.

Des Pres, T. (1976), *The Survivor: An Anatomy Of Life in the Death Camps*. New York: Oxford University Press.

Eagle, M. (1984), *Recent Developments in Psychoanalysis*. Cambridge, MA: Harvard University Press.

Edelman, G. M. (2004), *Wider Than the Sky: The Phenomenal Gift of Consciousness*. New Haven, CT: Yale University Press.

Eliot, T. S. (1943), *Four Quartets*. New York: Harcourt Brace, 1997.

Erikson, K. (1976), *Everything in its Path*. New York: Simon and Schuster.

_____. (1994), *A New Species of Trouble: The Human Experience of Modern Disasters*. New York: Norton.

Eshel, O. (2004), Let it be and become me: Notes on containing, identification and the possibility of being. *Contemp. Psychoanal.*, 40:323–352.

Fairbairn, W. R. D. (1952), *Psychoanalytic Studies of the Personality*. Boston, MA: Routledge Kegan Paul.

Fairfield, S. (2001), Analyzing multiplicity: A postmodern perspective on some current psychoanalytic theories of subjectivity. *Psychoanal. Dial.*, 11:221–251.

Felman, S., & D. Laub. (1992), *Testimony: Crises of Witnessing in Literature, Psychoanalysis, and History*. New York: Routledge.

Fenichel, O. (1954), The concept of trauma. In: *Collected Papers of Otto Fenichel, Series II*. H. Fenichel and D. Rapaport, eds. New York: Norton, pp. 60–84.

Ferenczi, S. (1933), The confusion of tongues between adults and children. In: *Final Contributions to the Problems and Methods of Psychoanalysis*, ed. M. Balint. London: Karnac Books, 1980, pp. 156–167.

Flax, J. (1996), Taking multiplicity seriously: Some consequences for psychoanalytic theorizing and practice. *Contemp. Psychoanal.*, 32:577–593.

Fonagy, P., G. Gergely, E. Jurst, & M. Target, eds. (2002), *Affect Regulation, Mentalization, and the Development of the Self*. New York: Other Press.

Frankel, J. (1998), Ferenczi's trauma theory. *American Journal of Psychoanalysis*, 58:41–61.

Frawley-O'Dea, M. (2003). When trauma is terrorism and the therapist is traumatized too: Working as an analyst since 9/11. *Psychoanalytic Perspectives*, 1:67-90.

Frederickson, J. (2000), There's something "youey" about you: The polyphonic unity of personhood. *Contemp. Psychoanal.*, 36:587–613.

Freedman, A. (1978), Psychoanalytic study of an unusual perversion. *J. Amer. Psychoanal. Assoc.*, 26:749–777

Freud, A. (1967), Comments on psychic trauma. In: *The Writings of Anna Freud* (Vol. 5), New York: International Universities Press, pp. 221–241.

Freud, S. (1914). The History of the Psychoanalytic Movement. *Standard Edition*, 14:3-66. London: Hogarth Press, 1963.

——— (1915). Thoughts for the Times on War and Death. *Standard Edition*, 14:275-300.

——— (1919). Introduction to Psychoanalysis and The War Neuroses. In Psychoanalysis and The War Neuroses. *Standard Edition*, 17:206-210. London: Hogarth Press, 1960.

——— (1920). Beyond the Pleasure Principle. *Standard Edition*, 18:7-64. London: Hogarth Press, 1955.

——— (1923). The Ego and the Id. *Standard Edition*, 19: 3-66. London: Hogarth Press, 1961.

——— (1926). Inhibitions, Symptoms and Anxiety. *Standard Edition*, 20:77-174. London: Hogarth Press, 1959.

——— (1933). New Introductory Lectures on Psychoanalysis. *Standard Edition*, 22:3-182. London: Hogarth Press, 1964.

——— (1937). Analysis Terminable and Interminable. *Standard Edition*, 23:211-253. London: Hogarth Press, 1964.

——— (1939). Moses and Monotheism. In *Standard Edition*, 23:3-127. London: Hogarth Press, 1964.

Fromm-Reichman, F. (1946), *Psychoanalysis and Psychotherapy.* Chicago, IL: University of Chicago Press, 1959.

Frommer, M. (2005), Living in the liminal space of mortality. *Psychoanal. Dial.*, 15:479–498.

Furst, S., ed. (1967), *Psychic Trauma*. New York: Basic Books.

Fussell, P. (1975/2000). *The Great War and Modern Memory.* New York: Oxford

Galea, S., J. Ahern, H. Resnick, D. Kilpatrick, M. Bucuvalas, J. Gold, & D. Vlahov. (2002), *New England Journal of Medicine.*, 346:982–986.

Gartner, R., ed. (1997), *Memories of Sexual Betrayal.* Northvale, NJ: Aronson

Galatzer-Levy, R. M. (2004), Chaotic possibilities: Toward a new model of development. *Int. J. Psychoanal.*, 85:419–442.

Gay, P. (1988), *Freud: A Life for Our Time.* New York: Doubleday.

Gedo, J. (1999), *The Evolution of Psychoanalysis.* New York: Other Press.

Gittleman, J. (2003, December 30). Green Beret on trial for cowardice. *The New York Times.*

Goldman, D., Rosenbach, N., Gensler, D., Goldman, D. S., Prince, R., Gordon, R. (2002). Voices from New York, September 11, 2001. *Contemp Psychoanal.*, 38:77-99.

Grand, S. (1997), Sexual betrayal and the persistence of nonlinguistic testimony. In: *Memories of Sexual Betrayal*, ed. R. Gartner. Northvale, NJ: Aronson, pp. 209–219.

———. (2000), *The Reproduction of Evil: A Clinical and Cultural Perspective.* Hillsdale, NJ: The Analytic Press.

Green, A. (October, 1997), Time and the other. Talk given at New York University.

Greenacre, P. (1967), The influence of infantile trauma on genetic patterns. In: *Psychic Trauma*, ed. S. Furst. New York: Basic Books, pp. 108–153.

Greenberg, J. (1991), *Oedipus and Beyond: A Clinical Theory.* Cambridge, MA: Harvard University Press.

Grinker, R., & J. Spiegel. (1945), *Men Under Stress*. Philadelphia, PA: Blakiston.

Grotstein, J. (1990), Nothingness, meaninglessness, chaos and the "black hole". *Contemp. Psychoanal.*, 26:257–290.

———. (1992), Commentary. *Psychoanal. Dial.*, 2:61–73.

———. (1994), Foreword. In *Affect Regulation and the Origin of the Self,* ed. A. Schore. Hillsdale, NJ: Lawrence Erlbaum Associates, Inc., pp. xxi-xxxi.

Hacking, I. (1995), *Rewriting the Soul: Multiple Personality and the Science of Memory*. Princeton, NJ: Princeton University Press.

Henry, V. (2004), The police, the World Trade Center attacks, and the psychology of survival: For clinical practice. *Psychoanal. and Psychotherapy*, 21:7–62.

Herman, J. (1992), *Trauma and Recovery*. New York: Basic Books.

Herbert, J. D., Lilienfeld, S., Kline, J., Montgomery, R., Lohr, J., Brandsma, L., Meadows,E., Jacobs, J., Goldstein, N., Gist, R., McNally, R., Acierno, R., Harris, M. Devilly, G., Bryant, R., Eisman, H., Kleinknecht, R., Rosen, G., Foa, E. (2001). Letter in *Monitor on Psychology* (p. 4). Washington, DC: American Psychological Association.

Hirsch, I. (2003). Reflections on clinical issues in the context of the national trauma of September 11. *Contemp. Psychoanal*, 39:665-681.

Hoffman, I. (1979), Death anxiety and adaptation to mortality in psychoanalytic theory. *The Annual of Psychoanalysis.*, 7:233–267.

———. (1991), Toward a social construction of reality. *Psychoanal. Dial.*, 1:74–105.

———. (1998), *Ritual and Spontaneity in the Psychoanalytic Process*. Hillsdale, NJ: The Analytic Press.

Hurvich, M. (1991), Annihilation anxiety: An introduction. In: *Psychoanalytic Reflections on Current Issues*, eds. H. Seigel, L. Barbanel, & I. Hirsch. New York: New York University Press, pp. 135–154.

Josephs, L. (2003), The analysis of meaningless. *Psychoanal. Psychol.*, 20:649–659.

Kadushin, C. (1986), The interpersonal environment and Vietnam veterans. In: *The Vietnam Veteran Redefined: Fact and Fiction*, eds. G. Boulanger & C. Kadushin. Hillsdale, NJ: Lawrence Erlbaum Associates, Inc., pp. 121–132.

———., G. Boulanger, & J. Martin. (1981), *The Legacies of Vietnam* (Vol. IV). Washington, DC: U.S. Government Printing Office.

Kardiner, A. (1969), Traumatic neuroses of war. In: *The American Handbook of Psychiatry*, ed. S. Arieti. New York: Basic Books.

Keane, T. (1995), The role of exposure therapy for the psychological treatment of PTSD. *NCP Clinical Quarterly*, 5(4).

Khan, M. (1975), *The Privacy of the Self*. London: Hogarth Press.

Klein,M. 1977. *Love, Guilt and Reparation & Other Works 1921-1945*. Delta, New York: Delta.

Knafo, D., ed. (2004), *Living With Terror: Working With Trauma: A Clinician's Handbook*. New York: Aronson.

Kogan, I. (2004), The role of the analyst and the analytic cure during times of chronic crises. *J. Amer. Psychoanal. Assoc.*, 52:735–757.

Kohut, H. (1977), *The Restoration of the Self*. New York: International Universities Press.

———. (1984), *How Does Analysis Cure?* Chicago, IL: University of Chicago Press.

Krystal, H., ed. (1968), *Massive Psychic Trauma*. New York: International Universities Press.

———. (1978), Trauma and affects. *The Psychoanalytic Study of the Child*, 33:81–116.

———. (1985), Trauma and the stimulus barrier. *Psychoanal. Inq.*, 5:121–161.

_____. (1988), *Integration and Self Healing: Affect, Trauma, Alexithymia*. Hillsdale, NJ: The Analytic Press.

Kulka, R. (1997), Quantum selfhood. *Psychoanal. Dial.*, 7:183–188.

Lacan, J. (1977), *Ecrits: A Selection*. New York: Norton.

Lachmann, F. (1996), How many selves make a person? *Contemp. Psychoanal*, 32:595–625.

Lakoff, G., & M. Johnson. (1999), *Philosophy in the Flesh*. New York: Basic Books.

Langer, L.(1991), *Holocaust Testimonies: The Ruins of Memory*. New Haven, CT: Yale University Press.

Langs, R. (2004): Death anxiety and the emotion-processing mind. *Psychoanal. Psychol.*, 21:31–53.

Laplanche, J., & J.-B. Pontalis. (1973), *The Language of Psychoanalysis*. New York: Norton

Laub, D., & S. Lee. (2003) Thanatos and massive psychic trauma: A psychoanalytic theory of remembering and forgetting. *J. Amer. Psychoanal. Assn.*, 51:433–463.

Laub, D., & N. Auerhahn. (1989), Failed empathy: A central theme in the survivor's holocaust experience. *Psychoanal. Psychol.*, 6:377–400.

Layton, L. (2005), Notes toward a nonconformist clinical practice. *Contemp. Psychoanal.*, 41:419–429.

Lear, J. (2000), Ed., *The Essential Loewald*. Hagerstown, MD: University Publishing Group.

LeDoux, J. (1996), *The Emotional Brain: The Mysterious Underpinnings of Emotional Life*. New York: Touchstone.

Levi, P. (1958). *Survival in Auschwitz: The Nazi Assault on Humanity*. New York: The Orion Press.

Lifton, R. (1967), *Death in Life*. New York: Random House.

_____. (1997), *Remembering Terrence Des Pres*. Paper presented at the Genocide and Memory Conference, January, Colgate University, Hamilton, N. Y.

_____. (2005), Americans as survivors. *New England Journal of Medicine*, 352:2263–2265.

Linenthal, E. T. (2001), *The Unfinished Bombing: Oklahoma City in American Memory*. New York: Oxford University Press.

Loewald, H. (1980), *Papers On Psychoanalysis*. New Haven, CT: Yale University Press.

Masson, J. M. (1984), *The Assault on the Truth: Freud's Suppression of the Seduction Theory*. New York: Farrar, Strauss & Giroux.

McCann, I., & L. Pearlman. (1992), Vicarious traumatization: A framework for understanding the psychological effects of working with victims. *J. Traumatic Stress*, 3:131–149.

Meyerson, A. (2001), Letter. *Newsletter of the Amer. Psychoanal. Assn.*, 35:4, p. 8.

Michaels, A. (1996), *Fugitive Pieces*. New York: Vintage.

Mills, J. (1998), Review of *Rewriting the Soul* by Ian Hacking. *Contemp Psychoanal.*, 4:157–169.

_____. (2005), A critique of relational psychoanalysis. *Pscyhoanal. Psych.*, 22:155–188.

Mitchell, J. T., & G. Everly. (1995), Critical incident stress debriefing (CISD) and prevention of work related traumatic stress among high risk occupational groups. In: *Psychotraumatology: key papers and core concepts in posttraumatic stress*, eds. G. Everly & J. Lating. New York: Plenum Press, pp. 159–169.

Mitchell, S. (1984), Object relations theory and the developmental tilt. *Contemp. Psychoanal*, 34:473–499.

_____. (1988), *Relational Concepts in Psychoanalysis: An Integration*. Cambridge, MA: Harvard University Press.

_____. (1993), *Hope and Dread In Psychoanalysis*. New York: Basic Books.

Mitrani, J. (2001), 'Taking the transference': Some technical implications in three papers by Bion. *Int. J. Psychoanal.*, 82:1085–1104.

_____. (2003), Notes on some transferential effects of the Holocaust: Unmentalized experience and the coincidence of vulnerability in the therapeutic couple. *Israeli Psychoanal. J.*, 25–37.

Modell, A. (1993), *The Private Self*. Cambridge, MA: Harvard University Press.

_____. (2002), Intentionality and the experience of time. *Kronoscope*, 2:21–39.

Moore, R. (1999), *The Creation of Reality in Psychoanalysis*. Hillsdale, NJ: The Analytic Press.

Moran, M. (2003), Trauma response strategies still missing in action. *Psychiatric News*, 38:23–24.

Muller, J.P. (1996). *Beyond the Psychoanalytic Dyad: Developmental Semiotics in Freud, Peirce, and Lacan*. New York: Routledge.

Murray, L. (1999), *Fredy Neptune*. New York: Farrar, Straus & Giroux.

National Public Radio (2005, August 31). All Things Considered.

Ogden, T. (1989), *The Primitive Edge of Experience*. Northvale, NJ: Aronson.

_____. (1990), *The Matrix of the Mind: Object Relations and the Psychoanalytic Dialogue*. Northvale, NJ: Aronson.

_____. (1997), *Reverie and Interpretation: Sensing Something Human*. Northvale, NJ: Aronson.

_____. (2003), On not being able to dream. *Int. J. Psychoanal*, 84:17–30.

Ornstein, A. (1986), Survival and recovery. *Psychoanal. Inq.*, 5:99–130.

_____. (2001), Survival and recovery: Psychoanalytic reflections: *Harvard Review of Psychiatry*, 9:48–64.

Pakman, M. (2004), The Epistemology of witnessing: Memory, testimony, and ethics in family therapy. *Family Process*, 43: 265–274.

Park, C., & C. Blumberg. (2002), Disclosing trauma through writing: Testing the meaning-making hypothesis. *Cognitive Therapy and Research*, 26:597–616.

Paulsen, S. (1995), Eye movement desensitization and reprocessing: Its cautious use in the dissociative disorders. *Dissociation*, 8:32–44.

Pennebaker, J. W. (1993), Putting stress into words: Health, linguistic, and therapeutic implications. *Behavior Research and Therapy*, 31: 539–48.

Perez Foster, R., M. Moskowitz, & R. A. Javier, eds. (1996), *Reaching Across Boundaries of Culture and Class: Widening the Scope of Psychotherapy*. Hillsdale, NJ: Aronson.

Peri, T. (2004), It was like the cartoons: From memory to traumatic memory and back. *Psychoanalysis and Psychotherapy*, 21:63–79.

Phillips, A. (1994), *On Flirtation*. Cambridge, MA: Harvard University Press.

Piers, C. (in press), Emergence: When a difference in degree becomes a difference in kind. In: *Self-Organizing Complexity in Psychological Systems*, eds. C. Piers, J. P. Muller, & J. Brent. Madison, CT: International Universities Press.

Poland, W. (2000), Witnessing and otherness. *J. Amer. Psychoanal. Assn.*, 48:17–34.

Priel, B. (1997), Time and self: On the intersubjective construction of time. *Psychoanal. Dial.*, 7:431–450.

Prince, R. (1985), Knowing the Holocaust. *Psychoanal. Inq.*, 5:51–61.

_____. (1998), Historical trauma: Psychohistorical reflections of the holocaust. In: *Children Surviving Persecution*, eds. J. Kestenberg & C. Kahn. New York: Praeger, pp. 42–53.

Protter, B. (1988), Ways of knowing in psychoanalysis: Some epistemic considerations for an autonomous theory of psychoanalytic praxis. *Contemp. Psychoanal.*, 24:498–526.

Pye, E. (1995), Memory and imagination: Placing imagination in the therapy of individuals with incest memories. In: *Sexual Abuse Recalled*, ed. J. Alpert. Northvale, NJ: Aronson, pp. 155–184

Rangell, L. (1967), The metapsychology of psychic trauma. In *Psychic Trauma*, ed. S. Furst. New York: Basic Books, pp. 51–84.

Reis, B. (1993), Toward a psychoanalaytic understanding of multiple personality disorder. *Bulletin of the Menninger Clinic.*, 57:25–35.

_____. (1995), Time as the missing dimension in traumatic memory and dissociative subjectivity. In: *Sexual Abuse Recalled*, ed. J. Alpert. Northvale, NJ: Aronson, pp. 215–234.

_____. (2005), The self is alive and well and living in relational psychoanalysis. *Psychoanal. Psychol.*, 22:86–95.

Reisner, S. (2003a), Psychic trauma and the seductions of a painful past. *Studies in Gender and Sexuality*, 4:263–286,

_____. (2003b), Trauma: The seductive hypothesis. *J. Amer. Psychoanal. Assn.*, 51:381–413.

Remarque, E. (1928), *All Quiet On the Western Front*. New York: Fawcett.

Rose, J. (1982), Introduction—II. In: *Feminine Sexuality: Jacques Lacan and the Ecole Freudienne*, eds. J. Rose and J. Mitchell. New York: Norton, pp. 27–58.

Rustin, J., & C. Sekaer. (2004), From the neuroscience of memory to psychoanalytic interaction, clinical implications. *Psychoanal. Psychol.*, 21:70–82

Saakvitne, K. (2002), Shared trauma: The therapist's increased vulnerability. *Psychoanal. Dial.*, 12:443–449.

Schermer, V. (2003), Terror and groups: Updating psychoanalytic group psychology for a new era. *Psychoanal. And Psychotherapy*, 20:199–222.

Schore, A. (1994), *Affect Regulation and the Origin of the Self: The Neurobiology of Emotional Development*. Hillsdale, NJ: Lawrence Erlbaum Associates, Inc.

Seeley, K. (2005b), The psychological treatment of trauma and the trauma of psychological treatment. In: *Wounded City: The Social Impact of 9/11*, ed. Nancy Foner. New York: Russell Sage Foundation, pp. 263–289.

_____. (2005a), Trauma as metaphor: The politics of psychotherapy after September 11, 2001. *Psychotherapy and Politics International*, 3:17–27.

Seligman, S. (2005), Dynamic systems theories as a metaframework for psychoanalysis. *Psychoan. Dial.*, 15:285–319

Shalev, A. (1996), Stress versus traumatic stress: From acute homeostatic reactions to chronic psychopathology. In: *Traumatic Stress: The Effects of Overwhelming Experience On Mind, Body, and Society*, eds. B. van der Kolk, A. McFarlane, & L. Weisaeth. New York: Guilford, pp. 77–101.

Shapiro, F., ed. (1995), *Eye Movement Desensitization and Reprocessing: Basic principles, Practices and Procedures*. New York: Guilford.

Shatan, C. (1973), The grief of soldiers: Vietnam combat veterans' self-help movement. *American Journal of Orthopsychiatry*, 43:640–653.

Silverman, L. (2004), Shared Meaning and the Language of Disaster. Presented at Division 39 of the American Psychological Association, April, New York.

Slavin, J. (1997), Memory, dissociation, and agency in sexual abuse. In: *Memories of Sexual Betrayal,* ed. R. Gartner. Northvale, NJ: Aronson.

_____., & L. Pollock. (1997), The poisoning of desire: The destruction of agency and the recovery of psychic integrity in sexual abuse. *Contemp. Psychoanal.,* 33:573–593.

Slochower, J. (2006), *Psychoanalytic Collision.* Mahwah, NJ: The Analytic Press.

Solomon, Z., N. Larror, & A. McFarlane. (1996), Acute posttraumatic reactions in soldiers and civilians. In: *Traumatic Stress: The Effects of Overwhelming Experience On Mind, Body, and Society,* eds. B. van der Kolk, A. McFarlane, & L. Weisaeth. New York: Guilford, pp. 102–114.

Sontag, S (2003), *Regarding the Pain of Others.* New York: Farrar, Straus and Giroux.

Stern, D. B. (1997), *Unformulated Experience: From Dissociation to Imagination in Psychoanalysis.* Hillsdale, NJ: The Analytic Press.

_____. (2000), The limits of social construction. *Psychoanal. Dial.,* 10:757–769.

Stern, D. N. (1985), *The Interpersonal World of the Infant: A View from Psychoanalysis and Developmental Psychology.* New York: Basic Books.

Stimmel, B. (2003), Tragedy and technique: stability when the earth shakes. *Psychoanalysis and Psychotherapy,* 20:97–118.

Stolorow, R. (1999), The phenomenology of trauma and the absolutisms of everyday life: A personal journey. *Psychoanal. Psychol.,* 16:380–386

Strozier, C. (2002), The World Trade Center disaster and the apocalyptic. *Psychoanal. Dial.,* 12:361–380.

_____. (2005), Trauma and poetry: On the World Trade Disaster. In: *On the Ground After September 11,* eds. Y. Danieli, R. Dingman, & Zellner, J. New York, Haworth, pp. 565–569.

Tarantelli, C. B. (2003), Life within death. *Int. J. Psychoanal.,* 84:915–928.

Taylor, C. (1989), *Sources of the Self.* Cambridge, MA: Harvard University Press.

The Cochrane Library (2006, April 20). Psychological debriefing for preventing posttraumatic stress disorder. www.cochrane.org.

Thelen, E., & L. Smith, eds. (1993), *A Dynamic Systems Approach to Development: Applications.* Cambridge, MA: MIT Press.

_____. (1996), *A Dynamic Systems Approach to the Development of Cognition and Action.* Cambridge, MA: MIT Press.

Thomas, N. (2004), An eye for an eye: Fantasies of revenge in the aftermath of trauma. In: *Living With Terror, Working With Trauma: A Clinician's Handbook,* ed. D. Knafo. New York: Aronson, pp. 297–311.

_____. (2005), The use of the hero. In: *On the Ground After September 11,* eds. Y. Danieli, R. Dingman, & X. Zellner. New York: Haworth, pp. 394–400.

Timerman, J. (2002), *Prisoner Without a Name, Cell Without a Number.* Madison, WI: University of Wisconsin Press.

Tomasch, S. (2004). Editing as Palinode: The invention of love and the text of the Canterbury Tales. *Exemplaria,* 16:457–476.

Tutte, J. (2004), The concept of psychical trauma: A bridge to interdisciplinary space. *Int. J. Psycho-Anal;* 85:897–921.

Ulman, R., & D. Brothers. (1988), *The Shattered Self.* Hillsdale, NJ: The Analytic Press.

Van der Kolk, B. (2002), Posttraumatic therapy in the age of neuroscience. *Psychoanal. Dial.,* 12:381–392.

_____, A. McFarlane, & L. Weisaeth, eds. (1996), *Traumatic Stress: The Effects of Overwhelming Experience on Mind, Body, and Society.* New York: Guilford.

Vedantam, S. (2005, December 27). Spiraling costs of PTSD treatment. *The Washington Post.*

Vinar, M. (2005), The specificity of torture as trauma: The human wilderness when words fail. *Int. J. Psycho-Anal.*, 86: 311–333.

Wachtel, P. L. (2002), EMDR and psychoanalysis. In: *EMDR as an Integrative Psychotherapy Approach: Experts of Diverse Orientations Explore the Paradigm Prism*, ed. F. Shapiro. Washington, DC: American Psychological Association, pp. 123–150.

Weil, S. (1940), *The Iliad or the Poem of Force.* New York: New York Review of Books Classics, 2005.

Wigren, P. (1999), As hardly killed, as easily wounded: Posttraumatic challenges to the working alliance. *Contemp. Psychoanal.*, 35:253–269.

Willoughby, R. (2001), The dungeon of thyself: The claustrum as pathological container. *Int. J. Psychoanal.*, 82:917–931.

Winnicott, D. (1958), *Collected Papers: Through Pediatrics to Psychoanalysis.* New York: Basic Books.

_____. (1965), *Maturational Processes and the Facilitating Environment.* New York: International Universities Press.

_____. (1974), Fear of breakdown. *Internat. Rev. Psycho-Anal.*, 1:103–107.

Yorke, C. (1986), Reflections on the problem of psychic trauma: *The Psychoanalytic Study of the Child* 41: 221–236, New Haven, CT: Yale University Press

Zizek, S.(1989), *The Sublime Object of Ideology,* London: Verso.

Index